Studies in Digital History and Hermeneutics

Edited by
Andreas Fickers, Valérie Schafer, Sean Takats,
and Gerben Zaagsma

Volume 1

Max Kemman
Trading Zones of Digital History

Max Kemman

Trading Zones of Digital History

—

ISBN 978-3-11-068196-3
e-ISBN (PDF) 978-3-11-068210-6
e-ISBN (EPUB) 978-3-11-068225-0
ISSN 2629-4540
DOI https://doi.org/10.1515/9783110682106

Library of Congress Control Number: 2021941687

Bibliographic information published by the Deutsche Nationalbibliothek
The Deutsche Nationalbibliothek lists this publication in the Deutsche Nationalbibliografie;
detailed bibliographic data are available on the Internet at http://dnb.dnb.de.

© 2021 Max Kemman, published by Walter de Gruyter GmbH, Berlin/Boston.
The book is published open access at www.degruyter.com.

Cover image: graphics © Max Kemman and Nick Jelicic; typewriter: © Graphisterie Générale
Typesetting: Integra Software Services Pvt. Ltd.
Printing and binding: CPI books GmbH, Leck

www.degruyter.com

MIX
Papier aus verantwor-
tungsvollen Quellen
FSC® C083411

Contents

Introduction

> Like Hamlet, historians have now reached the crossroads of "to be or not to be;" either they accept the challenge and attain to new heights of achievement or else reject it and be swamped by the tidal wave of accumulated and expanding knowledge as was the art savant in "Penguin Island."[1]

> [I]f we do not wake up soon to the new realities of big data, computer scientists will leave us behind, biting the dust in this road to knowledge.[2]

The Urgency of Digital History

As long as there have been computers, there have been scholars pulling at historians, challenging them to use these computers for historical research. Historians need to adapt to the new technological possibilities, otherwise they risk becoming irrelevant. The reason for such calls is not just to become a modern profession, but because historians are supposedly faced with ever increasing amounts of sources, big data, or even knowledge. These challenges are then argued to require computational approaches. Such calls have largely gone unanswered, as can be seen from the two quotes above, which are 70 years apart, yet pose a similar challenge to historians. Already in 1948, the historian Murray G. Lawson stated that "historians have not been sufficiently conscious of the benefits to be derived from the technological revolution which has transformed contemporary society."[3] In 1968, the historian Emanuel Le Roy Ladurie made the (in)famous statement that "the historian will be a programmer or he will be nothing".[4] In 1990, the historians Onno Boonstra, Leen Breure and Peter Doorn wrote that "[t]he historian who refuses to use a computer as being unnecessary, ignores vast areas of historical research and will not be taken serious anymore".[5]

---

1 Murray G. Lawson, "The Machine Age in Historical Research," *American Archivist* 11, no. 2 (1948): 149.
2 Roberto Franzosi, "A Third Road to the Past? Historical Scholarship in the Age of Big Data," *Historical Methods: A Journal of Quantitative and Interdisciplinary History* 50, no. 4 (2017): 14, https://doi.org/10.1080/01615440.2017.1361879.
3 Lawson, "The Machine Age in Historical Research," 142.
4 Quoted in Lawrence Stone, "The Revival of Narrative: Reflections on a New Old History," *Past & Present* 85, no. 85 (1979): 13.
5 Onno Boonstra, Leen Breure and Peter Doorn, "Past, Present and Future of Historical Information Science," *Historical Social Research / Historische Sozialforschung* 29, no. 2 (2004): 4.

Fourteen years later, they were disappointed, and although a group of enthusiasts in history had formed, computational methods had far from diffused in the historical profession.

This lack of diffusion was partially due to critical responses from historians. Especially the first wave of computational methods in history, consisting of quantitative analyses, was criticised since "almost all important questions are important precisely because they are not susceptible to quantitative answers".[6] Yet turning to qualitative data did not lead to much more enthusiasm. The historian Peter Denley instead noted that "we have sacrificed at the altar of the microchip the thirteenth century fief rolls of Champagne and the fifteenth century baptismal records of Pisa, the naturalisation lists of fourteenth century Freiburg in Switzerland and tenth century Cluniac charters".[7] Yet more important than such critical exchanges was the lack of engagement; historians interested in computational approaches simply failed to convince their peers.[8]

This is not to say that historians have entirely missed the so-called "digital turn". Every historian nowadays has a computer on their desk, writes their monograph in word processing software and searches for information on Google or some specific online database.[9] A renewed interest in digital methods has arisen now that libraries and archives are increasingly publishing sources in online databases. Vast quantities of sources have been digitised in the large-scale digitisation projects of the past decades. Yet although historians and archives are highly interdependent, historians have largely remained silent about questions regarding the consequences of digitisation.[10] The digitisation of sources

---

6 Arthur Schlesinger, "The Humanist Looks at Empirical Social Research," *American Sociological Review* 27, no. 6 (1962): 770, https://doi.org/10.2307/2090404, cited in Stephan Thernstrom, "The Historian and the Computer," in *Computers in Humanistic Research: Readings and Perspectives*, ed. Edmund A. Bowles (1967), 73–81.

7 Quoted in William A. Speck, "History and Computing: Some Reflections on the Achievements of the Past Decade," *History and Computing* 6, no. 1 (1994): 30.

8 Boonstra, Breure and Doorn, "Past, Present and Future of Historical Information Science," 85–59; Speck, "History and Computing."

9 Max Kemman, Martijn Kleppe and Stef Scagliola, "Just Google It," in *Proceedings of the Digital Humanities Congress 2012*, ed. Clare Mills, Michael Pidd and Esther Ward (Sheffield, UK: HRI Online Publications, 2014).

10 Ian G. Anderson, "Are You Being Served? Historians and the Search for Primary Sources," *Archivaria* 58 (2004): 81–129; Andreas Fickers, "Veins Filled with the Diluted Sap of Rationality: A Critical Reply to Rens Bod," *BMGN – Low Countries Historical Review* 128, no. 4 (2013): 155–63; Andreas Fickers, "Update Für Die Hermeneutik. Geschichtswissenschaft Auf Dem Weg Zur Digitalen Forensik?," *Zeithistorische Forschungen – Studies in Contemporary History* 17, no. 1 (2020): 157–68; Tim Hitchcock, "Confronting the Digital: Or How Academic History Writing Lost the Plot," *Cultural and Social History* 10, no. 1 (2013): 9–23,

and workflows and the introduction of search engines are often thought of as practical revolutions, while the effect on research is treated as a secondary by-product.[11] The speedup of archival exploration is perceived as an advantage, mainly because it leaves more time for close reading.[12]

Such interpretations treat the digital form as an equivalent surrogate to the original source, merely more accessible. Computers are, however, envisioned to allow much more comprehensive interaction with the historical material. Historians that subscribe to this vision have gathered under the signifier of "digital history". They experiment with tools, concepts and methods from other disciplines, mostly computer science and computational linguistics, to benefit the discipline of history, constituting methodological interdisciplinarity.[13]

In digital history, therefore, historians collaborate with computational experts to try and adjust tools and methods from other disciplines to fit the needs of historians. The ambition is that, at some point, such digital methods might eventually diffuse to the broader field of history and be adopted by historians who do not collaborate with computational experts. These cross-disciplinary interactions are what interests me in this book. Historians in digital history try to innovate historical research in a way that is methodologically and epistemologically acceptable to the values and norms of their discipline.[14] At the same time, computational experts are interested in what is computationally feasible when confronted with the heterogeneous, imperfect and incomprehensive collections that historians have been working with for centuries. Computational methods are not yet adapted to such issues, and how to extract valuable information from historical datasets is a matter of active research.

Digital history thus creates uncertainty for both sides; historians are uncertain how they as historians should use digital methods, and computational experts are

---

https://doi.org/10.2752/147800413X13515292098070; Frank M. Bischoff and Kiran Klaus Patel, "Was Auf Dem Spiel Steht. Über Den Preis Des Schweigens Zwischen Geschichtswissenschaft Und Archiven Im Digitalen Zeitalter," *Zeithistorische Forschungen – Studies in Contemporary History* 17, no. 1 (2020): 145–56.

11 Bob Nicholson, "The Digital Turn," *Media History* 19, no. 1 (2013): 59–73, https://doi.org/10.1080/13688804.2012.752963.

12 Adrian Bingham, "'The Digitization of Newspaper Archives: Opportunities and Challenges for Historians,'" *Twentieth Century British History* 21, no. 2 (2010): 225–31, https://doi.org/10.1093/tcbh/hwq007.

13 Julie Thompson Klein, *Interdisciplining Digital Humanities: Boundary Work in an Emerging Field*, online (University of Michigan Press, 2014), https://doi.org/10.3998/dh.12869322.0001.001.

14 Wolfgang Kaltenbrunner, "Reflexive Inertia: Reinventing Scholarship through Digital Practices" (PhD thesis, Leiden University, 2015).

uncertain how digital methods should work with historical datasets. The opportunity that arises from this uncertainty is that historians and computational experts need to negotiate the methods and concepts under development. Historians need to adapt their practices to what is computationally feasible, but the methods that are being developed need to be adapted to what is of interest to historians. How historians can influence the development of digital methods, and how digital methods affect the methodology and epistemology of the historical discipline, has thus far been underexplored.[15] In this book, I explore these issues by following digital history scholars and understanding their practices, responding to the call to action from the information scientist Christine Borgman.[16] As such, this book is inspired by the well-known social studies of science, applied to digital history in practice.[17] Through a mixed-methods, multi-sited ethnographic approach, I provide a critical view on digital history grounded in how it is conducted and negotiated.

To support this analysis, I develop a model to analyse digital history collaborations as trading zones. This concept was developed by the historian of science Peter Galison to describe how two communities with vastly different practices and discourses can interact and negotiate a joint enterprise. He defined a trading zone as "an arena in which radically different activities could be *locally*, but not globally, coordinated."[18] While historians and computational experts in general employ different discourses and practices, and publish in different formats and venues, locally it is possible to coordinate practices toward a shared objective. Through such coordination a trading zone emerges which I analyse according to three dimensions. First, engagement as the extent to which the two communities come together to meet and interact. That is, a trading zone where historians and computational experts share an office and meet daily is different from one where communication is done per email once a month. Second, power relations as the extent to which

---

15 Hinke Piersma and Kees Ribbens, "Digital Historical Research: Context, Concepts and the Need for Reflection," *BMGN – Low Countries Historical Review* 128, no. 4 (2013): 78–102; Bernhard Rieder and Theo Röhle, "Digital Methods: Five Challenges," in *Understanding Digital Humanities*, ed. David Berry (Palgrave Macmillan, 2012), 67–84; Gerben Zaagsma, "On Digital History," *BMGN – Low Countries Historical Review* 128, no. 4 (2013): 3–29, https://doi.org/10.18352/bmgn-lchr.9344.
16 Christine L. Borgman, "The Digital Future Is Now: A Call to Action for the Humanities," *DHQ: Digital Humanities Quarterly* 3, no. 4 (2009).
17 Karin Knorr Cetina, *Epistemic Cultures: How the Sciences Make Knowledge* (Harvard University Press, 1999); Bruno Latour and Steve Woolgar, *Laboratory Life: The Social Construction of Scientific Facts* (SAGE Publications, 1979).
18 Peter Galison, "Computer Simulations and the Trading Zone," in *The Disunity of Science: Boundaries, Contexts, And Power*, ed. Peter Galison and David J. Stump (Stanford University Press, 1996), 119, emphasis in original.

one community has a stronger negotiating power to decide goals and practices than the other community. For example, computational experts may push a tool for historians while historians remain unable to adapt the tool to their needs. Finally, changing practices as the extent to which the trading zone remains an interaction of distinct communities, or merges into a singular community of shared practices. That is, whether these trading zones remain distinct historians and computational experts, or blend into a community of digital historians.

Following arguments that digital history is to be positioned between the traditionally historical and the computational or digital, I focus on practices between these two ends.[19] I argue that digital history does not occupy a singular position between the digital and the historical. Instead, historians continuously move across this dimension, choosing (or finding themselves in) different positions as they construct different trading zones through cross-disciplinary engagement, negotiation of research goals and individual interests.

This book is thereby aimed at scholars interested in digital history and its relations to the historical discipline and to digital humanities. At the heart of my investigation are the processes of negotiating and exchanging of disciplinary practices, and how such trading affects the way historians practice historical research. Furthermore, this book will be of interest to scholars working on interdisciplinary collaborations towards digital research infrastructures.

Structure of the Book

In the rest of this chapter, I contextualise digital history by discussing its relationship to digital humanities and exploring its origins in histories of library sciences, archival sciences and historiography. I argue that for many decades historians have been able to trust librarians and archivists to facilitate historical research, without deeply engaging with these communities. However, with digital infrastructures, the structure of databases affects what historians can do and what questions can be pursued. I argue that this change of infrastructure for historical research is what necessitates cross-disciplinary collaborations, so that historians steer these infrastructures into directions suitable for historians.

In Chapter 2, I develop a theoretical model for analysing cross-disciplinary collaborations, basing my work on the concept of trading zones. I elaborate this

---

19 Jennifer Edmond, "The Role of the Professional Intermediary in Expanding the Humanities Computing Base," *Literary and Linguistic Computing* 20, no. 3 (2005): 367–80, https://doi.org/10.1093/llc/fqi036; Patrik Svensson, "The Digital Humanities as a Humanities Project," *Arts and Humanities in Higher Education* 11, no. 1–2 (2011): 42–60, https://doi.org/10.1177/1474022211427367.

concept according to the three aforementioned dimensions. Based on the work of the sociologists Harry Collins, Robert Evans and Michael Gorman, trading zones are conceptualised according to the first two dimensions of changing practices and power relations. The dimension of changing practices describes the extent to which practices in a trading zone remain heterogeneous, conducted by two distinct communities, or homogeneous, conducted by a unified community without distinction. The dimension of power relations describes who is in control of practices in trading zones, where I build upon the work of the philosopher Michel Foucault. I extend this two-dimensional model of trading zones with the framework of communities of practice by the educational theorist Étienne Wenger to better describe how the communities in trading zones engage with one another. Following the elaboration of the theoretical model, I discuss how the concept of trading zones has been applied in digital humanities literature thus far, noting that this literature has not sufficiently considered local variations in digital humanities practices. Finally, I elaborate how my method of research is based in ethnographic work as described by Clifford Geertz.

In Chapter 3, I explore the first dimension of engagement by analysing how historians in digital history collaborations engage with historical peers and cross-disciplinary collaborators. Such engagements include interdisciplinary boundary crossing, where historians cross disciplinary boundaries to engage with computational experts. Yet by doing so historians may develop new practices and vocabularies that hinder discussion with historical peers, leading to intradisciplinary boundary construction where historians become separated. Finally, I explore how digital history collaborations may cross institutional boundaries, through collaborations between different institutes, or construct such boundaries, through the institutionalisation of centres and labs. I elaborate such mechanisms of engagement by an analysis of ethnographic observations and interviews about digital history as conducted at the University of Luxembourg. This university established the Luxembourg Centre for Contemporary and Digital History (C^2DH) in 2016 and the Digital History Lab in 2015.

In Chapter 4, I explore the second dimension of power relations by analysing how participants in digital history collaborations coordinate tasks and goals. I describe four case studies of digital history collaborations of which I have interviewed multiple participants to gain differing perspectives of the goals of the collaborations. I analyse these interviews building upon the work of the information scientist Judith Weedman who described incentives for collaborating as related to 1) reasons for joining a project, 2) individual goals for a project, and 3) expected effects of participation after the project has ended. Through this analysis I identify six categories of incentives: 1) funding, 2) digital history/humanities, 3) data, 4) tool development, 5) historical research and 6) computational research.

In the second half of the chapter, I juxtapose these incentives to analyse how in-centives conflicted in collaborations and how such conflicts were resolved, leading to power asymmetries and detachment of individual practices from the collaboration.

In Chapter 5, I explore the final dimension of changing practices. In this concluding chapter I analyse the extent to which the historians in my studies adopted new practices that altered how they conducted historical research. By reviewing the findings of chapters 3 and 4 I show that the changes of practices are not uniform for all historians participating in digital history. Instead, the professors in history who led the institutional units (chapter 3) and collabora-tions (chapter 4) served as what I call digital history brokers who connect and translate between the historical and computational communities in digital his-tory trading zones. I argue that digital history brokers are essentially performing infrastructuring to resolve the tensions that arise when digital infrastructures are developed and negotiated between historians and computational experts. I conclude this chapter with a set of recommendations for future digital history collaborations.

Positioning Digital History

In studying practices and negotiations of digital history it is necessary to demar-cate which practices and negotiations count as examples of digital history. Digital history and digital humanities more broadly are underdefined, and volumes have been dedicated to questions of whether "digital humanities" refers to a discipline, field, or something else, who is part of it, and how it must further be defined.[20] The website https://whatisdigitalhumanities.com/ demonstrates this in an ironic fashion by providing a different definition from a scholar every time the visitor refreshes the page. The scholar of digital media Smiljana Antonijević tellingly groups her discussion of the terminology, boundary work and communities of digital humanities under the section *Controversies in Digital Humanities*.[21]

Rather than definitions of what should and should not count, the digital humanist Roopika Risam suggests "accents" to recognise and respect that prac-tices are localised, and may be different between geographical, linguistic, or

---

20 For example, see Melissa Terras, Julianne Nyhan and Edward Vanhoutte, eds., *Defining Digital Humanities* (Ashgate, 2013).
21 Smiljana Antonijević, *Amongst Digital Humanists: An Ethnographic Study of Digital Knowl-edge Production*, pre-print (Basingstoke New York, NY: Palgrave Macmillan, 2015), 16–29.

disciplinary communities.[22] Rather than a singular global model of digital humanities that highlights certain practices at the expense of others, digital humanities may be considered a global field of diverse, bordering areas where no area is central to all.[23] Since my study is empirically based within the context of the Netherlands, Belgium and Luxembourg, my accent of digital history emphasises practices present in this region and its geographical, linguistic or epistemic neighbours. Therefore, my positioning of digital history is not meant as a global definition, but as a characterisation of the practices that I investigate.[24]

To start from a broader view, I see digital history within the scope of digital humanities. This view is not uncontested. Some authors argue that the two have different topical emphases.[25] Furthermore, digital humanities is commonly traced to the Italian Jesuit priest Roberto Busa, while digital history is traced to quantitative history and public history.[26] Yet the terms overlap in several significant ways. Digital history is arguably one of the dominant strands within digital humanities and is strongly represented at digital humanities conferences.[27] Both furthermore

---

22 Roopika Risam, *New Digital Worlds: Postcolonial Digital Humanities in Theory, Praxis, and Pedagogy* (Northwestern University Press, 2018), https://doi.org/10.2307/j.ctv7tq4hg.

23 Amy E. Earhart, "Digital Humanities Within a Global Context: Creating Borderlands of Localized Expression," *Fudan Journal of the Humanities and Social Sciences* 11, no. 3 (2018): 357–69, https://doi.org/10.1007/s40647-018-0224-0.

24 Vered Amit, "Introduction," in *Constructing the Field: Ethnographic Fieldwork in the Contemporary World*, ed. Vered Amit (Routledge, 2000), 1–18.

25 Stephen Robertson, "The Differences between Digital History and Digital Humanities," in *Debates in the Digital Humanities* (University of Minnesota Press, 2016).

26 For origins of digital humanities, see Susan Hockey, "The History of Humanities Computing," in *A Companion to Digital Humanities*, ed. Susan Schreibman, Ray Siemens and John Unsworth, online (Blackwell, 2004), 3–19; Steven E. Jones, *Roberto Busa, S. J., and the Emergence of Humanities Computing: The Priest and the Punched Cards* (2018); for origins of digital history, see Edward L. Ayers, "The Pasts and Futures of Digital History," *History News* 56, no. 3 (2001): 5–9; Stephen Brier, "Confessions of a Premature Digital Humanist," *The Journal of Interactive Technology & Pedgagoy*, no. 11 (2017); Shawn Graham, Ian Milligan and Scott Weingart, *Exploring Big Historical Data: The Historian's Macroscope* (Imperial College Press, 2015); the historian Jane Winters, however, draws the origins of digital history to Busa, arguing that his work was "very clearly an exercise in historical research" Jane Winters, "Digital History," in *Debating New Approaches to History*, ed. Marek Tamm and Peter Burke (Bloomsbury Academic, 2018), 277.

27 A number of analyses of DH conferences show history as a strong strand within the field. Scott Weingart has analysed submissions to the ADHO DH conference in 2017, with historical studies as the fifth discipline "Submissions to DH2017 (Pt. 1)," *The Scottbot Irregular* (blog), November 10, 2016, http://scottbot.net/submissions-to-dh2017-pt-1/; Eetu Mäkelä and Mikko Tolonen analysed submissions to DHN2018, finding historical studies as the top discipline,

share important commonalities. Digital humanities and digital history emerge in the meeting between computational approaches to historical or humanistic subjects.[28] Both share dispositions towards texts.[29] Therefore, I regularly place digital history in the wider context of discussions about digital humanities, providing a much wider ground for what constitutes digital humanities and how it affects practices within the humanities.

In characterising digital history, several authors have argued that it involves approaching (preferably big) data with tools to create a narrative or other representation of the past.[30] It has furthermore been argued that digital history is also about the reflection on these practices and understanding how the digital changes the way historians work.[31] Finally, digital history has been said to be an interdisciplinary collaboration, not only using available datasets and tools but developing them.[32] This emphasis on development is resonated in debates about the digital humanities, with scholars emphasising practices such as modelling, building, or even creating infrastructures for large datasets.[33] What these authors share is that

"DHN2018 – an Analysis of a Digital Humanities Conference" (Proceedings of the Digital Humanities in the Nordic Countries 3rd Conference, CEUR-WS, 2018), 1–9; in my own analysis of DHBenelux 2019 submissions, I found "history" and "historical" to be among the top words in abstracts "DHBenelux 2019 Submissions," *Max Kemman* (blog), September 3, 2019, http://www.maxkemman.nl/2019/09/dhbenelux-2019-submissions/.

28 Edmond, "The Role of the Professional Intermediary in Expanding the Humanities Computing Base"; Svensson, "The Digital Humanities as a Humanities Project."

29 Antonijević, *Amongst Digital Humanists*; Erik M. Champion, "Digital Humanities Is Text Heavy, Visualization Light, and Simulation Poor," *Digital Scholarship in the Humanities* (2016), https://doi.org/10.1093/llc/fqw053; Kasper Risbjerg Eskildsen, "Leopold Ranke's Archival Turn: Location and Evidence in Modern Historiography," *Modern Intellectual History* 5, no. 3 (2008): 425–53, https://doi.org/10.1017/S1479244308001753.

30 Graham, Milligan and Weingart, *Exploring Big Historical Data: The Historian's Macroscope*; Jo Guldi and David Armitage, *The History Manifesto*, online (Cambridge: Cambridge University Press, 2014), https://doi.org/10.1017/9781139923880; Toni Weller, "Introduction: History in the Digital Age," in *History in the Digital Age*, ed. Toni Weller (Routledge, 2013), 1–20.

31 Zaagsma, "On Digital History."

32 Daniel J. Cohen et al., "Interchange: The Promise of Digital History," *The Journal of American History* 95, no. 2 (2008): 452–91; Andreas Fickers, "Towards A New Digital Historicism? Doing History In The Age Of Abundance," *VIEW Journal of European Television History and Culture* 1, no. 1 (2012): 19–26.

33 John Unsworth, "What Is Humanities Computing and What Is Not?," in *Defining Digital Humanities*, ed. Melissa Terras, Julianne Nyhan and Edward Vanhoutte, Digital Research in the Arts and Humanities (Routledge, 2002), 51–63; Stemphen Ramsay, "On Building," *Stephenramsay.Us* (blog), January 11, 2011, https://web.archive.org/web/20170704144620/http://stephenramsay.us:80/text/2011/01/11/on-building/; Richard Rogers, *Digital Methods* (MIT Press, 2013), 259.

simply using digital means in humanities scholarship by itself does not constitute digital humanities work.[34]

My focus is on the cross-disciplinary collaboration through which digital history development is performed. Yet, some scholars might argue that digital history is most interesting when conducted by individuals, when historians learn how to write software code themselves. Reflections on how understanding code shapes practices exist as well for the digital humanities more broadly.[35] Yet, here too, historians depend on utilising a language developed by computational experts. Furthermore, programming largely depends on importing packages developed by others and combining these in appropriate flows.[36] There is thus still an indirect interaction as historians import concepts and tools developed by computational experts. Since my interest is in how the import of methods and practices affects historians, an individual view of digital history makes these methodological and epistemological tensions internal. It is not a coincidence that essays that consider how historians are affected as users of technology have taken the form of reflective pieces of internal tensions.[37] By studying collaborations instead, I aim to make these tensions, the uncertainty of digital history and the process of negotiation explicit and observable.

But what is it that is being developed in these digital history collaborations? I argue that this can be characterised as the development of infrastructures, where the goal is that the product of the collaboration may underlie historical research, during the project or in the future. This future historical research then need not be conducted through cross-disciplinary collaborations, nor does it demand advanced technical proficiency. I understand these infrastructures as the constellation of technologies and practices required to access, collect and analyse sources for historical research. Now that more and more aspects of historical scholarship are becoming digital, the need for digital infrastructures that

---

34 Antonijević, *Amongst Digital Humanists*; Anne Burdick et al., *Digital_Humanities* (MIT Press, 2012).

35 Joris van Zundert and Ronald Haentjens Dekker, "Code, Scholarship, and Criticism: When Is Code Scholarship and When Is It Not?," *Digital Scholarship in the Humanities* 32, no. suppl_1 (2017): i121–33, https://doi.org/10.1093/llc/fqx006.

36 Églantine Schmitt, "Des Humains Dans La Machine: La Conception d'un Algorithme de Classification Sémantique Au Prisme Du Concept d'objectivité," *Sciences Du Design* 2, no. 4 (2016): 83–97.

37 Lara Putnam, "The Transnational and the Text-Searchable: Digitized Sources and the Shadows They Cast," *The American Historical Review* 121, no. 2 (2016): 377–402, https://doi.org/10.1093/ahr/121.2.377; Julia Laite, "The Emmet's Inch: Small History in a Digital Age," *Journal of Social History* (2019), https://doi.org/10.1093/jsh/shy118.

facilitate the scholarly cycle becomes increasingly urgent.[38] The development of digital infrastructures depends on collection experts, computational linguists and computational researchers to collaborate on physical technology, digital technology and user interfaces. Historians have started to become aware of this, with some historians criticising their profession for their silence on the impact of digitisation.[39] Others furthermore called for historians to become actively involved:

> It was previously enough to take a thing – a printed volume, or an archival box – and place it upon a scholar's desk; there was no need to know what was being done with it in order to deliver it correctly. Now, as material is delivered digitally, every design decision taken when building new user interfaces allows some kinds of use but may exclude others. [. . .] This is then a call to historians to be there at the beginning of that process, to help design those systems to meet our needs.[40]

As a result, the hidden infrastructures underlying historical practices have become visible. The historians I study in this book have joined collaborations to shape the infrastructures to their disciplinary needs, so that other historians may benefit from the new technological means without the requirement of learning how to code or collaborate with computational experts themselves. My study of how digital history affects historical practices thereby follows the approaches developed in the field of social construction of technology:

> Technology is not an independent, non-social variable that has an 'impact' on society or culture. On the contrary, any technology is a set of social behaviours and a system of meanings. To restate the point: when we examine the 'impact' of technology on society, we are talking about the impact of one kind of social behaviour on another.[41]

The "impact of one kind of social behaviour on another" in my case is the impact of collaborative negotiations of digital history on practices of the wider history discipline.

In short, I position digital history in the negotiations and practices between historians and computational experts in the development of digital infrastructures to the benefit of historical research more broadly. Yet infrastructures are

---

38 Jennifer Edmond et al., "Springing the Floor for a Different Kind of Dance – Building DARIAH as a Twenty-First-Century Research Infrastructure for the Arts and Humanities," in *Digital Technology and the Practices of Humanities Research*, ed. Jennifer Edmond (Open Book Publishers, 2020), 207–34, https://doi.org/10.11647/obp.0192.09.
39 Fickers, "Veins Filled with the Diluted Sap of Rationality: A Critical Reply to Rens Bod."
40 Peter Webster, "Digital Contemporary History: Sources, Tools, Methods, Issues," *Temp: Tidsskrift for Historie* 14 (2017): 37.
41 Bryan Pfaffenberger, "Fetishised Objects and Humanised Nature: Towards an Anthropology of Technology," *Man* 23, no. 2 (1988): 42, https://doi.org/10.2307/2802804.

not a new phenomenon to historical scholarship. In the next section I therefore position digital history in historiography, by tracing its roots in developments in historical research and its infrastructures of archives and libraries.

Origins of Digital History

As I argue above, historians have been called to use computers since the 1940s. This raises the question of what makes digital history different from earlier periods. In order to understand the current state of digital history, it is useful to consider the debates that led to what is now called digital history. These debates surround how to search, collect and analyse source material, especially when confronted with overabundant source material.[42] To provide insights into the shifting practices and arguments, I start from the 1940s, the period in which modern computers and practices of computing were invented. From there on, I consider several developments in the history of history as a profession, and its relationship with closely related professions. History as a community of historians with shared practices and concepts cannot be described without considering the archives and libraries that are central to historical research. As such, this history considers the "inside", the history of the historical discipline, as well as the "outside", the history of developments in work practices and infrastructures in general over many fields.[43] I thus synthesise the "inside" historiography of historical practices, with the "outside" developments of archives, libraries and information technology as infrastructural to historical practices.

The historian Ernst Breisach distinguishes between two forms of historiography.[44] The first approach is to provide an overview of perspectives and debates, without assuming historiography has a certain direction or that historical research improves over time. The second approach, in contrast, is to discuss historiography as the development of history as a science, giving preference to historians who aided that development, while neglecting arguments that did not endure. I take

---

42 E.g., Fickers, "Towards A New Digital Historicism? Doing History In The Age Of Abundance"; Ian Milligan, *History in the Age of Abundance?: How the Web Is Transforming Historical Research* (2019); Roy Rosenzweig, "Scarcity or Abundance? Preserving the Past in a Digital Era," *The American Historical Review* 108, no. 3 (2003): 735–62, https://doi.org/10.1086/529596.

43 Geoffrey C. Bowker, "The History of Information Infrastructures: The Case of the International Classification of Diseases," *Information Processing and Management* 32, no. 1 (1996): 49–61, https://doi.org/10.1016/0306-4573(95)00049-M.

44 Ernst Breisach, *Historiography: Ancient, Medieval & Modern*, 2nd ed. (Chicago: University of Chicago Press, 1994), 3–4.

the latter approach, focusing on the development of the boundaries and boundary practices of history as a community of practice. For ease of reading, I thereby describe a more or less linear path of developments leading towards the current state of digital history.

Continuing the view of disciplines as communities sharing practices and concepts, I describe the historiographical developments as boundary work.[45] That is, there is a continuous debate about what it means to be an academic historian, what a good historical analysis is and what the role of sources must be in historical research. Historians thus draw boundaries within which a historian must operate to remain recognisable as a historian. To fall outside of that boundary would mean their work is no longer recognised as historical scholarship. Such boundary work is similarly prevalent in the archival and library professions, as I show. Yet in order to develop this boundary work, the three communities simultaneously cross boundaries in their interdependency on one another. I, therefore, show how archives and libraries are infrastructural to historical scholarship.

1940s–1970s: Expansion & Automation

As noted in the introduction, perhaps the first historian who argued historians should use computers for scholarship was Murray Lawson, who presented his paper at the annual meeting of the American Historical Association in 1946.[46] In this paper, he described how a combination of punched cards and microfilm would enable historians to counter the abundance of source material. His vision of historical research using machines was based on the earlier writing of the engineering scientist Vannevar Bush who published his famous *As We May Think* in 1945, in which he proposed a hypothetical *memex* device which combined microfilms and punched cards to store literature and provide quick access to the individual scientist faced with an abundance of publications.[47] In a similar problem statement, the librarian Fremont Rider (1885–1962), a student of Melvil Dewey, published *The Scholar and the Future of the Research Library, a Problem and Its Solution* in 1944.[48] In this book, Rider extrapolated the growth of libraries

---

45 Thomas F. Gieryn, "Boundary-Work and the Demarcation of Science from Non-Science: Strains and Interests in Professional Ideologies of Scientists," *American Sociological Review* 48, no. 6 (1983): 781–95, https://doi.org/10.2307/2095325.

46 Lawson, "The Machine Age in Historical Research."

47 Vannevar Bush, "As We May Think," *The Atlantic Monthly* 176, no. 1 (1945): 101–8.

48 Fremont Rider, *The Scholar and the Future of the Research Library, a Problem and Its Solution* (N.Y.: Hadham Press, 1944).

to predict unmanageable amounts requiring vast library storage space.[49] Moreover, the Library of Congress provided the catalogue information for other libraries by selling catalogue cards, yet was itself falling behind in its efforts so that catalogue cards were created with a delay, or not at all.[50]

While concerns of abundant collections were not new to their field, archivists of the 1940s too deemed existing approaches no longer sufficient.[51] The archivist and scholar of archival theory Terry Cook described the development at the US National Archives as follows:

> When the National Archives in Washington was created in 1934, it inherited an awesome backlog of about one million metres of federal records, with a growth rate of more than sixty thousand metres annually. By 1943, under the expansion of the state to cope with the Great Depression and World War II, that growth rate had reached six hundred thousand metres annually.[52]

In short, the US National Archives saw the number of new to be added records rise by tenfold within a decade. Librarians and archivists developed diverging ideas about how to confront these problems. Some archivists rejected the increasingly impractical ideas of the archivist Hilary Jenkinson, who had argued in 1922 that archivists must not perform any interpretation, but keep all records produced by archived administrations, so that the archive would remain as objective evidence.[53] The archivist Margaret Cross Norton, who co-founded the Society of American Archivists in 1936, stated that "it is obviously no longer possible for any agency to preserve all records which result from its activities. The emphasis of archives work has shifted from preservation of records to selection of records for preservation".[54]

Archivists increasingly needed to select what should be archived, and what should otherwise be discarded. The appraisal of documents, earlier rejected by Jenkinson on the grounds of it being a subjective exercise tainting the objectivity of the archive, was inevitable, but needed to be systematised so as to retain a

---

49 Rolland E. Stevens, "The Microform Revolution," *Library Trends* 19, no. 3 (1971): 379–95.

50 Barbara B. Tillett, "Catalog It Once for All: A History of Cooperative Cataloging in the United States Prior to 1967 (Before MARC)," *Cataloging & Classification Quarterly* 17, no. 3–4 (1994): 3–38, https://doi.org/10.1300/J104v17n03_02.

51 Cf. Ann Blair, *Too Much to Know: Managing Scholarly Information before the Modern Age* (New Haven, Conn: Yale University Press, 2010).

52 Terry Cook, "What Is Past Is Prologue: A History of Archival Ideas Since 1898, and the Future Paradigm Shift," *Archivaria*, no. 43 (1997): 26.

53 Hilary Jenkinson, *A Manual of Archive Administration Including the Problems of War Archive Making* (The Clarendon Press, 1922); Cook, "What Is Past Is Prologue."

54 Quoted in Cook, "What Is Past Is Prologue," 26.

professional status. The archivist Theodore Schellenberg synthesised the rules for appraisal, and thus became "the father of appraisal theory in the United States".[55] In 1956 Schellenberg published *Modern Archives: Principles and Techniques*, in which he argued documents had primary and secondary values.[56] The primary value referred to the value for the original creator of a document. The secondary value referred to the unforeseen use in the future by others, due to evidential or informational values. Evidential value is the historical value for researchers, as a trace of the functioning of the organisation in which the document was created. Informational value is the research value of the contents of a document as traces of the societal context in which the document was created. Of interest to note here is the close relationship between Schellenberg's principles of appraisal, and the historical profession:

> Since Schellenberg's generation also coincided in its upbringing with the widespread professionalization of academic history in the universities, it is also not surprising to find in his work the close identification of archivists with historians, and archival "informational value" with historical themes and interpretations.[57]

Future use by historians consequently became a central criterion for the selection of documents for American archivists. After Schellenberg there was thus arguably a true mutual dependency between historians and archivists; where historians had been dependent on archivists since the historian Leopold von Ranke had emphasised the systematic study of archival sources, archivists were now becoming dependent on historians to determine what should be archived in the first place.[58] However, this "use-based approach" to appraisal was also criticised for being non-transparent, as well as for introducing a theory of appraisal dependent on contexts unrelated to the creation and use of the original document.[59] Although appraisal would thus become a core practice for archivists, how to appraise documents remained a matter of debate.

Librarians in contrast did not debate the extent to which documents could be selected or discarded. With respect to the problem of cataloguing running

---

55 F. Gerald Ham, *Selecting and Appraising Archives and Manuscripts* (The Society of American Archivists, 1993), 7.
56 Theodore R. Schellenberg, *Modern Archives. Principles and Techniques* (F.W. Cheshire, 1956).
57 Cook, "What Is Past Is Prologue," 29.
58 Rens Bod, *De Vergeten Wetenschappen: Een Geschiedenis van de Humaniora* (Prometheus, 2010); Georg G. Iggers, "The Crisis of the Rankean Paradigm in the Nineteenth Century," *Syracuse Scholar (1979–1991)* 9, no. 1 (1988); Georg G. Iggers, "The Professionalization of Historical Studies and the Guiding Assumptions of Modern Historical Thought," *A Companion to Western Historical Thought*, 2007, 225–42, https://doi.org/10.1002/9780470998748.ch12.
59 Cook, "What Is Past Is Prologue."

behind the addition of books, rules for standardisation were suggested in 1940 by the Library of Congress (LoC) with the aim of simplifying the process. On the one hand, librarians needed to develop social practices to create trust in the co-operation between LoC and other libraries:

> As for accepting the work of others, [Andrew Osborn] noted catalogers cannot even accept uncritically the cataloging from the Library of Congress, but must add, subtract, and modify the records, until they might as well have cataloged it themselves. He said not just large libraries, but also small libraries did this.[60]

On the other hand, librarians relied on technological solutions to combat the growth of the collection. Two technologies are of interest in this history; microphotography and punched cards.

In the 1940s, microphotography was hardly an innovative technology, having been invented in 1839 by John Dancer. Yet, at that time there was no clear use case for microphotographs. It took until the 1920s before microfilms, the most commonly used format of microphotography, became prevalent, and until the 1930s before it was used seriously by historians and librarians.[61] From 1935–1942 American historians participated in the *Historical Records Survey*, a New Deal program in which historians surveyed records in archives and libraries of historical value. While inventorying, historians were asked to microfilm these records. The main goals for microfilm were preservation of fragile material, as well as to provide wider access, as microfilms could be copied and distributed more widely than the original documents. Yet these two goals ultimately failed within the programme, as microfilms were of poor quality, unreadable and the microfilms themselves ended up being as inaccessible as the original records.[62] However, as an experimental trial, it was successful in innovating the methods of microfilming, as well as in proving the utility of the technology.

Librarians were soon convinced of the wonderful promises of microfilm, with some hailing it as the most important innovation since Gutenberg's printing press. Microfilms were discussed to such an extent that it seemed almost an end in itself.[63] Several reasons drove the enthusiasm for microfilming, notably access (to obtain rare books), preservation (to replace items on deteriorating paper), usability (to replace large volumes such as newspaper volumes that were difficult to handle) and

---

60 Tillett, "Catalog It Once for All," 29.

61 Stevens, "The Microform Revolution."

62 Clifton D. Foster, "Microfilming Activities of the Historical Records Survey, 1935–42," *The American Archivist* 48, no. 1 (1985): 45–55.

63 Susan A. Cady, "The Electronic Revolution in Libraries: Microfilm Déjà Vu?," *College & Research Libraries* 51, no. 4 (1990): 374–86.

saving space (to replace print material with much smaller microforms).[64] However, despite the warnings of Fremont Rider about unmanageable collections, librarians did not initially deem saving space a primary reason for microfilming. When they did so, it was mainly done for large bound volumes such as newspapers. Many libraries held newspapers, creating a large market for microfilms. Books in contrast only rarely ended up being microfilmed.[65] Instead, preservation and access were the main reasons for microfilming. Yet, not everyone was as enthusiastic about microfilm. Readers found it difficult to use the microfilms, as documents were put on microfilm at a higher pace than the development of usable microfilm readers. Cost-savings were a reason for microfilming, and the quality of the images was not always considered as much as should have been.[66] Microfilm then failed to fulfil the promise of greater usability. The enthusiasm of librarians for microfilm was consequently not shared by scholars and historians. Once beyond the peak of the technology's hype in the 1970s, the primary purpose moved from preservation and access to saving storage space, but with less excitement than during the hype of the 1940s–50s.[67] Microfilm thus did not end up transforming the library. The technology's potential advantages did not convince the community to accept the disadvantages.

It could, however, be argued that microfilm did end up transforming archives. Although seemingly not as heavily debated in literature, microfilm introduced a significant possibility for archives. Many of the collections in archives are unique to that archive, contrary to most library collections. Historians need to visit a specific archive to read a unique document. With microfilm, archives could duplicate parts of their collections and make these available in archives elsewhere, even on other continents. The access that microfilm could provide to source material located elsewhere was a significant transformation of infrastructure. Historians gladly accepted a cumbersome microfilm reader if this allowed them to find a piece of information they could not have consulted otherwise. Overall, it is of interest that with microfilm, the first attempts at transforming the collections of infrastructures are seen; first for reasons of access and preservation, and later for financial reasons of cheap material and saving storage space. This process would later be repeated with the digitisation of collections.

---

64 Stevens, "The Microform Revolution."
65 Stevens.
66 Cady draws a parallel between the advantages and disadvantages of microfilms and of modern-day digital texts, in saving space but introducing issues of readability: "The Electronic Revolution in Libraries."
67 Cady.

The other technology of interest to librarians was punched cards. This, too, was hardly an innovative technology, invented in 1887 and first used on a large scale for computing the results of the 1890 US Census.[68] This census was one of the early situations in which there was too much data to handle, requiring technological innovations, and as such punched cards became the "big data" technology of the late nineteenth and early twentieth century. Yet, it took several decades before scientists and librarians became invested in the technology. Librarians started experimenting with punched cards in the 1930s, but throughout the 1940s were more excited about microfilm instead. However, in the 1940s, scientists became increasingly interested in punched cards for the use of information processing and retrieval.[69] It nonetheless took until the 1960s before punched cards became systematically used in libraries. With the advent of computer systems, libraries became increasingly invested in using these systems, with punched cards as the input mechanism for entering data. At first, automation of library systems focused on library circulation and keeping track of inventories, but later on libraries turned to computer systems for the creation and maintenance of catalogues. Libraries had already grown accustomed to using catalogue cards to describe and maintain their collections.[70] Therefore, it was a small step to recreate these cards as punched cards.

In 1965, the Library of Congress started investigating the use of computer systems for library processes, leading to the MARC (Machine-Readable Cataloging) format in 1968, then named MARC II.[71] It took another decade for the MARC format to be fully recognised by libraries, but then became such an important standard that machine-readable formats, in contrast with microfilms, arguably did transform libraries, laying the groundwork for later digitisation projects. Punched cards were not an end in itself the way microfilm was perceived to be, but was a necessary medium in the first steps to moving library catalogues to computer systems. The librarian Sally McCallum concluded there were three reasons why MARC became a central piece of libraries.[72] First, it was innovative. Second, it was developed collaboratively, by engineers with participation of librarians. And third, the

---

68 Robert V. Williams, "The Use of Punched Cards in US Libraries and Documentation Centers, 1936–1965," *IEEE Annals of the History of Computing* 24, no. 2 (2002): 16–33, https://doi.org/10.1109/MAHC.2002.1010067.
69 Williams.
70 Markus Krajewski, *Paper Machines: About Cards & Catalogs, 1548–1929*, trans. Peter Krapp (MIT Press, 2011), https://doi.org/10.7551/mitpress/9780262015899.001.0001; Tillett, "Catalog It Once for All."
71 Sally H. McCallum, "MARC: Keystone for Library Automation," *IEEE Annals of the History of Computing* 24, no. 2 (2002): 34–49, https://doi.org/10.1109/MAHC.2002.1010068.
72 McCallum.

Library of Congress, which already was a central institute in the creation and distribution of catalogue cards in the USA, adopted the format immediately for its catalogues, so that other libraries could benefit from this.

During the 1960s, historians became invested in computer systems as well. In this decade, universities established computer centres featuring a mainframe computer, which required punched cards for both input and output. Despite historians being called conservative by Lawson, there are several examples of historians who quickly adopted mainframes for research. For example, the historian Tito Orlandi already experimented with punched cards for the creation of a critical edition during his doctoral research in 1960.[73] More generally for the humanities, this is the period where the founding of "humanities computing", a forerunner of digital humanities, is traced back to. While the founding myth of digital humanities starts in 1949 when the Jesuit priest Father Roberto Busa approached IBM with the request to collaborate on an automated concordance of the works of St. Thomas Aquinas on punched cards, it took until the 1960s before humanities computing became more established.[74] In 1963 the University of Cambridge founded the Centre for Literary and Linguistic Computing, in 1966 the University of Tübingen appointed a research officer for computer applications in the humanities and in that same year the journal *Computers and the Humanities* was founded.[75]

Historians in this period engaged with university computer centres, but not under the flag of humanities computing. After 1945, historians became more involved with the social sciences for the adoption of theoretical theories as well as methods. In Europe, and especially France, this happened mainly within the Annales school, while in the USA this happened under the flag of quantitative history, also known as cliometrics. This latter movement became more fully established in the 1960s, with the founding of journals such as *Historical Methods* and the *Journal of Social History* in 1967, the *Journal of Interdisciplinary History*

---

73 Julianne Nyhan and Andrew Flinn, "Hic Rhodus, Hic Salta: Tito Orlandi and Julianne Nyhan," in *Computation and the Humanities*, Springer Series on Cultural Computing (Cham: Springer International Publishing, 2016), 75–86, https://doi.org/10.1007/978-3-319-20170-2.

74 Hockey, "The History of Humanities Computing"; Jones, *Roberto Busa, S. J., and the Emergence of Humanities Computing*; this founding myth of digital humanities is increasingly debated and contested, c.f. Rachel Sagner Buurma and Laura Heffernan, "Search and Replace: Josephine Miles and the Origins of Distant Reading," *Modernism/Modernity* 3, no. 1 (2018).

75 Hockey, "The History of Humanities Computing"; Julianne Nyhan and Andrew Flinn, "The University Was Still Taking Account of Universitas Scientiarum: Wilhelm Ott and Julianne Nyhan," in *Computation and the Humanities*, Springer Series on Cultural Computing (Cham: Springer International Publishing, 2016), 55–73, https://doi.org/10.1007/978-3-319-20170-2.

in 1970, and *Social Science History* in 1976.[76] In 1967, a conference was held in the USA to discuss the then current state of quantitative history with three aims: 1) to present notable findings of earlier scholars, 2) to survey material that could be used for quantitative research, and 3) to raise hopes for the future.[77] Participants succeeded largely in the final part, with the (in)famous conclusion from the historian Emmanuel Le Roy Ladurie that "the historian will be a programmer or he will be nothing" in 1968.[78] The historian Theodore Rabb enthusiastically wrote that "[n]ot since the days of Leopold von Ranke and his followers has there been such joy and excitement about the discovery or the inventive new use of documentary evidence".[79]

Although this may in hindsight have been an exaggeration, it is fair to say quantitative history was a step further in the professionalisation of the field started by Von Ranke. It brought attention to the accumulation of datasets, making history a more cumulative science. Due to the emphasis on methods of statistics, analysis arguably became more transparent and open to debate.[80] One of the most prominent works in the field is *Time on the Cross* by the economic historians Robert Fogel and Stanley Engerman, published in 1974.[81] Fogel and Engerman studied the economics of slavery in southern states in the USA and tested the then commonly agreed belief that slavery was economically inefficient. After investigating economic and social factors, they concluded that slavery was economically viable and states with slavery were actually more efficient than states without. Its reception was generally positive at first, but their study was later denounced for containing too many errors to support the conclusions and questions were raised about whether a numerical view of a moral issue such as slavery was valid.[82] Yet the explicit methods, datasets and statistics allowed for a scholarly debate to emerge that would have been difficult otherwise.

---

76 John F. Reynolds, "Do Historians Count Anymore?: The Status of Quantitative Methods in History, 1975–1995," *Historical Methods: A Journal of Quantitative and Interdisciplinary History* 31, no. 4 (1998): 141–48, https://doi.org/10.1080/01615449809601196.

77 Theodore K. Rabb, "The Development of Quantification in Historical Research," *Journal of Interdisciplinary History* 13, no. 4 (1983): 591–601.

78 Quoted in Stone, "The Revival of Narrative," 13.

79 Rabb, "The Development of Quantification in Historical Research," 596.

80 Morgan Kousser, "Quantitative Social-Scientific History," in *The Past before Us: Contemporary Historical Writing in the United States*, ed. M. Kammen (Cornell University Press, 1980).

81 Robert W. Fogel and Stanley L. Engerman, *Time on the Cross: The Economics of American Negro Slavery* (1974; repr., New York; London: W.W. Norton, 1995).

82 Michiel Leezenberg and Gerard de Vries, *Wetenschapsfilosofie Voor Geesteswetenschappen*, 5th ed. (Amsterdam University Press, 2001).

This transparency was, however, simultaneously one of the weaknesses of the field. It opened studies to criticism, leading to more rejections from reviewers and thus fewer successful publications.[83] Another problem was that quantitative history did not always fit within the boundary work of historians, argued to consist of:

> [A] concern for the understanding and explanation of situations, processes, or events, *more than* for the theoretical means by which such understand and explanation are reached [. . .]; a willingness to relate one's findings to the classic questions of history [. . .]; an emphasis on temporal causation.[84]

Quantitative history arguably strayed too far from these characteristics. It consequently did not maintain momentum after the mid 1980s.[85] Quantitative history separated from the dominant branch of the historical community, yet it did not disappear.[86] In contrast, with the advent of computers and online sources, as I detail in the next section, in recent years quantification has steadily increased not as a goal in itself but as a part of historical analysis.[87]

Instead, the narrative method was revived, starting in the 1950s among a small group of historians, gaining prominence in the 1970s and arguably becoming the dominant form of history from the 1990s onward. In this revival, the methods of sociology and economics were replaced with methods of anthropology, with which historians would study the culture of a time. This movement is consequently regularly referred to as the cultural turn. Historians shifted their efforts to the analysis of power relations, mentalities and presenting these results in narrative form. The movement furthermore included the investigation of the meaning of words and ideas in their historical context, and as such led to the so-called linguistic turn.[88] According to the historian Lawrence Stone, the revival of narrative marked the end of the attempts to "produce a coherent

---

83 Reynolds, "Do Historians Count Anymore?"
84 Rabb, "The Development of Quantification in Historical Research," 598, emphasis in original.
85 Reynolds, "Do Historians Count Anymore?"
86 Robert Whaples, "Is Economic History a Neglected Field of Study?," *Historically Speaking* 11, no. 2 (2010): 17–20, https://doi.org/10.1353/hsp.0.0109.
87 Pat Hudson and Mina Ishizu, *History by Numbers: An Introduction to Quantitative Approaches*, Second edition (Bloomsbury Academic, 2017); Steven Ruggles, "The Revival of Quantification: Reflections on Old New Histories," *Social Science History* 45, no. 1 (2021): 1–25, https://doi.org/10.1017/ssh.2020.44.
88 James Vernon, "Who's Afraid of the 'Linguistic Turn'? The Politics of Social History and Its Discontents," *Social History* 19, no. 1 (1994): 81–97, https://doi.org/10.1007/s13398-014-0173-7.2.

scientific explanation of change in the past".[89] History instead gained a renewed attention toward the role of interpretation in historical research, and thus reinforced hermeneutics as the core method.[90]

The perceived downfall of quantitative history leads to an interesting problem of self-identification for digital history as a profession. Within the digital humanities, some historians argue that digital history has a long tradition parallel to the literary-oriented digital humanities, starting with social and quantitative history, as well as public history, in the 1970s.[91] In contrast, outside of the digital humanities, historians emphasise that digital history is not a continuation of quantitative history, but actually embedded in the cultural turn.[92]

Notable with the cultural turn is the attention towards the general people, and the required new sources to investigate these people (reasons 1 and 3 above). This signifies another step in the shifting attention from elites to the general population, which had arguably started with the economic theories of Karl Marx and was refined with quantitative history with social and economic models and sources, and thus continued as part of the narrative method with anthropological interpretation of sources.[93]

This shift in attention by historians coincided with a shift in the archival profession, where from the 1960s onward archivists too became more concerned with records of the general population.[94] This meant that not only the traditional records from governments or institutions should be considered. Already in 1944, one of the Annales' most prominent historians, the historian Marc Bloch, contended that in the pursuit of a historical account of a society, all types of sources are relevant for study.[95] However, this exponentially enlarged the problem of archival overload. Not only had the amount of traditional archival documents increased, now too the number of institutions, organisations, or

---

89 Stone, "The Revival of Narrative," 19.

90 Hans-Georg Gadamer, *Truth and Method* (1960; repr., Bloomsbury Academic, 2014); Hayden White, "The Question of Narrative in Contemporary Historical Theory," *History and Theory* 23, no. 1 (1984): 1–33, https://doi.org/10.2307/2504969.

91 Brier, "Confessions of a Premature Digital Humanist."

92 Ayers, "The Pasts and Futures of Digital History."

93 Bod, *De Vergeten Wetenschappen*; Lynn Hunt, "French History in the Last Twenty Years: The Rise and Fall of the Annales Paradigm," *Journal of Contemporary History* 21, no. 2 (1986): 209–24, https://doi.org/10.1177/002200948602100205; Leezenberg and de Vries, *Wetenschapsfilosofie Voor Geesteswetenschappen*.

94 Patrick M. Quinn, "Archivists and Historians: The Times They Are a-Changin'," *The Midwestern Archivist* 2, no. 2 (1977): 5–13.

95 Marc Bloch, *The Historian's Craft*, trans. Peter Putnam, Repr (Manchester: Manchester Univ. Press, 2004).

individuals from which to select documents increased. This required new methods of appraisal, and from the 1980s on several theorists argued for a "societal approach" of appraisal to replace the "use-based approach". Where the latter meant archivists selected records that ought to be of importance for future historical research, the "societal approach" meant archivists should select records that best reflect the society in which they were created.[96] In the terminology of Schellenberg, this meant archives shifted emphasis from sial value, the historical value to researchers, to informational value, the research value to investigate the societal context. The scope of expertise required by archivists thus broadened even further. Not only would an archivist need to know about archival practices, but they also needed to understand historical practices to know how to provide records of importance to historical research, and now they required knowledge of sociological practices to reflect society in their archives. Furthermore, from the 1980s onward, they would have to learn new skills related to information technology.

1980s–2010s: Digitalisation

Although computers had been under development for several decades, the 1970s saw the first examples of personal computers. These were aimed at hobbyists, as they required assemblage by the owner, but in the 1980s the computer industry was transformed by computers from IBM and Apple that worked out of the box.[97] Many scholars soon had a computer standing on their desk and learned how to use this device. Scholars who previously wrote their articles and books by hand or with typing machines moved to word processing software.[98] Research too increasingly required a computer, as archives and libraries started moving their collections to digital formats.

Libraries had prepared for this "digital revolution". The aforementioned MARC standard meant libraries already had much of their catalogue available in machine-readable form. A major actor in moving libraries into the digital period was the American Ohio College Library Center, founded in 1967, which was later renamed the Online Computer Library Center as it broadened its services outside of Ohio College, and is nowadays more commonly known simply as the OCLC. In the 1980s and 1990s, libraries started digitising their collections and

---

96 Cook, "What Is Past Is Prologue."

97 Walter Isaacson, *The Innovators: How a Group of Hackers, Geniuses and Geeks Created the Digital Revolution* (Simon & Schuster, 2014).

98 Matthew Kirschenbaum, *Track Changes: A Literary History of Word Processing* (Harvard University Press, 2016).

publishing these in "digital libraries" with the aim of providing access.[99] By the 1990s, most libraries had moved from card catalogues to digital systems for item retrieval in the form of OPACs (Online Public Access Catalogues). While the card catalogue was maintained for existing items, new items would only be added to the OPAC.[100] In 1998, OCLC launched WorldCat, an online catalogue where anyone can find items in any library connected to the WorldCat system.[101] Digitisation of library collections thereby followed similar arguments as those around microfilms, as I discuss above. At first, catalogues and documents were digitised to provide access. In libraries with fragile materials digitisation occurred for preservation. Other libraries, such as the digital research library JSTOR, which was established in 1995, digitised with the aim of saving storage space; if libraries could provide access to a digital copy of a journal, they would be able to discard the physical copy.[102]

Archivists saw a rougher transition to the new medium. At first, some wondered anxiously whether archivists would be replaced by computer specialists or information managers.[103] Early digital archives emphasised what was digitally available and could be put into the databases of the time. This mainly concerned statistical data, coinciding with the developments toward quantitative history. Yet in the mid-1980s this changed, as relational databases became available that were more compatible with existing non-digital archival practices. As archivists became more involved with the digital medium, these digital archives were also organised increasingly according to the rules of the profession. The earlier so-called "library-oriented, discrete-item approach" came under discussion from archivists that demanded more context and provenance to be embedded in the systems.[104] In other words, although at first some form of technological determinism provided the conditions within which archival material could be digitally stored, later on the boundary work of archivists became more active to structure digital archives according to the norms of the profession. A remaining challenge for archivists is to

---

99 Christine L. Borgman, "What Are Digital Libraries? Competing Visions," *Information Processing and Management* 35, no. 3 (1999): 227–43, https://doi.org/10.1016/S0306-4573(98)00059-4; Marilyn Deegan and Kathryn Sutherland, *Transferred Illusions: Digital Technology and the Forms of Print* (Ashgate, 2009).

100 Deegan and Sutherland, *Transferred Illusions*.

101 "WorldCat", accessed May 12, 2021, https://www.worldcat.org/.

102 Deegan and Sutherland, *Transferred Illusions*.

103 Cook, "What Is Past Is Prologue."

104 Terry Cook, "Easy To Byte, Harder To Chew: The Second Generation of Electronic Records Archives," *Archivaria* 33 (1991): 206.

develop practices for the digital society, i.e. to create infrastructures for archiving born-digital material such as websites or social media.[105]

Relational databases also enabled historians to employ qualitative research digitally. In 1980, the historian Manfred Thaller released the relational database management system CLIO.[106] This software has been argued to have initiated "history and computing" as a precursor to digital history, as it was the first database system specifically designed for historical sources and research.[107] The 1980s subsequently saw the establishment of the *Association for History and Computing* in 1983, of the *Nederlands Historisch Data Archief* (Dutch Historical Data Archive) in the Netherlands in 1988, and the initiation of the *Vereniging voor Geschiedenis en Informatica* (Association for History and Informatics) between Belgium and the Netherlands in 1987.[108] Yet, while several history programmes started including computation in their curricula, history and computing remained a small community. Practices hardly diffused to the wider discipline, despite the activities within a group of enthusiasts.[109]

In the wider digital humanities, similar groups of enthusiasts established research centres to allow sustainable interactions between computational experts and humanities scholars, supported by third-party funding.[110] From the mid-1980s onward, the Netherlands saw a field called *alfa-informatica* (alpha-informatics) enjoy a short peak, in which humanities students learned how to use computers and write code. However, alfa-informatics was deemed a mere support service for helping scholars use powerful but complex computers. With the advent of more usable software the field's potential to establish humanities computing widely in the Netherlands soon drifted away in budget cuts.[111] Rather

---

105 Kimberly Barata, "Archives in the Digital Age," *Journal of the Society of Archivists* 25, no. 1 (2004): 63–70, https://doi.org/10.1080/0037981042000199151; Christine L. Borgman, *Big Data, Little Data, No Data* (MIT Press, 2015); Niels Brügger and Niels Ole Finnemann, "The Web and Digital Humanities: Theoretical and Methodological Concerns," *Journal of Broadcasting & Electronic Media* 57, no. 1 (2013): 66–80, https://doi.org/10.1080/08838151.2012.761699; Milligan, *History in the Age of Abundance?*

106 Manfred Thaller, "Automation on Parnassus Clio – a Databank Oriented System for Historians," *Historical Social Research* 5, no. 3 (1980): 40–65.

107 Boonstra, Breure and Doorn, "Past, Present and Future of Historical Information Science."

108 Boonstra, Breure and Doorn.

109 Speck, "History and Computing."

110 Peter Robinson, "Digital Humanities: Is Bigger, Better?," in *Advancing Digital Humanities*, ed. Paul Longley Arthur and Katherine Bode (London: Palgrave Macmillan UK, 2014), 243–57, https://doi.org/10.1057/9781137337016_16.

111 Joris van Zundert and Karina van Dalen-Oskam, "Digital Humanities in the Netherlands," *H-Soz-Kult* (2014).

than historians developing software themselves for their specific purposes, they moved to generally available commercial software such as Microsoft Access. In contrast with Le Roy Ladurie's claim that historians would need to become programmers, thanks to database software, they only needed to learn to press the right buttons.[112] However, this move was not uncontested:

> [A] wonderful big lie, with respect to the complexities of database design. It was wonderful because of its user-friendly interface. It rapidly swept away its stubborn predecessors like dBASE and Paradox. If a historical dataset was not too complicated, database design and querying were easy. Finally, the computer seemed to have reached the stage of development of the modern car: the mechanic with his oilcan was no longer needed. Built-in 'wizards' compensated for lack of theoretical knowledge and querying a database could be as simple as searching for words in a text processor. One could even successfully complete certain tasks without knowing exactly what had happened.[113]

Besides a move away from custom humanities software to generic commercial software, Manfred Thaller noticed a wider move away from using the computer for historical research in the 1990s. He reflected on this, perhaps somewhat cynically, as follows in an interview:

> [T]he more serious disappointment, which I still think is something which has damaged parts of the Humanities, is that in the 1990s there was a move away from working with formalised results. And I have a strong suspicion that that simply relates to the fact that if you want to study a phenomenon formally – I do not say quantitatively because my own work had moved far away from quantification by the late 1980s – computers have the obnoxious habit of telling you time and time again that your data may contain errors, while what may actually be going on is that your data contains something that does not fit your hypothesis. So, it's a long and painstaking process. However, it is much, much faster, and much less frustrating to go into an archive and find a document with a human appeal and publish it and add a clever interpretation to it. Historical research has certainly fallen into what I consider a trap by getting away from doing the types of research that are harder to do.[114]

While his interpretation is debatable, it signifies that even while computers could do more than quantification, computational approaches were difficult to align with the cultural turn.

This coincides with to the so-called archival turn in the 1990s, in which historians and other scholars started to consider the archive not just as a provider

---

112 Speck, "History and Computing."
113 Boonstra, Breure and Doorn, "Past, Present and Future of Historical Information Science," 27.
114 Julianne Nyhan and Andrew Flinn, "It's Probably the Only Modestly Widely Used System with a Command Language in Latin: Manfred Thaller and Julianne Nyhan," in *Computation and the Humanities* (Springer International Publishing, 2016), 205, https://doi.org/10.1007/978-3-319-20170-2_13.

of research material, but as an object of study in itself.[115] The first step towards this archival turn among historians was taken by the philosopher Michel Foucault, who argued that archives should not only be considered as physical spaces containing documents. Instead, archives constitute structures of power that keep documents in a particular order, thereby structuring what can be said about the past.[116] The second step, which truly started this archival turn, was taken by the philosopher Jacques Derrida, who built upon the work by Foucault. He argued that archives are structures of power that determine what is preserved and what is destroyed, so that the past is not just preserved but constructed by archives.[117] On the one hand, these arguments led to an acknowledgement of archival work that was not prevalent before. Historians consequently became interested in studying the ethnography of archives, leading to critical, postcolonial and feminist perspectives on archives as political actors.[118] On the other hand, historians developed methods to counter the construction of the past by archives, by focusing on individuals that did not fit the general narrative of their time. In accordance with the quote from Manfred Thaller, this method has been described as follows:

> [To] search the archive for eccentric anecdotes and enigmatic fragments as the basis for constructing counterhistories that interrupt the homogenizing forces of previous grand historical narratives and archival order by grounding themselves in the contingent and "the real," all the while acknowledging that "the real" is never accessible as such.[119]

Newly developed narratives are thereby set in contrast with the narrative of the archive, while still requiring archival sources on which counternarratives are based.

Yet the historical archival turn has been criticised for not engaging with archivists. The work of archivists still remained invisible to many historians.[120]

---

115 Eric Ketelaar, "Prolegomena to a Social History of Dutch Archives," in *A Usable Collection: Essays in Honour of Jaap Kloosterman on Collecting Social History*, ed. Aad Blok, Jan Lucassen and Huub Sanders (Amsterdam University Press, 2014), 40–55.
116 Michel Foucault, *The Archaeology of Knowledge And the Discourse on Language*, trans. A.M. Sheridan Smith (Pantheon Books, 1972).
117 Jacques Derrida, "Archive Fever: A Freudian Impression," *Diacritics* 25, no. 2 (1995): 9–63.
118 Alexandra Walsham, "The Social History of the Archive: Record-Keeping in Early Modern Europe," *Past & Present* 230, no. suppl 11 (2016): 9–48, https://doi.org/10.1093/pastj/gtw033; Elizabeth Yale, "The History of Archives: The State of the Discipline," *Book History* 18, no. 1 (2015): 332–59, https://doi.org/10.1353/bh.2015.0007.
119 Jaimie Baron, *The Archive Effect: Found Footage and the Audiovisual Experience of History* (Routledge, 2014), 3.
120 Terry Cook, "The Archive(s) Is a Foreign Country: Historians, Archivists, and the Changing Archival Landscape," *The American Archivist* 74, no. 2 (2011): 600–632, https://doi.org/10.17723/aarc.74.2.xm04573740262424.

While historians studied the archive as a structure of power, archivists where not included and consulted. Arguably, although historians thus became more aware of archives, making archival structures visible in their work, some features of archival practices remained hidden from view in an infrastructural role.

Despite an apparent move away from the computer for more advanced tasks than word processing software, the 1990s brought another technology that nonetheless established the computer as an indispensable tool. In 1990, the computer scientist Tim Berners-Lee developed the HTTP protocol that laid the foundation for the World Wide Web.[121] With the HTTP protocol, a document could create a link to another document, so that related documents could easily be retrieved. Reminiscent of the *memex* device by Vannevar Bush, the web transformed scientific communication and communication in general, by making it much easier to quickly retrieve documents from anywhere, as well as disseminate documents to others.[122] In 1993, Tim Berners-Lee published the first proposal for a specification for HTML, while the software developer Marc Andreessen announced the Mosaic browser as a first easy to install and easy to use web browser with support for images.[123]

One of the earliest examples of disseminating historical research via the web is work by the historian Edward Ayers and his collaborators. Their *The Valley of the Shadow* project on the American Civil War was published as a web page in 1993 containing maps, letters and other documents.[124] While another notable project of historical publishing including multimedia, the *Who Built America?* project, used CD-ROM for dissemination, the web page of *The Valley of the Shadow* facilitated a form of public access that proved more advantageous.[125] Although at first the project was criticised, historians soon recognised "that the digital medium allowed Ayers to create a thoroughly captivating, technically savvy, and wholly unexpected comparative approach to the Civil War, one so complex and interconnected that such a thing seemed impossible in more linear media such as film and books."[126]

---

121 Tim Berners-Lee and Mark Fischetti, *Weaving the Web: The Original Design and Ultimate Destiny of the World Wide Web by Its Inventor* (Harper San Francisco, 1999); Isaacson, *The Innovators*.

122 Bush, "As We May Think."

123 Tim Berners-Lee and Daniel Connolly, "Hypertext Markup Language (HTML) A Representation of Textual Information and MetaInformation for Retrieval and Interchange," w3.org (W3, 1993); Isaacson, *The Innovators*.

124 This project is still available online: "The Valley of the Shadow: Two Communities in the American Civil War", accessed May 12, 2021, http://valley.lib.virginia.edu/.

125 William G. Thomas, "Computing and the Historical Imagination," in *A Companion to Digital Humanities*, ed. Susan Schreibman, Ray Siemens and John Unsworth, online (Blackwell, 2004), 116–32.

126 Thomas, 62.

As such, the project showed the first example of a historical publication online, providing easy access to sources and updates, as well as a rich media offering of images, maps and different ways of browsing the publication. From this web project came the first explicit notion of digital history, when Edward Ayers and William G. Thomas III founded the *Virginia Center for Digital History* in 1998, later defining the term as "an approach to examining and representing the past that works with the new communication technologies of the computer, the Internet network, and software systems."[127] Interestingly, this use of the term digital history thereby predates the starting point for the popularisation of the term digital humanities with the book *A Companion to Digital Humanities* published in 2004.[128]

A difficulty of the early 1990s web was that it could prove difficult to find information of interest. Although there is a history of web search engines or web portals with collections of links, of interest to my discussion is the founding of Google in 1998.[129] Google started as a digital library project and is interesting for several reasons.[130] First, Google provides a single point of access to all kinds of information, originating from libraries, archives, governments etc. This is what the media scholar Siva Vaidhyanathan calls the Googlization of everything, so that Google is "the lens through which we view the world."[131] This raises the question to what extent Google provides the lens to the past when historians use Google's services to explore libraries and read books or articles.[132] Second, Google demonstrates the importance of the physical technical infrastructure, i.e. the machines underlying the digital infrastructure, for providing access: "they deployed far more bandwidth, processing power, and storage capacity to the task than any rival."[133] Although this book does not focus on these physical, technical infrastructures, it is important to note that digital libraries are not "virtual" intangible entities. Digital libraries are embedded in physical infrastructures that introduce a power relation, as not every institution will have the funds to deploy such a technical infrastructure.[134] Finally, apart from the famous Google Search that

---

127 William G. Thomas in Cohen et al., "Interchange: The Promise of Digital History."

128 Susan Schreibman, Ray Siemens and John Unsworth, eds., *A Companion to Digital Humanities*, online (Oxford: Blackwell, 2004); for a history of the digital humanities terminology, see Matthew Kirschenbaum, "Digital Humanities As/Is a Tactical Term," in *Debates in the Digital Humanities*, ed. Matthew K. Gold, online (University of Minnesota Press, 2012).

129 For a more elaborate history of the web, see Isaacson, *The Innovators*.

130 David Hart, "On the Origins of Google," National Science Foundation (2004).

131 Siva Vaidhyanathan, *The Googlization of Everything (And Why We Should Worry)* (Berkeley: University of California Press, 2011), 7.

132 Kemman, Kleppe and Scagliola, "Just Google It."

133 Isaacson, *The Innovators*, 476.

134 Vaidhyanathan, *The Googlization of Everything*.

now dominates web search for billions of people, Google provides two services of interest that have successfully infiltrated the work of historians. These services provide an interface to the digital infrastructures of archives and libraries: Google Scholar and Google Books.

Google Scholar launched in 2004 as a search engine specifically for academic literature. Although to my knowledge no comprehensive study has been undertaken on how exactly historians use Google Scholar and how this impacts their usage of secondary literature, it has been shown that many historians frequently use Google Scholar.[135] Google Scholar has proved such a successful search tool that the discovery tools that were provided by university libraries have come under pressure. The Utrecht University Library was notably the first to remove their own discovery tool in 2013, instead pointing users to online search tools such as Scopus and Google Scholar.[136] Interestingly, although the library did not receive major complaints, especially scholars from the humanities were disappointed as they did not consider search tools such as Google Scholar to be apt solutions. By helping these users find specific databases for the humanities, such as JSTOR, these complaints were alleviated. This indicates that humanities scholars did not appreciate a generic, catch-all search tool, but demanded specific discovery systems tailored to their disciplines. In 2018, Utrecht University Library completed the next step to fully integrate their book catalogue in WorldCat.[137]

Kortekaas and Kramer state they believe that "the OPAC is dead."[138] This means that the library is essentially receding from the front-end, retiring the search systems developed in-house, to a back-end task of ensuring the collections are discoverable in other search systems. Moreover, journals are increasingly consulted online rather than in print, so that users are sent directly from the search tool to the journal website.[139] In other words, while the library was visible in the search user interface or in the collection, it increasingly takes on an infrastructural role of invisibly connecting other search interfaces to licensed online material, including journals and ebooks. As before with Microsoft Access, here too we might speak of a trading zone, including scholars, librarians and commercial technology firms,

---

135 Kemman, Kleppe and Scagliola, "Just Google It."

136 Simone Kortekaas and Bianca Kramer, "Thinking the Unthinkable – Doing Away with the Library Catalogue," *Insights: The UKSG Journal* 27, no. 3 (2014): 244–48, https://doi.org/10. 1629/2048-7754.174.

137 Interview with Coen Wilders, head of academic services Utrecht University Library, April 15, 2020.

138 Kortekaas and Kramer, "Thinking the Unthinkable," 248.

139 Peter Boyce et al., "How Electronic Journals Are Changing Patterns of Use," *The Serials Librarian* 46, no. 1–2 (2004): 121–41, https://doi.org/10.1300/J123v46n01_14.

notably Google. The technology firms introduce a power asymmetry here, as Google is providing search tools on which librarians and scholars have no influence, but that are so enticing that they push out the existing search systems. Within this trading zone then, librarians are challenged to take on new roles.

Google Books also launched in 2004, then under the name of Google Print. Google Books shifted the practice and purpose of mass digitisation to such an extent that one might ask whether the earlier efforts could rightly be called mass digitisation. Before Google, digitisation efforts emphasised precision and preventing duplication. Librarians were able to complete projects in which a million pages were digitised, but Google promised to digitise 4.5 billion pages in a period of six years.[140] In other words, "it took the most aggressive and technologically advanced library digitizers a decade to scan less than what Google was able to scan each week."[141] Preferring speed over precision, Google Books contains a lot of books, but with a lot of errors. Users in general, and historians specifically, were critical (and still are) about technical issues of quality in the scans, the metadata, or wrongly stated copyrights.[142] Research based on the digitised sources has consequently been characterised as investigating a historical record that never existed.[143] Furthermore, Google Books was found to contain a surplus of academic rather than popular literature, diminishing its value in representing a society or time period.[144]

Google Books was, moreover, criticised for socio-political issues. Robert Darnton, the director of the Harvard University Library between 2007 and 2016, criticised Google Books for establishing a monopoly, since Google was the only one to possess the means for such large-scale digitisation and copyright related trials in court.[145] Furthermore, Google did this as a for-profit company, not as a library whose purpose is to provide access to knowledge. In Europe, Jean-Noël Jeanneney, the president of the *Bibliothèque nationale de France* between 2002

---

140 Deegan and Sutherland, *Transferred Illusions*.

141 Alissa Centivany, "The Dark History of HathiTrust," *Proceedings of the 50th Hawaii International Conference on System Sciences* (2017), 2361.

142 E.g., Robert Townsend, "Google Books: What's Not to Like?," American Historical Association blog (2007).

143 Johan Jarlbrink and Pelle Snickars, "Cultural Heritage as Digital Noise: Nineteenth Century Newspapers in the Digital Archive," *Journal of Documentation* 73, no. 6 (2017): 1228–43, https://doi.org/10.1108/JD-09-2016-0106.

144 Eitan Adam Pechenick, Christopher M. Danforth and Peter Sheridan Dodds, "Characterizing the Google Books Corpus: Strong Limits to Inferences of Socio-Cultural and Linguistic Evolution," ed. Alain Barrat, *PLOS ONE* 10, no. 10 (2015), https://doi.org/10.1371/journal.pone.0137041.

145 Robert Darnton, *The Case for Books: Past, Present, and Future* (New York: PublicAffairs, 2009).

and 2007, criticised Google Books for imposing Anglo-Saxon cultural values and knowledge.[146] He argued European cultural heritage should not depend on American industries for preservation and access. These authors consequently pushed for public competitors to Google Books, respectively the Digital Public Library of America and Europeana.[147]

Some of these criticisms can be explained by the observation that these mass digitisation efforts were pushed mainly by computer scientists and engineers, whereas the efforts around microfilm 60 years earlier were pushed by librarians. As such, these efforts arguably constitute trading zones including technologists, librarians and expected users. I might again speak of a power asymmetry with powerful technology firms, as other projects "are overshadowed by mass digitisation, whose intoxicating claims appear to fuel our voracious appetite for digital media, making us ever more impatient of obstacles to the seamless integration of content with commercial search engines – and ever more reluctant to engage closely and critically with what we find electronically."[148] While the boundary work of librarians traditionally emphasised precision of material and metadata and carefulness to prevent duplication, the values of speed and efficiency prevailed in mass digitisation projects. Furthermore, the speed of mass digitisation limited the material that could be digitised. For example, medieval manuscripts required much more careful handling, requiring different practices of digitisation, thereby creating a bias for certain types of library sources.[149]

Libraries had incentives to participate though, as Google did not keep the books to themselves. Participating libraries received digital copies of the scanned books that they were free to distribute for non-commercial use. The University of Michigan Library was the first to join Google's efforts, following several reasons that together led to the decision to collaborate.[150] One reason was that Google would cover the costs and would return digitised books within an alluring time frame. Second, collaborating with Google was deemed to possible increase the university's reputation. Third, digitisation was deemed moral, to make the collection accessible to society. The final two reasons show that while I might speak of a trading zone of librarians and technologists, librarians were already rather aligned

---

146 Jean Noël Jeanneney, *Google and the Myth of Universal Knowledge: A View from Europe*, trans. Teresa Lavender Fagan (Chicago: University of Chicago Press, 2007).
147 Nanna Bonde Thylstrup, *The Politics of Mass Digitization* (Cambridge, MA: The MIT Press, 2018).
148 Deegan and Sutherland, *Transferred Illusions*, 160.
149 Andrew Prescott and Lorna Hughes, "Why Do We Digitize? The Case for Slow Digitization," *Archive Journal*, 2018.
150 Centivany, "The Dark History of HathiTrust."

with the aims of Google: mass digitisation was deemed inevitable, as something that libraries were just supposed to do. Finally, librarians wanted to make a statement regarding copyright. The University of Michigan Library therefore set out to digitise its entire holdings, while other participating libraries digitised material that was out of copyright.

Issues surrounding copyright eventually led Google into several court cases. While Google ultimately won the legal battle, the Books project had lost its momentum and currently does not seem to receive significant attention for further development anymore, leaving "a database containing 25-million books and nobody is allowed to read them."[151] Yet the feeding back of digitised material challenged librarians to develop their own digital infrastructures. The librarians at the University of Michigan soon recognised they needed to collaborate with other institutes to be able to develop and maintain a sufficiently powerful digital infrastructure. Consequently, while Google Books' development stalled, libraries formed national infrastructures such as HathiTrust in the US (established in 2008) and Delpher in the Netherlands (established in 2013).

Some worried early on about the sustainability of Google Books. As an alternative, the Internet Archive, established in 1996, announced the Open Content Alliance (OCA) in 2005 as a consortium effort, including Microsoft amongst others. Despite this different institutional structure, the two efforts ended up being not too dissimilar in procedure and results.[152] Both services "black boxed" the exact procedures of digitisation. Both permitted the libraries that provided the original works to redistribute the digitised material for non-commercial use. Finally, both offered a web interface to read the books. Yet comparing Google Books and the OCA provides insight into the flexibility digitisation allows for functionality. As both projects focused on scanning books, the procedures for handling and scanning were consequently similar. However, the databases of the two projects are very different, leading to significantly different practices.

Both Google Books and the OCA provide full-text search within a book in the web interface, but only Google Books provides full-text search on the entire collection of books.[153] While the OCA maintained a relatively classic model of searching by metadata and reading a book by flipping through the pages, Google

---

151 James Somers, "Torching the Modern-Day Library of Alexandria," The Atlantic (2017). Interestingly, after years of silence, the Google Ngram Viewer received an update in 2020 to include data up to 2019; "Google Ngram Viewer", accessed May 12, 2021, https://books.google.com/ngrams/info.

152 Kalev Leetaru, "Mass Book Digitization: The Deeper Story of Google Books and the Open Content Alliance," *First Monday* 13, no. 10 (2008).

153 Leetaru.

enabled entirely new forms of interacting with books. First and foremost, Google Books allows a user to search for a specific question and find a single passage in a book that answers this question, without needing to read the rest of the book. At this level, some scholars have criticised Google Books, and digital libraries in general, as providing something that is similar to libraries, but worse. It is debatable whether it is desirable that people search for bits and pieces within books, rather than consulting a book as a comprehensive work in itself.[154] Moreover, keyword search assumes a scholar already knows what they are looking for and only retrieves those relevant parts. This leaves historians to worry about the loss of the context of the library, as well as of serendipity as an important factor in knowledge discovery.[155]

Since Google keeps the full-texts of collected books in a database, in contrast with the OCA, this furthermore allowed new forms of research on the entire corpus. This has famously been demonstrated with the Google Ngram Viewer.[156] In this approach, the full-texts of books are used to investigate the texts through n-grams, where "n" refers to the length in number of words that follow one another in a text. For example, "archive" is a 1-gram, "digital history" a 2-gram, and "the history of infrastructures in" a 5-gram. This way the development of a specific term, or a combination of terms, can be analysed over a long period of time, and compared with the evolution of other terms (see Figure 1). This user interface

---

154 Vaidhyanathan, *The Googlization of Everything*; in this sense, the understanding of books as being valuable for containing information has been argued to reflect a scientific rather than humanistic perspective. The information scientist Ronald E. Day argues: "The contrast between science and humanities scholarship, when it does exist today, at least in terms of hermeneutics, is between documents as containers of information, which are consulted for the information that they representationally contain, and texts, understood through close readings and a type of understanding that involves both a bridging of hermeneutic horizons and a critical and sometimes formally performative questioning of their topics by the style of these very texts". Google Books then elevates a scientific understanding of books. *Indexing It All: The Subject in the Age of Documentation, Information, and Data*, History and Foundations of Information Science (Cambridge, Massachusetts: MIT Press, 2014), 24.
155 Kim Martin and Anabel Quan-Haase, "Are E-Books Replacing Print Books? Tradition, Serendipity, and Opportunity in the Adoption and Use of e-Books for Historical Research and Teaching," *Journal of the American Society for Information Science and Technology* 64, no. 5 (2013): 1016–28, https://doi.org/10.1002/asi.22801; Kim Martin and Anabel Quan-Haase, "The Role of Agency in Historians' Experiences of Serendipity in Physical and Digital Information Environments," *Journal of Documentation* 72, no. 6 (2016): 1008–26, https://doi.org/10.1108/JD-11-2015-0144.
156 Erez Aiden and Jean-Baptiste Michel, *Uncharted: Big Data as a Lens on Human Culture* (Riverhead Books, 2013); "Google Ngram Viewer", accessed May 12, 2021, https://books.google.com/ngrams.

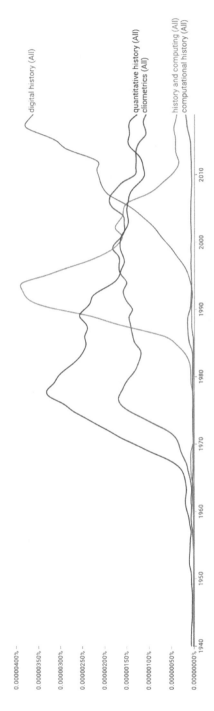

Figure 1: Google Ngram Viewer comparing occurrences of digital history, quantitative history, cliometrics, history and computing and computational history between 1940 and 2019. This chart shows in one simple overview the rise and fall of communities preceding digital history, notably quantitative history and history and computing.

has since been replicated for other text corpora, such as the Dutch National Library's newspaper corpus.[157] These differences in functions are notably not because the OCA could not offer similar functions to Google Books in theory, but because the OCA chose not to offer such functions; a decision that may have been informed by considerations of technological feasibility or path-dependency.

Mass digitisation contains interesting similarities as well as contrasts to the previously described practices of microfilming. Both efforts seemingly have similar goals and require a person in combination with a machine to transform a document into another format. This new format then requires, or allows, new practices for consultation. As a contrast, where microfilm was a good technology for preservation, but not optimal for distribution and access, Google Books and the OCA are instead good for distribution and access, but essentially bad at preservation.[158]

Yet Google Books took digitisation even further, into datafication.[159] That is, Google Books offered functionality beyond a digital surrogate of the original object. Google aggregated the collections of books from multiple libraries and turned this into one big dataset of words (or n-grams), which then facilitated new practices. Such datafication of humanities sources underlies much large-scale analysis in the digital humanities, with prominent scholars calling for macroanalysis or the more commonly used term distant reading.[160] In these approaches, scholars are challenged not to "close read" the sources one by one, but to provide an overview of the corpus, and with statistical analyses contextualise data points. In the terminology of Schellenberg, Google transformed books to give informational value; not as information containers in themselves, but as containers of language that signify the societal context within which they were written, published and maintained.[161]

This is not to say Google Books caused these approaches. The term "digital humanities" was coined in 2004, and "distant reading" was coined by the literary historian Franco Moretti in 2000 already, four years before Google Books and ten years before the Google Ngram Viewer.[162] Still, Google Books fit in what, in the

---

157 "PoliticalMashup KB ngramviewer", accessed May 12, 2021, http://ngramviewer.kbre search.nl/.

158 Deegan and Sutherland, *Transferred Illusions*; Leetaru, "Mass Book Digitization."

159 Viktor Mayer-Schönberger and Kenneth Cukier, *Big Data: A Revolution That Will Transform How We Live, Work, and Think* (Houghton Mifflin Harcourt, 2013).

160 Matthew L. Jockers, *Macroanalysis: Digital Methods and Literary History* (University of Illinois Press, 2013); Franco Moretti, *Distant Reading* (Verso Books, 2013).

161 The digital humanist Frédéric Kaplan critically argued that Google not only datafied but essentially commodified linguistic expression, using linguistic data to develop and improve sales of advertisements. "Linguistic Capitalism and Algorithmic Mediation," *Representations* 127, no. 1 (2014): 57–63, https://doi.org/10.1525/rep.2014.127.1.57.

162 Franco Moretti, "Conjectures on World Literature," *New Left Review*, no. 1 (2000): 54–68.

terminology of the philosopher of science Thomas Kuhn, has been called the fourth paradigm: research based on data-intensive computing.[163] While Google Books is not the cause of this turn to data-intensive humanities research, it did arguably make it more prominent.

With such large-scale datasets and digital methods, it has been argued that historians can return to *longue durée* historical investigations.[164] For example, the historian Jo Guldi experimented with the Google Ngram Viewer and other databases to investigate the history of walking over three centuries, and especially the apparent rise of walking between 1800–1850.[165] Such investigations require counting of terms over long periods of time, introducing issues of concept drift.[166] That is, the meaning of terms may change over time and context to describe different concepts, or other terms might be used to describe the same concept. Linguistics is consequently an important subject of digital history. This is arguably a continuation of the linguistic turn that started with the cultural turn described above, embedded in computational technologies.

The computational linguistic approach to large unstructured datasets requires expertise that is not part of the work of historians and, therefore, invites collaboration with computational linguists.[167] Furthermore, the subsequent systems required to store and provide access to this data and the user interfaces to retrieve and consult this data in whatever form require computational expertise in knowledge modelling, database design, user interface design and human-computer interaction. The digital infrastructures of digital history thus require cross-disciplinary collaborations on a level not seen before in archives and libraries.

---

163 Thomas S. Kuhn, *The Structure of Scientific Revolutions*, 2nd ed., International Encyclopedia of Unified Science Foundations of the Unity of Science (Chicago University Press, 1994); Tony Hey, Stewart Tansley and Kristin Tolle, eds., *The Fourth Paradigm: Data-Intensive Scientific Discovery*, 2nd ed. (Microsoft Research, 2009).

164 Guldi and Armitage, *The History Manifesto*.

165 Jo Guldi, "The History of Walking and the Digital Turn: Stride and Lounge in London, 1808–1851," *The Journal of Modern History* 84, no. 1 (2012): 116–44.

166 Shenghui Wang, Stefan Schlobach and Michel Klein, "Concept Drift and How to Identify It," *Web Semantics: Science, Services and Agents on the World Wide Web* 9, no. 3 (2011): 247–65, https://doi.org/10.1016/j.websem.2011.05.003.

167 Michael Piotrowski, *Natural Language Processing for Historical Texts*, ed. Graeme Hirst, *Synthesis Lectures on Human Language Technologies*, vol. 5 (Morgan and Claypool, 2012), https://doi.org/10.2200/S00436ED1V01Y201207HLT017; Barbara McGillivray, Thierry Poibeau and Pablo Ruiz Fabo, "Digital Humanities and Natural Language Processing: Je t'aime . . . Moi Non Plus," *Digital Humanities Quarterly* 14, no. 2 (2020).

As the case of Google Books demonstrates, the way the database is structured affects what a historian can do with the data. A full-text search on the level of a book is significantly different from a full-text search on the level of the entire library. How data is processed may introduce biases or limitations not immediately recognisable to historians.[168] On top of this, the user interface affects even further what a historian can do with the data; a search box returning a list of results is a significantly different tool than an Ngram Viewer, leading to different questions. The archival turn led to an understanding of archives as structuring the perspective on the past. Likewise, the user interfaces of archives and libraries act as an interface to the past, shaping perspectives on the past.[169] The infrastructures directly influence the possible practices of historians and the knowledge that may be generated. Therefore, historians are collaborating in digital history projects with the goal of steering these infrastructures into directions suitable for historians. It is through these collaborations that historians, computational linguists, computer scientists, archivists and librarians negotiate how digital infrastructures will facilitate future practices of historians.

To understand how these negotiations takes place, I develop a model to critically examine collaborations as trading zones in which concepts, methods and tools are shared and exchanged. In the next chapter, I elaborate this model and discuss how I apply the trading zones concept to digital history collaborations. Readers who prefer to skip directly to my studies of digital history collaborations may instead prefer to move on to Chapter 3. In the third chapter I examine digital history collaborations at the University of Luxembourg by means of the first dimension of my model, engagement, to consider how historians engage with one another and with cross-disciplinary collaborators.

---

168 Antske Fokkens et al., "BiographyNet: Methodological Issues When NLP Supports Historical Research," in *Proceedings of the Ninth International Conference on Language Resources and Evaluation (LREC'14)*, ed. Nicoletta Calzolari et al. (Reykjavik, Iceland: European Language Resources Association (ELRA), 2014), 3728–35.

169 Margaret Hedstrom, "Archives, Memory, and Interfaces with the Past," *Archival Science* 2, no. 1 (2002): 21–43, https://doi.org/10.1007/BF02435629.

The Trading Zones Model

Dimensions of Trading Zones

The concept of trading zones was introduced by the historian of science Peter Galison to describe how two communities with vastly different practices and discourses can interact and negotiate a joint enterprise. As I briefly introduced in the previous chapter, the concept describes how two communities that do not coordinate practices on a global scale may be able to do so on a local scale. He considered the practices of scholarly communities as "language", building upon the work of the philosopher of science Thomas Kuhn.[170] Different scholarly communities can consequently be conceptualised as employing incommensurable languages.[171]

By considering the practices of a scholarly community as a language, the differences between scholarly communities can be described as when people from two cultures with different languages meet. Imagine the difficulty between someone who solely speaks German when they have to coordinate with someone who solely speaks French. From this problem follows the core concept of trading zones, namely the formation of inter-language as a language between languages. Galison distinguishes between two phases of inter-language. At first, a pidgin may develop so that two communities can exchange goods, specialised just to enable that coordination. Participants do not use the pidgin outside of an exchange, but return to their native languages when the interaction is over. Over time, a pidgin may develop into a creole, where an inter-language becomes complex enough to allow a wide variety of practices beyond the exchange and is able to serve as a native language by itself. In the case of scholarly communities, scholars can then sustain activity within this new creole language. The community becomes one on its own, without it being an extension of another discipline.[172]

The extent of exchanges is described by Galison as follows: "it is possible to share a local understanding of an entity without sharing the full apparatus of meanings, symbols, and values in which each of us might embed it."[173] This means that historians can share local understandings of concepts from computer science that are relevant to a task, without needing to understand the

---

170 Kuhn, *The Structure of Scientific Revolutions*.
171 Peter Galison, "Trading with the Enemy," in *Trading Zones and Interactional Expertise: Creating New Kinds of Collaboration*, ed. Michael E. Gorman (MIT Press, 2010), 25–52.
172 Peter Galison, *Image and Logic: A Material Culture of Microphysics* (The University of Chicago Press, 1997).
173 Galison, "Trading with the Enemy," 44.

entirety of computer science or become computer scientists themselves. This can also be said in the opposite direction for computer scientists with respect to history. The concept of "trading" is thus not meant to denote an economic exchange or a *quid pro quo*, but refers to the shallow sharing and exchanging of concepts and practices in different local settings.[174] Instead, the concept of trading zones demands a deeper probe into digital history, to investigate not just what is coordinated, but how the coordination of practices takes place.

Galison's original use of the concept was in his study of the interactions between experimental and theoretical physicists, who arguably came from the same discipline despite their different practices. Digital history might instead be characterised as a meeting from particularly distant positions, as a bridging of the Two Cultures divide between the humanities and hard sciences.[175] Yet besides the meeting of two different communities, what Galison's study and mine furthermore share is the transforming role of computers. The meeting between experimental and theoretical physicists was significantly altered by the introduction of computers, which increasingly replaced physicists to perform tasks. At first, computers took over the demanding task of data reduction, the cleaning and selecting of data from a large dataset. Later, computers were used to automate analysis, interpreting data to create visualisations and charts. Finally, computers replaced physical experiments with simulation, reproducing experiments in mathematical models.[176] Throughout this process, physicists continuously negotiated the roles of computers and physicists; what it means to be a scholar, to do an experiment and how science relates to reality.[177]

In short, digital humanities and digital history are not unique in their renegotiation of practices following the introduction of computational methods. It is

---

174 Galison, "Trading with the Enemy."

175 Julie Thompson Klein, "A Taxonomy of Interdisciplinarity," in *The Oxford Handbook of Interdisciplinarity*, ed. Robert Frodeman et al. (Oxford University Press, 2010), 15–30; C.P. Snow, *The Two Cultures and the Scientific Revolution* (Cambridge University Press, 1959).

176 While simulation does not play a significant role yet in digital history, some authors have explored agent-based modelling for simulating historical events; see Marten Düring, "The Potential of Agent-Based Modelling for Historical Research," in *Complexity and the Human Experience: Modeling Complexity in the Humanities and Sociol Sciences*, ed. Paul A. Youngman and Mirsad Hadzikadic (Pan Stanford Publishing, 2014), 121–37; Michael Gavin, "Agent-Based Modeling and Historical Simulation," *DHQ: Digital Humanities Quarterly* 8, no. 4 (2014); digital history may benefit from synergies with digital archaeological research, where experiments with simulation have a longer history, see Timothy A. Kohler and George G. Gumerman, *Dynamics in Human and Primate Societies: Agent-Based Modeling of Social and Spatial Processes* (Oxford University Press, 2000).

177 Galison, *Image and Logic*.

a common assumption that other disciplines, especially from STEM, do not need digital labels. Yet the period that Galison describes as the "pidginization" of computers in physics might as well have been called "digital physics" as a transitional term, similar to "digital history".[178] The trading zones concept is therefore highly relevant to digital history, as a description of exchanging practices between two communities that are both affected by the introduction of computers.

Yet a limitation of the concept is that Galison's original study only considered one trading zone between communities, and as such he did not elaborate a comparative analysis between different trading zones. Therefore, the sociologists Harry Collins, Robert Evans and Michael Gorman extended the concept by describing trading zones according to two dimensions.[179] First, homogeneous-heterogeneous (the extent to which two communities become alike or stay apart). Second, coercive-collaborative (the extent to which one community forces the other community to trade).

Changing Practices: Homogeneous-Heterogeneous

The first dimension, changing practices, touches directly upon the most common questions in digital history; will historians become like programmers? Will historians lose touch with some of the core values of the discipline? As a historian of science, Galison wrote about the temporal process of trading, with periods of negotiation, resistance and acceptance. A collaboration continuously moves across the changing practices dimension between homogeneous and heterogeneous, where it is likely that a collaboration will be more heterogeneous at the beginning but might end up more homogeneous.

Heterogeneity, especially at the start of a collaboration, might become apparent in a number of different ways. The first problem might be that of language in the literal sense. Terminology between scholarly communities is a common issue. Especially in the beginning of a collaboration a participant might be unaware of what the other means with certain words.[180] For example, in one collaboration in

---

178 Zaagsma, "On Digital History."

179 Harry Collins, Robert Evans and Michael Gorman, "Trading Zones and Interactional Expertise," *Studies in History and Philosophy of Science* 38, no. 4 (2007): 657–66, https://doi.org/10.1016/j.shpsa.2007.09.003.

180 Lynne Siemens, "'It's a Team If You Use "Reply All"': An Exploration of Research Teams in Digital Humanities Environments," *Literary and Linguistic Computing* 24, no. 2 (2009): 225–33, https://doi.org/10.1093/llc/fqp009.

which I participated, there was a debate about whether a digital archive could automatically create metadata for items. The historians contended that this was not possible, as they understood "metadata" to mean descriptions of an object as an archivist would do. The computer scientists did not understand the problem, since they understood "metadata" to mean descriptions such as file format, encoding, or date of upload. Once this confusion was understood, the collaboration decided to use the term "annotation" for the metadata as desired by the historians, to denote the manual effort in creating such descriptions.

Another important difference between scholars may be publication strategies.[181] In digital history, for example, the contrast between historians commonly publishing books and computer scientists commonly publishing conference papers introduces different desires about the speed of publication, co-authorship and how to determine prestige.

Finally, the aim of a research project can be fundamentally different. As the political scientists Gary King and Daniel Hopkins put it: "computer scientists may be interested in finding the needle in the haystack (such as a potential terrorist threat or the right web page to display from a search), but social scientists are more commonly interested in characterizing the haystack."[182] Following this metaphor, historians could be said to be interested in characterising how the needle is part of the haystack, individually unique but part of a greater whole.[183] Interdisciplinary collaborations therefore require coordination to align participants with respect to the project's goals, terminology, and desired results. I elaborate this aspect of coordination in Chapter 4.

Such differences between scholars or scholarly communities may emerge through different disciplinary backgrounds, as scholars are part of the historical discipline or the computer science discipline. The sociologist Karin Knorr Cetina describes disciplines as epistemic cultures: "those amalgams of arrangements and mechanisms – bonded through affinity, necessity, and historical coincidence – which, in a given field, make up *how we know what we know*."[184] She describes epistemic cultures as self-referential systems. That means that, for example, historians are trained by other historians at history departments, read

---

181 De Jonge Akademie, "Grensverleggend: Kansen En Belemmeringen Voor Interdisciplinair Onderzoek" (KNAW, 2015); Eric T. Meyer and Ralph Schroeder, *Knowledge Machines: Digital Transformations of the Sciences and Humanities* (MIT Press, 2015).

182 Gary King and Daniel J. Hopkins, "A Method of Automated Nonparametric Content Analysis for Social Science," *American Journal of Political Science* 54, no. 1 (2010): 230, https://doi.org/10.1111/j.1540-5907.2009.00428.x.

183 Tim Hitchcock, "Big Data, Small Data and Meaning," Historyonics, 2014.

184 Knorr Cetina, *Epistemic Cultures*, 1, emphasis in original.

work from other historians, are supervised by a historian during their PhD and when staying in the academy usually try to end up at a history department at some university. The concept not only intends to describe the practices of scholars, but how those practices are guided by systems of culture. That is, the notion of culture goes beyond the mere behavioural repertoire, to describe the "control mechanisms" that govern behaviour, which may help understand why scholars act differently between disciplinary communities.[185]

In this line, the scholar of higher education Tony Becher spoke of disciplinary cultures and investigated specifically the shared repertoire of language and taboos present in disciplinary communities.[186] For example, within the history discipline, words of praise include "scholarly" and "original", while words of condemnation are "trivialising" and "thin". A taboo would be to misuse evidence to prove one's point, rather than to try and gain alternative perspectives. Despite the wide array of subfields of history related to different periods or geographical areas, historians still maintain there is a unified field of history. Yet Becher also noted deeper disagreements in the field. Historians looked down on historical biographies or narrative history. At the margins of the discipline he found a distrust of quantification, modelling and economic history. Arguably, these results have changed over time. Becher published this work in 1981, shortly after the hype of quantitative history, around the shift toward cultural history and narrative.

I might, therefore, investigate history and computer science by these aspects of disciplines and gain an understanding of their differences or common interests. A question might then be how the disciplines relate to one another within digital history, and what form of cross-disciplinarity is performed:[187]
- multidisciplinarity (historians and computer scientists work in parallel or serially on a shared problem, applying their own disciplinary perspective and analysis),
- interdisciplinarity (historians and computer scientists work together on a shared problem and coordinate their practices to join their disciplinary perspectives),

---

185 Clifford Geertz, *The Interpretation of Cultures: Selected Essays* (Basic Books, Inc., 1973), 44.
186 Tony Becher, "Towards a Definition of Disciplinary Cultures," *Studies in Higher Education* 6, no. 2 (1981): 109–22, https://doi.org/10.1080/03075078112331379362.
187 Bernard C.K. Choi and Anita W.P. Pak, "Multidisciplinarity, Interdisciplinarity and Transdisciplinarity in Health Research, Services, Education and Policy: 1. Definitions, Objectives, and Evidence of Effectiveness," *Clinical and Investigative Medicine* 29, no. 6 (2006): 351–64; Patricia L. Rosenfield, "The Potential of Transdisciplinary Research for Sustaining and Extending Linkages between the Health and Social Sciences," *Social Science & Medicine*, Special Issue Building Research Capacity for Health Social Sciences in Developing Countries 35, no. 11 (1992): 1343–57, https://doi.org/10.1016/0277-9536(92)90038-R.

– transdisciplinarity (historians and computer scientists create a shared understanding and approach towards a problem, each no longer within their own disciplinary boundaries).

Multidisciplinary interactions are the least significant form, in the sense that historians and computer scientists still mainly perform traditional practices and require little mutual coordination. In contrast, transdisciplinary interactions require significant coordination to establish joint practices and perspectives. While combining multiple disciplinary perspectives, the outcome may be described as a single unity of knowledge.[188] This model of synthesis has been popularised especially due to the argument that it is necessary in order to address real-world problems, rather than theoretical ones.[189] Comparing this typology to that of trading zones, it could be argued that transdisciplinary research constitutes a homogeneous and power symmetric trading zone, or creole. Interdisciplinary research might constitute a heterogenous trading zone. Multidisciplinary research finally might constitute a heterogeneous trading zone without any real sharing of expertise.[190]

The scholar of interdisciplinary studies Julie Thompson Klein characterises the digital humanities as methodological interdisciplinarity.[191] Methodological interdisciplinarity encompasses the borrowing of tools, concepts and methods from other disciplines to improve one's own research questions or results. In this sense, digital humanities can be described as importing tools, concepts and methods from computational sciences to improve humanities scholarship. The dimension of changing practices then considers the extent to which practices of scholars in digital history remain heterogeneous, historians with historical practices and computational experts with computational practices, or homogeneous, historians and computational experts no longer distinguishable by their practices.

188 Thierry Ramadier, "Transdisciplinarity and Its Challenges: The Case of Urban Studies," *Futures* 36, no. 4 (2004): 423–39, https://doi.org/10.1016/j.futures.2003.10.009.
189 Michael Gibbons, "Introduction," in *The New Production of Knowledge: The Dynamics of Science and Research in Contemporary Societies*, ed. Zaheer Baber et al., vol. 24 (SAGE Publications, 1994), 1–19, https://doi.org/10.2307/2076669.
190 Harry Collins, Robert Evans and Michael Gorman, "Trading Zones Revisited," in *The Third Wave in Science and Technology Studies*, ed. David S. Caudill et al. (Cham: Springer International Publishing, 2019), 275–81, https://doi.org/10.1007/978-3-030-14335-0_15.
191 Klein, *Interdisciplining Digital Humanities*.

Power Relations: Symmetric-Asymmetric

The second dimension of trading zones, power relations, describes the extent to which one party or community has control over the other party or community. Within digital history collaborations historians and computational experts both need to negotiate the goals of the collaboration and the individual tasks of participants. This process is called coordination, which may be defined as "the integration or linking together of different pieces of a project to accomplish a collective task."[192] Coordination is a continuous process, enduring as long as the collaboration does. Throughout a collaboration, participants are in constant negotiation of the project goal or goals, while mutually accountable towards one another to fulfil their individual tasks.

Yet a collaboration does not exist in a vacuum; negotiations are positioned in a broader system that influences the collaboration, such as the institutes where collaborators are employed, their disciplinary backgrounds, funding structures, etc. Furthermore, negotiations are not necessarily level, although this would be the preferred situation, but can be conducted through different power relations. In the history of the trading zones of physics, Peter Galison discussed three metaphors employed by physicists who feared a loss of control.[193] First, the metaphor of prostitution, to critique physicists selling out to engineering, focusing on applied rather than basic research. Second, the metaphor of handmaidens, to describe the relationship between a boss and a servant, with physicists demanding engineers perform certain tasks. Third, the metaphor of flies and spiders, to describe the danger of physicists following engineers for too long, after which they end up trapped and unable to return.

Control, and specifically who is in control, is an aspect of great significance to the participants of trading zones, leading to desirable or less desirable results. In the model from Collins et al., a significant aspect of coercive trading zones is that they lack a mutual exchange of practices and concepts. They consequently describe two types of coercive trading zones, along the dimension of changing practices. In the first type, coercive-heterogeneous, two communities ultimately do not trade practices at all. The dominant community protects its expertise against the subordinate community and is not interested in learning from the weaker community either. For example, computational experts might dictate how a tool will work and what the goal of a project should be, without teaching historians anything

---

192 Jonathon N. Cummings and Sara Kiesler, "Collaborative Research Across Disciplinary and Organizational Boundaries," *Social Studies of Science* 35, no. 5 (2005): 704, https://doi.org/10. 1177/0306312705055535.
193 Galison, *Image and Logic*.

about the internal workings, nor trying to understand how historians would want to use the tool. Or vice versa, historians might demand certain features to be developed by computational experts, without communicating the tacit knowledge of historical practice or trying to understand what software development entails. In the second type, coercive-homogeneous, the dominant community replaces the practices of the subordinate community. For example, computational practices might end up replacing historical practices, emphasising programming at the expense of reading, or data processing at the expense of hermeneutics.

A problem with the term "coercion" may be, however, that it too strongly implies that one party is unable to make their own choices. It is no surprise that digital history collaborations are emphasised to be collaborative rather than coercive, since historians are part of collaborations out of their own choice.[194] Yet concluding trading zones are fully collaborative merely because practices are insufficient to count as coercive would be a simplification. Instead, I propose that trading zones should be analysed as embedding power asymmetries as consisting of mutual, but not necessarily equivalent, power relations.

The philosopher Michel Foucault defined a power relation as "a mode of action which does not act directly and immediately on others. Instead, it acts upon their actions: an action upon an action, on existing actions or on those which may arise in the present or the future."[195] A power relation is thereby understood not an act directly on another person, but on their actions. Furthermore, Foucault argued that "[t]o govern, in this sense, is to structure the possible field of action of others."[196] Thus, a power relation consists of one party shaping the possibilities of behaviour of the other party. Yet this latter party might resist, in forms of opposing a power relation or disconnecting the relationship. An individual's autonomy then exists in their resistance to imposed power relations. It is in this resistance that power relations become visible for analysis.

The political scientist Clarissa Hayward takes autonomy a step further.[197] Not only can a person resist a shaping of their field of action, they can act upon the boundaries and shape their field of action themselves. Building on the work of Foucault, she makes a number of characteristics of power relations between two (or more) parties explicit that aid my discussion. Both parties are affected by power mechanisms, so that there is no possibility to discern between "authentic"

---

194 E.g., Svensson, "The Digital Humanities as a Humanities Project."
195 Michel Foucault, "The Subject and Power," *Critical Inquiry* 8, no. 4 (1982): 789, https://doi.org/10.1086/448181.
196 Foucault, 790.
197 Clarissa Rile Hayward, *De-Facing Power*, Contemporary Political Theory (Cambridge: Cambridge University Press, 2000).

action and actions resulting from power relations. Both parties have some form of power, and encounter constraints in their practices. Furthermore, power relations need not always be intended, but might follow from unintended consequences of actions or decisions. Finally, power not only constrains, but simultaneously enables practices.

To illustrate, a digital history collaboration defines a certain project goal and establishes a group of participants. The project goal prescribes the field of action of what each participant should do in the collaboration. The computational expert might be envisioned to develop a computer algorithm for the historical texts of interest to the historian, rather than some other dataset. Simultaneously, the historian might be envisioned to do historical research with the computational expert's algorithm to analyse these historical texts, rather than through traditional methods of close reading. Such requirements are the trading zone's boundaries of action that both confine and enable the practices in the collaboration. Throughout the project, participants coordinate with one another about specific implementations of the project's goal. This is where one can investigate the power relations. The computational expert might actively shape the field of action of the historian, enabling practices of distant reading, while preventing possible research questions or conclusions. Vice versa, the historian might instead not only choose their own research questions, but perhaps even resist the project's goal of adopting the algorithm for their research, pushing the boundaries of their field of action to include practices of historical research without the algorithm.

I am, therefore, interested in investigating two different dynamics of power relations. First, the extent to which participants in a trading zone constrain or enable the actions of other participants. Second, the extent to which participants in a trading zone are able to define their own boundaries of action. Power asymmetries in trading zones are thereby defined as the extent to which some participants are less able to shape their own field of action, and where one party is able to shape the field of action of the other party to a greater extent than vice versa.

Engagement: Connected-Disconnected

Finally, a limitation of the work on trading zones by Galison and Collins et al. is that they did not investigate the extent to which two communities interact with one another. Engagement is assumed, since without exchanges or trades there is no trading zone to speak of. Yet, this does not cover differences between deep or shallow engagement, such as the extent to which trading occurs on a daily basis in an office or on a much sparser basis via email. That the physical organisation influences cross-community engagement was shown by the information scientists Susan Leigh Star and Karen Ruhleder, who found that the adoption of a digital information system was affected by the physical access of users to the required computers.[198]

To better understand engagement within and between communities, one aspect to consider is the configuration of people participating in digital history. Because digital history is commonly described as an interdisciplinary activity, one approach would be to consider the interactions between different disciplines such as history and computer science. Disciplines have been classified according to two general aspects: first, the cognitive aspect, the general topical area of expertise and established research methods and resources. For example, history can be described as a discipline topically concerned with events in the past, with hermeneutics and source criticism as established research methods, and archives and libraries as resources. The second aspect is the social, predominantly defined by institutional incorporation such as history departments at universities.[199] Other aspects with which individual disciplines can be described are discourses and methods of communication in journals, the founding myth of a discipline and the construction of the boundaries of a discipline.[200] This final aspect is better known as boundary work, i.e. defining what falls within scope by contrasting it with what falls outside scope of a discipline.[201]

Yet viewing digital history on the level of global disciplines poses several limitations. Describing historians and computer scientists by their discipline does not cover the different practices within a single department, even if I were to take a more granular level of computer science into knowledge modelling, information retrieval, or artificial intelligence.[202] Another limitation is that in collaborations where collaborators come from industry, computer engineers building tools, this

---

198 Susan Leigh Star and Karen Ruhleder, "Steps Toward an Ecology of Infrastructure: Design and Access for Large Information Spaces," *Information Systems Research* 7, no. 1 (1996): 111–34, https://doi.org/10.1287/isre.7.1.111.

199 Tony Becher and Sharon Parry, "The Endurance of the Disciplines," in *Governing Knowledge*, ed. Ivar Bleiklie and Mary Henkel, vol. 9 (Springer, 2005), 133–44, https://doi.org/10.1007/1-4020-3504-7_9.

200 Cassidy R. Sugimoto and Scott Weingart, "The Kaleidoscope of Disciplinarity," *Journal of Documentation* 71, no. 4 (2015): 775–94, https://doi.org/10.1108/JD-06-2014-0082.

201 Gieryn, "Boundary-Work and the Demarcation of Science from Non-Science: Strains and Interests in Professional Ideologies of Scientists."

202 Juha Tuunainen, "When Disciplinary Worlds Collide: The Organizational Ecology of Disciplines in a University Department," *Symbolic Interaction* 28, no. 2 (2005): 205–28, https://doi.org/10.1525/si.2005.28.2.205.

is not covered by the concept of disciplines.[203] Especially in considering the digital of digital humanities as a single heterogeneous community consisting of computer scientists, software engineers, computational linguists and others, this cannot accurately be described as a discipline.[204]

Rather than disciplines, I describe collaborators according to their membership of communities of practice. This framework describes communities according to three dimensions:[205]

1. mutual engagement (involving regular interaction),
2. joint negotiated enterprise (mutual goal and accountability),
3. shared repertoire of negotiable resources (such as jargon and practices).

Note that the shared repertoire is congruent with the earlier dimensions of changing practices. Furthermore, the joint negotiated enterprise is dependent on the power relations dimension, insofar as the negotiation of this enterprise is shaped by power relations.

Communities of practice (COP) can take shape in a wide variety of situations, such as projects, needs for standards and virtual networks.[206] Disciplines too arguably constitute communities of practice. For example, the historical discipline covers mutual engagement through conferences and journals, a joint enterprise in studying the past and a shared repertoire in hermeneutics, source criticism, archival research and discourses. Yet a COP is not necessarily homogeneous, containing both core and peripheral members, or encompassing multiple configurations of nested communities.[207] Continuing my example, while the entire history discipline might be described as a community of practice, this contains nested COPs for subfields interested in different periods such as ancient, pre-modern, modern, contemporary history, or in different geographical areas such as French, German, or European history.

Rather than their institutional embedding, communities of practice are defined by, as the name suggests, their practices: "doing in a historical and social

---

203 Becher and Parry, "The Endurance of the Disciplines."

204 I therefore employ the generic term "computational experts" to refer to computer scientists, computational linguists, software engineers, or other computational collaborators of digital history trading zones.

205 Etienne Wenger, *Communities of Practice: Learning, Meaning, and Identity* (Cambridge University Press, 1998), 73.

206 Harriett E. Green, "Facilitating Communities of Practice in Digital Humanities: Librarian Collaborations for Research and Training in Text Encoding," *The Library Quarterly* 84, no. 2 (2014): 219–34, https://doi.org/10.1086/675332; Klein, *Interdisciplining Digital Humanities.*

207 Wenger, *Communities of Practice*; Etienne Wenger, "Communities of Practice and Social Learning Systems," *Organization* 7, no. 2 (2000): 225–46, https://doi.org/10.1177/135050840072002.

context that gives structure and meaning to what we do."[208] It is, therefore, congruent with the description of scholarship as the weaving of social, intellectual and technical practices.[209] These practices include both explicit and tacit knowledge. Sharing tacit knowledge among members tends to involve face-to-face interactions to achieve enculturation; gradually acting in accordance to the norms of a COP.[210] The framework thereby puts local rather than global communities at the forefront, enabling alignment with the locality of trading zones. Insofar as knowledge can be disseminated explicitly, this knowledge can become part of a delocalised, global community of practice, such as a discipline, the difference being that knowledge that one should do something might be encoded globally, while how one should do something is exposed locally.[211]

The third dimension of engagement describes the extent to which collaborators engage with one another. An important aspect of this is what Wenger calls the "geography of practice". This concept describes the distance between collaborators within a trading zone. Although physical distance by itself is a fairly straightforward metric, the distance in meters between collaborators, it has a diverse set of consequences.[212] Distance has an impact on communication; when collaborators are closer together, communication has lower cost (e.g. of travelling), higher quality, and higher frequency.[213] When collaborators are closer, it is easier to communicate face-to-face, which in turn has been found to improve coordination.[214] Distance affects the awareness about other collaborators, following the "out of sight is out of mind" adage. The effect of this distance may be experienced very soon already: "if two people reside more

---

208 Wenger, *Communities of Practice*, 47.

209 Latour and Woolgar, *Laboratory Life*; Andrew Pickering, "From Science as Knowledge to Science as Practice," in *Science as Practice and Culture*, ed. Andrew Pickering (The University of Chicago Press, 1992), 1–26.

210 John Seely Brown, Allan Collins and Paul Duguid, "Situated Cognition and the Culture of Learning," *Educational Researcher* 18, no. 1 (1989): 32–42, https://doi.org/10.3102/0013189X018001032; Paul Duguid, "'The Art of Knowing': Social and Tacit Dimensions of Knowledge and the Limits of the Community of Practice," *The Information Society* 21, no. 2 (2005): 109–18, https://doi.org/10.1080/01972240590925311.

211 Duguid, "'The Art of Knowing.'"

212 Sara Kiesler and Jonathon N. Cummings, "What Do We Know about Proximity and Distance in Work Groups? A Legacy of Research," in *Distributed Work*, ed. Pamela Hinds and Sara Kiesler (MIT Press, 2002), 57–82.

213 Robert Kraut and Carmen Egido, "Patterns of Contact and Communication in Scientific Research Collaboration," in *Proceedings of the 1988 ACM Conference on Computer-Supported Cooperative Work* (ACM, 1988), 1–12, https://doi.org/10.1145/62266.62267.

214 Kiesler and Cummings, "What Do We Know about Proximity and Distance in Work Groups?"

than 30 meters apart, they may as well be across the continent."[215] Finally, distance affects the social grouping of collaborators. Groups located close together develop a group culture distinct from groups located elsewhere, leading to collaborators speaking in terms of "us" and "them". Though not quite as dramatic as to occur after 30 meters, this was found to happen in collaborations involving multiple institutes, so that a national inter-institutional collaboration is similar to an international collaboration.[216] Considering this final aspect, a collaboration between historians from one institute and computational researchers from another institute would be expected to lead to group identities in their disciplinary background and their institute, limiting the ability to develop shared practices and become more homogeneous. While heterogeneity by itself does require coordination to align the collaborators, these disciplinary differences have not been found to increase problems of coordination, as physical distance does.[217]

This is not to say that physical distance is merely a negative aspect, nor does physical proximity guarantee a better collaboration. Too many collaborators in too close proximity might even lead to negative experiences. For collaborations within a university, the number of collaborators was found to correlate with negative collaborative experiences. Yet this correlation was not found for collaborations between different universities.[218] When placed together in a single space, close proximity might even lead to less engagement in order not to disturb others in the same space, as has been found for "open office" spaces.[219] Allowing a larger physical distance introduces advantages, such as the ability to find the most fitting collaborators, rather than being limited to who is available nearby.[220] Physical distance in

---

215 Judith S. Olson et al., "The (Currently) Unique Advantages of Collocated Work," in *Distributed Work*, ed. Pamela Hinds and Sara Kiesler (MIT Press, 2002), 114.

216 David J. Armstrong and Paul Cole, "Managing Distances and Differences in Geographically Distributed Work Groups," in *Distributed Work*, ed. Pamela Hinds and Sara Kiesler (MIT Press, 2002), 167–86.

217 Cummings and Kiesler, "Collaborative Research Across Disciplinary and Organizational Boundaries"; John P. Walsh and Nancy G. Maloney, "Collaboration Structure, Communication Media, and Problems in Scientific Work Teams," *Journal of Computer-Mediated Communication* 12, no. 2 (2007): 378–98, https://doi.org/10.1111/j.1083-6101.2007.00346.x.

218 Chin-Chang Tsai, Elizabeth A. Corley and Barry Bozeman, "Collaboration Experiences across Scientific Disciplines and Cohorts," *Scientometrics* 108, no. 2 (2016): 505–29, https://doi.org/10.1007/s11192-016-1997-z.

219 Ethan S. Bernstein and Stephen Turban, "The Impact of the 'Open' Workspace on Human Collaboration," *Philosophical Transactions of the Royal Society B: Biological Sciences* 373, no. 20170239 (2018), https://doi.org/10.1098/rstb.2017.0239.

220 Lynne Siemens and Elisabeth Burr, "A Trip around the World: Accommodating Geographical, Linguistic and Cultural Diversity in Academic Research Teams," *Literary and Linguistic Computing* 28, no. 2 (2013): 331–43, https://doi.org/10.1093/llc/fqs018.

a collaboration can moreover be a strategy to disseminate knowledge beyond one's own local network.[221] Despite the arguments opposing physical distance, collaborations are increasingly conducted on a large distance using digital communication technologies. Studies on such "virtual teams" show these are successful, in contrast with predictions from earlier literature. However, the formation of mutual trust was found to be impaired in virtual teams.[222] Face-to-face communication was, furthermore, found to be stronger related to team performance than virtual communication.[223] Yet "hybrid teams" may prove to be advantageous, where complex problems are coordinated face-to-face, while clearer tasks may be coordinated via communication technology such as email. Establishing trust and coordinating ill-defined problems, which are common in digital history, thus benefits from face-to-face meetings throughout a collaboration, while other tasks may be coordinated otherwise.[224]

From the above literature, geography of practice is less about the exact distance in meters between collaborators, but rather about how people may be divided into distinct groups. I consequently consider distance in terms of institutional space. That is, distance is discussed in terms of sharing an office, being in the same building, being at different institutes etc. I regard collaborations where the main participants are located in a single space as one end of this dimension. In contrast, collaborations where the main participants are located in different institutes in different countries are the other end of this dimension. The dimension of engagement, therefore, ranges from connected engagement to disconnected engagement.

I consider the main participants of collaborations, since I observed that collaborations are often officially led by professors who have their own offices, but mainly conducted by researchers in PhD or postdoc positions, who might be sharing an office together. It is the interactions of these main participants that are of interest for the development of shared practices. While this is not to deny that professors may be among the main participants of a collaboration, not all individuals on a collaboration are equally engaged.

---

221 Alex H. Poole, "Now Is the Future Now? The Urgency of Digital Curation in the Digital Humanities," *Digital Humanities Quarterly* 7, no. 2 (2013).
222 Radostina K. Purvanova, "Face-to-Face versus Virtual Teams: What Have We Really Learned?," *The Psychologist-Manager Journal* 17, no. 1 (2014): 2–29, https://doi.org/10.1037/mgr0000009.
223 Shannon L. Marlow et al., "Does Team Communication Represent a One-Size-Fits-All Approach?: A Meta-Analysis of Team Communication and Performance," *Organizational Behavior and Human Decision Processes* 144 (2018): 145–70, https://doi.org/10.1016/j.obhdp.2017.08.001.
224 Siemens and Burr, "A Trip around the World."

Expanding the Trading Zones Model

In summary, in this book I conceptualise digital history as a meeting of two communities of practice. Digital history can be described as consisting of the digital and of the history; the computational domains and the historical discipline.[225] Both communities are defined by their practices and perform boundary work to distinguish practices that fall within and outside the interests of their communities. To investigate the cross-disciplinary practices of digital history, I consider how boundary work is combined with practices to cross and negotiate those boundaries within trading zones. My main interest is how this affects the practices of historians, in learning computational practices or unlearning traditional historical practices.

In order to investigate trading zones of digital history, I propose to expand the trading zones matrix by Collins et al. with the third dimension of engagement, in order to better understand how trading occurs. This leads to the updated trading zones model in Figure 2, describing six different types of trading zones according to three dimensions (see Table 1). I elaborate these types of trading zones in the next section by applying the model to discussions surrounding digital humanities.

By adding the third dimension of engagement the symmetric-heterogeneous trading zones, what Collins et al. called "fractioned" trading zones, as well as the asymmetric-homogeneous trading zones, what they called "subversive", are both split into connected and disconnected types. A significant effect is that this model reflects the split that Collins et al. made in fractioned trading zones between boundary objects and interactional expertise.[226] In my model, scholars are not in close connection in a disconnected fractioned trading zone, so that each develops their own perspective on the objects under investigation. These objects are what holds the collaboration together, but need no continuous negotiation towards a shared framework, thereby constituting boundary objects.[227] Boundary objects have been described as "objects which are both plastic enough to adapt to local needs and the constraints of the several parties employing them, yet robust enough to maintain a common identity across sites."[228] As such, the same object can be interpreted as a different thing by the different communities. For example,

---

225 Edmond, "The Role of the Professional Intermediary in Expanding the Humanities Computing Base"; Svensson, "The Digital Humanities as a Humanities Project."
226 Collins, Evans and Gorman, "Trading Zones and Interactional Expertise."
227 Susan Leigh Star and James R. Griesemer, "Institutional Ecology, `Translations' and Boundary Objects: Amateurs and Professionals in Berkeley's Museum of Vertebrate Zoology, 1907–39," *Social Studies of Science* 19, no. 3 (1989): 387–420, https://doi.org/10.1177/030631289019003001.
228 Star and Griesemer, 393.

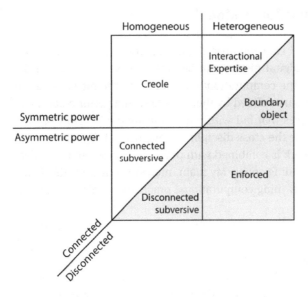

Figure 2: Three-dimensional overview of trading zones. The first dimension of changing practices (homogeneous-heterogeneous) is represented by the left and right halves of the figure. The second dimension of power relations (symmetric-asymmetric) is represented by the upper and lower halves of the figure. The third dimension of engagement (connected-disconnected) is represented by the white and grey halves of the figure.

Table 1: Typology of trading zones according to the three dimensions.

TITLE	ENGAGEMENT	POWER RELATIONS	CHANGING PRACTICES
Creole	Connected	Symmetric	Homogeneous
Interactional Expertise	Connected	Symmetric	Heterogeneous
Connected subversive	Connected	Asymmetric	Homogeneous
Disconnected subversive	Disconnected	Asymmetric	Homogeneous
Boundary object	Disconnected	Symmetric	Heterogeneous
Enforced	Disconnected	Asymmetric	Heterogeneous

a letter might serve as a source on which to build a narrative for a historian yet be a data point to train a language model for a computational linguist.

In contrast, in a connected fractioned trading zone, the culturally separated sides of the collaboration engage with one another through one or more interactional experts who are able to broker between the two communities. Brokers learn enough about the interacting communities to be able to understand their practices, and can discuss in the language of each community, while not becoming contributing experts. For example, a historian might learn to read and discuss publications from computer science, without the ability to publish computer science work themselves. According to Collins et al., fractioned trading zones, and especially interactional expertise, are the most common type of trading zones.

Two types of trading zones are not shown in this model, since I do not consider these compatible with the literature. First, disconnected-symmetric-homogeneous trading zones. This would constitute a creole community of scholars not engaging with one another. However, without engagement, there is no opportunity to develop such an inter-language.[229] Without mutual engagement, a community of practice cannot be sustained.[230] The second type not in the model is the exact opposite; connected-asymmetric-heterogeneous trading zones. This would constitute what Collins et al. called an "enforced" trading zone, yet with scholars actively engaging with one another. However, this type was described to lack cultural exchanges, thus without true engagement.[231] I consequently do not consider these to be possible trading zones and have left them out of the model.

The Digital Humanities Trading Zone

The literature on digital humanities offers a broad range of characterisations of the interactions between humanists and computational experts. In some cases, these refer explicitly to trading zones, while in others the characterisation may be fit into one of the types of trading zones. This section thus serves a double purpose. First, it elaborates the model by considering what each trading zone type looks like. Second, it reflects on characterisations of digital humanities in terms of the model. Note that this discussion does not include the dimension of engagement, since the literature tends to discuss digital humanities as a global phenomenon of existing engagement.

The upper-left quadrant, symmetric-homogeneous (creole) trading zone, describes the situation where two communities have become deliberately homogeneous. The communities that started the trading zones do not preserve their cultures, but instead establish a new disciplinary culture. Some scholars have argued that digital humanities constitutes such a community, as a discipline separate from computer science or any specific humanities discipline. Digital humanities would have its own practices, resources and discourse serving as creole. Scholars that have argued for this include Willard McCarty, who described

---

229 Olson et al., "The (Currently) Unique Advantages of Collocated Work"; Siemens, "'It's a Team If You Use "Reply All"': An Exploration of Research Teams in Digital Humanities Environments."
230 Wenger, *Communities of Practice*.
231 Collins, Evans and Gorman, "Trading Zones and Interactional Expertise."

"humanities computing" as a third space, neither one culture nor the other, and Melissa Terras who argued digital humanities is a discipline in its own right.[232]

The upper-right quadrant, symmetric-heterogeneous (fractioned) trading zone, describes the situation where two communities deliberately remain distinct while interacting. The communities that started the trading zones preserve their cultures, so that a continuous coordination is necessary to establish a pidgin to enable exchanges. Collins et al. stated that this is the most common type of trading zone, which is reflected in the literature on digital humanities. Most authors refer to Patrik Svensson, who described digital humanities as a meeting place, an "inbetween" the two cultures of humanities and computational research.[233] In this line, Andrea Hunter described digital humanities as a bridge or translation between two cultures.[234] Bernhard Rieder and Theo Röhle argued that not the language in terminology should be coordinated, but the practices in methods.[235] Finally, Joris van Zundert questioned whether the formation of methodological creole truly happens.[236] In his study of a digital humanities collaboration he found scholars and computational experts exchanged jargon only superficially. While he observed scholars appropriating technology in their existing practices, he did not find a deeper exchange of theoretical concepts, indicating the collaboration constituted a fractioned rather than a creole trading zone.

The lower-left quadrant, asymmetric-homogeneous (subversive) trading zone, describes the situation where two communities become homogeneous through one community shaping the practices of the other. This means that one-sided convergence takes place, where one community becomes more like the other, yet without acquiring the expertise of the dominant community. For example, historians might adopt methods from computer science, without acquiring the expertise to understand and influence these methods. Several authors point to the use of ready-made tools as such a trading zone. When a historian uses a digital tool for research, the user interface prescribes how the software should be used and how an object

---

232 Willard McCarty, *Humanities Computing* (Palgrave Macmillan, 2005); Melissa Terras, "Disciplined: Using Educational Studies to Analyse 'Humanities Computing,'" *Literary and Linguistic Computing* 21, no. 2 (2006): 229–46, https://doi.org/10.1093/llc/fql022.

233 Svensson, "The Digital Humanities as a Humanities Project."

234 Andrea Hunter, "Digital Humanities as Third Culture," *MedieKultur: Journal of Media and Communication Research* 30, no. 57 (2014): 18–33.

235 Bernhard Rieder and Theo Röhle, "Digital Methods: Five Challenges," in *Understanding Digital Humanities*, ed. David Berry (Palgrave Macmillan, 2012), 67–84.

236 Joris van Zundert, "The Case of the Bold Button: Social Shaping of Technology and the Digital Scholarly Edition," *Digital Scholarship in the Humanities* 31, no. 4 (2016): 898–910, https://doi.org/10.1093/llc/fqw012.

should be understood.[237] When the software generates certain results, a historian needs to trust that these results are adequate.[238] A historian as end-user thereby has no power to change the user interface or options to fit their needs.[239] Johanna Drucker in this context writes about graphical tools as trojan horses.[240] Pierre Mounier furthermore suggested that digital humanities brings research in the form of projects and short-term competitive funding to the humanities.[241] He later added the characterisation of digital humanities as contaminating humanistic attitudes toward research objects, methods and labour.[242] E-Science more broadly, and the spread of digital technologies in research, has similarly been characterised as computer science "invading" other disciplines.[243] Moreover, it could be argued that the many warnings to humanities scholars to adapt or become marginalised, as discussed in the previous chapter, would fit in this quadrant as arguments that historians need to adopt the methods from digital humanities or computer science, whether they want to or not.

Finally, the lower-right quadrant, asymmetric-heterogeneous (enforced) trading zone, describes the situation where the two communities remain distinct, while one community shapes the practices of the other. This may occur when the dominant community protects its expertise against the subordinate community and does not want to learn from the latter either.[244] For example, computer scientists might dictate how a tool will work and what the goal of a digital humanities project should be, without teaching historians anything about the internal workings, nor trying to understand how historians would want to use the tool. Or vice versa, historians might demand certain features to be developed by computer scientists, without informing computer scientists about the tacit knowledge of historical practice or trying to understand what software development entails. Such a power struggle of respectively technology-push or technology-pull strategies is not

---

237 Mel Stanfill, "The Interface as Discourse: The Production of Norms through Web Design," *New Media & Society* 17, no. 7 (2014): 1059–74, https://doi.org/10.1177/1461444814520873.
238 Rebecca Sutton Koeser, "Trusting Others to 'Do the Math,'" *Interdisciplinary Science Reviews* 40, no. 4 (2016): 376–92, https://doi.org/10.1080/03080188.2016.1165454.
239 Lev Manovich, *Software Takes Command* (Bloomsbury Academic, 2013).
240 Johanna Drucker, "Humanities Approaches to Graphical Display," *Digital Humanities Quarterly* 5, no. 1 (2011): 1–21.
241 Pierre Mounier, "Une «utopie Politique» Pour Les Humanités Numériques?," *Socio* 4 (2015): 97–112, https://doi.org/10.4000/socio.1338.
242 Pierre Mounier, *Les humanités numériques: Une histoire critique*, online (Éditions de la Maison des sciences de l'homme, 2018), https://doi.org/10.4000/books.editionsmsh.12006.
243 Meyer and Schroeder, *Knowledge Machines*, 207.
244 Collins, Evans and Gorman, "Trading Zones and Interactional Expertise."

uncommon in software development.[245] Yet, within digital humanities this would usually be seen as a worst-case scenario of a failed collaboration. I consequently did not encounter authors that characterised digital humanities as such. However, digital humanities collaborations regularly include software engineers rather than computational researchers, as participants who do not have their own research agenda and do not appropriate the expertise of historians. Such cases, as well as collaborations that are multidisciplinary rather than interdisciplinary, arguably constitute asymmetric-heterogenous trading zones.[246]

As noted above, it is of interest that in discussing digital humanities as a trading zone, the literature seems to describe the digital humanities as a unitary trading zone that acts as a global coordination.[247] This goes against the original description of trading zones as local coordination, exactly because of global incommensurability. Furthermore, coordination and becoming a homogeneous community is a long-term process. A trading zone is thus not a static state of being, but collaborations can change over time and switch from one type to another. By investigating digital history projects as local and temporal trading zones, this book provides insights into how different practices of coordination lead to different trading zones and thereby to different outcomes.

Method

To approach the question of how historians interact in and are affected by digital history collaborations, I need to unpack the collaborations and untangle the interactions among participants. I am, therefore, mostly interested in the people practising the negotiation of digital history. Focusing on practitioners allows me to move beyond the common scholarly debates between proponents and opponents of digital history. This problem of untangling practices from debates was previously described by the anthropologist Clifford Geertz.[248] Analogous to his study of religion, digital history has its preachers, those scholars who claim that without digital history the profession shall be lost, and its "atheists" (or "Luddites"), those scholars who oppose digital history as dangerous to the values of

---

245 Jan van den Ende and Wilfred Dolfsma, "Technology-Push, Demand-Pull and the Shaping of Technological Paradigms – Patterns in the Development of Computing Technology," *Journal of Evolutionary Economics* 15, no. 1 (2005): 83–99, https://doi.org/10.1007/s00191-004-0220-1.
246 Collins, Evans and Gorman, "Trading Zones Revisited."
247 This same assumption of digital humanities as a global monolithic community arguably underlies much of the controversy around defining the field as well.
248 Geertz, *The Interpretation of Cultures*.

historical discipline. If I were to limit my investigation to such debates, it would be easy to follow conclusions to one end of the spectrum that digital history is a necessity for otherwise historians will not be taken seriously anymore, or to the other end that digital history is a neo-liberal enterprise that endangers scholarly values.[249] Yet my aim is not to make claims about whether digital history is good or bad, but to come to an understanding of how it is performed and experienced.

Furthermore, my interest is mainly in how historians are affected by digital history. Above I characterise digital history as the meeting between the digital and the history. Yet my focus of attention lies on how the digital affects the history; how computational practices affect historical practices. This focus follows existing debates around digital humanities. The literature discussed thus far has mainly originated from humanities scholars reflecting on the digitalisation of their profession. For this reason, Julie Thompson Klein described methodological interdisciplinarity in digital humanities as importing computational methods into the humanities.[250] The digital humanist Patrik Svensson moreover characterised "digital humanities as a humanities project."[251] In one study, the computer scientist Stefan Jänicke and his collaborators followed the diffusion of a digital humanities concept back into the computer science community.[252] They reviewed literature on distant reading visualisations and compared growth in the digital humanities and computer science communities between 2005 and 2015. While the topic grew steadily within digital humanities, from two papers in 2005 to 23 in 2015, the topic remained stable in the computer science domain at two to four papers per year. This suggests that trading of practices in digital humanities is mainly in the direction from the computational to the humanistic, rather than vice versa.

Fitting with my focus, my heuristic for selecting case studies was the participation of academic historians, with a PhD in history or at a history department, who collaborate with computational experts. Moreover, I conducted this research as a member of a history department myself. My results are therefore biased towards the perspectives of historians and consider the direction of shifting practices from the computational to the historical.

---

249 As argued by respectively Boonstra, Breure and Doorn, "Past, Present and Future of Historical Information Science"; Mounier, "Une «utopie Politique» Pour Les Humanités Numériques?"
250 Klein, *Interdisciplining Digital Humanities*.
251 Svensson, "The Digital Humanities as a Humanities Project."
252 Stefan Jänicke et al., "Visual Text Analysis in Digital Humanities: Visual Text Analysis in Digital Humanities," *Computer Graphics Forum* 36, no. 6 (2017): 226–50, https://doi.org/10.1111/cgf.12873.

My approach to these practices is that of ethnographic research, as has been defined in the work of Clifford Geertz.[253] He described ethnography not as a set of methods, like interviews or observations, but as thick description. Whereas "thin description" is the mere description of what someone is doing, thick description aims to describe the structures in which those actions take place and have meaning. For example, in my study of a digital history collaboration, I am not just interested in observing that a computational expert delivered a technology and that a historian responds in a positive or negative way. Instead, I aim to uncover the cultural structures that lead to tensions of how computational experts design technology or how historians build up particular expectations of technology.

To this epistemology of thick description, the anthropologist Michael Agar added that ethnography works in an iterative and recursive way.[254] The investigation of a different culture leads to so called "rich points", where the ethnographer does not understand what the participant says or does. Here the ethnographer must assume coherence, that the point of confusion makes sense in the context of the participant's culture. For example, I might observe a historian criticising digital history on grounds that could be dismissed as "Luddite". Yet it is far more enlightening to investigate how this criticism is coherent within the context of the epistemic culture of that historian. This way I can pursue how such criticisms play a role in the alignment of computational methods with historical values. My approach is thereby influenced by the approaches related to social studies of science, investigating scholarship as social practices. My emphasis on local observations of social practices is hence inspired from the seminal work in lab studies.[255]

Yet a criticism of local studies is that, while they reveal certain mechanisms, they obscure others, particularly mechanisms that lie outside the local scope but shape it from "outside".[256] I therefore employ triangulation to collect observations of digital history practices at different sites and scales.[257] This

---

253 Geertz, *The Interpretation of Cultures*.

254 Michael Agar, "An Ethnography By Any Other Name . . . ," *Forum Qualitative Sozialforschung / Forum: Qualitative Social Research* 7, no. 4 (2006), https://doi.org/10.17169/fqs-7.4.177; Michael Agar, "Ethnography," in *Culture and Language Use*, ed. Gunter Senft, Jan-Ola Östman and Jef Verschueren (John Benjamins Publishing Company, 2009), 110–20.

255 Knorr Cetina, *Epistemic Cultures*; Bruno Latour, *Science in Action* (Harvard University Press, 1987); Latour and Woolgar, *Laboratory Life*.

256 Peter Galison, "Limits of Localism: The Scale of Sight," in *What Reason Promises*, ed. Wendy Doniger, Peter Galison and Susan Neiman (Berlin, Boston: De Gruyter, 2016), 155–70, https://doi.org/10.1515/9783110455113-020.

257 Helena Karasti and Jeanette Blomberg, "Studying Infrastructuring Ethnographically," *Computer Supported Cooperative Work* 27, no. 2 (2018): 233–65, https://doi.org/10.1007/s10606-017-9296-7.

triangulation of perspectives is conducted by juxtaposing the views and practices of historians and computational experts, and by comparing between a number of collaborations that serve as case studies. I moreover contextualise these case studies in studies with a wider selection of scholars. I thus adopt a "multi-sited ethnography" approach to study multiple trading zones of digital history and find differences and similarities.[258] Through this strategy, I aim to generalise my findings of the case studies and gain not just a local understanding of an observed trading zone, but a view of trading zones in digital history more broadly.

In the next chapter, I start with my ethnographic observations at a single site, the University of Luxembourg, and examine the first dimension of trading zones, namely how participants of digital history collaborations engage with one another across disciplinary and institutional boundaries.

---

[258] George E. Marcus, "Ethnography in/of the World System: The Emergence of Multi-Sited Ethnography," *Annual Review of Anthropology* 24 (1995): 95–117.

Engaging in Collaboration

Collaboration

Collaboration is far from ubiquitous in the humanities, where the myth of the lone scholar is still a prevalent image. Collaboration has even been suggested as one of the practices dividing the Two Cultures, with the humanities as solitary scholarship and the sciences as teamwork.[259] This division is reinforced by a reluctance of scholars to adopt collaboration in opposition to a "science model" of their research, with practices of collaboration standing in contrast to established disciplinary cultures.[260] In this line, historical research has been said to require "'a single intellect to turn over the material'; 'ideas have to be shaped in the mind of the individual scholar'."[261]

And yet, within the digital humanities, collaboration is emphasised.[262] The different facets of digital history research and digital infrastructure development, such as computer technology, data management and historic inquiry, call for experts with different backgrounds to collaborate. In digital humanities collaborations, the most frequent reason for teamwork is the joining of different skill sets and expertise.[263] Consequently, digital humanities and digital history are accompanied by a proliferation of project-based work and institutionalisation in centres and labs to sustain interdisciplinary collaboration.[264] That is not

---

259 McCarty, *Humanities Computing*; Leslie A. Real, "Collaboration in the Sciences and the Humanities: A Comparative Phenomenology," *Arts and Humanities in Higher Education* 11, no. 3 (2012): 250–61, https://doi.org/10.1177/1474022212437310; Snow, *The Two Cultures and the Scientific Revolution*.
260 Jenny M. Lewis, Sandy Ross and Thomas Holden, "The How and Why of Academic Collaboration: Disciplinary Differences and Policy Implications," *Higher Education* 64, no. 5 (2012): 693–708, https://doi.org/10.1007/s10734-012-9521-8.
261 Tony Becher and Paul R. Trowler, *Academic Tribes and Territories: Intellectual Enquire and the Culture of Disciplines*, 2nd ed. (The Society for Research into Higher Education & Open University Press, 2001), 126.
262 Borgman, "The Digital Future Is Now"; Klein, *Interdisciplining Digital Humanities*; Lisa Spiro, "'This Is Why We Fight': Defining the Values of the Digital Humanities," in *Debates in Digital Humanities*, ed. Matthew K. Gold, online (University of Minnesota Press, 2012).
263 Lynne Siemens et al., "'More Minds Are Brought to Bear on a Problem': Methods of Interaction and Collaboration within Digital Humanities Research Teams," *Digital Studies / Le Champ Numérique* 2, no. 2 (2011).
264 Urszula Pawlicka-Deger, "The Laboratory Turn: Exploring Discourses, Landscapes, and Models of Humanities Labs," *Digital Humanities Quarterly* 14, no. 3 (2020); Robinson, "Digital Humanities: Is Bigger, Better?"; Edin Tabak, "A Hybrid Model for Managing DH Projects," *Digital Humanities Quarterly* 11, no. 1 (2017).

to say that collaboration in the humanities mirrors the practices of the sciences. For example, one study of a digital humanities network found that the network provided the exchange of information and insights, without necessarily leading to co-authoring papers or co-analysing data.[265] Within the network, scholars still mainly worked by themselves. Thus far, single-authored works remain the dominant form of authorship in the digital humanities.[266]

Collaborations in digital history can, therefore, be seen as a balancing of teamwork, such as jointly working towards the goal of a project, and individual scholarship. This balancing requires scholars to coordinate their goals and responsibilities with the team, so that the discrepancies between the ambitions of participants does not inhibit collaboration.[267] Considering the uncertainties posed by digital history, goals emerge through continuous negotiation, rather than being fully established prior to collaborating.[268] As such, collaborations require mutual trust to coordinate ill-defined goals.[269] As collaboration is not already entrenched in their disciplinary culture, humanities scholars have to learn how to collaborate, and tend to do so by trial-and-error through continued interactions between team members.[270]

The current chapter explores how historians collaborate with one another and with cross-disciplinary partners. I thereby explore the dimension of engagement and consider how disciplinary and institutional boundaries are simultaneously crossed and established. By crossing the boundaries between disciplines, as interdisciplinary boundary crossing, the question is how this affects the relationship with a historian's disciplinary community. It has been argued that participants drift away from their disciplinary culture following the adoption of new

---

265 Anabel Quan-Haase, Juan Luis Suarez and David M. Brown, "Collaborating, Connecting, and Clustering in the Humanities: A Case Study of Networked Scholarship in an Interdisciplinary, Dispersed Team," *American Behavioral Scientist* 59, no. 5 (2015): 565–81, https://doi.org/10.1177/0002764214556806.

266 Julianne Nyhan and Oliver Duke-Williams, "Joint and Multi-Authored Publication Patterns in the Digital Humanities," *Literary and Linguistic Computing* 29, no. 3 (2014): 387–99, https://doi.org/10.1093/llc/fqu018.

267 Lynne Siemens, "'It's a Team If You Use "Reply All"': An Exploration of Research Teams in Digital Humanities Environments," *Literary and Linguistic Computing* 24, no. 2 (2009): 225–33, https://doi.org/10.1093/llc/fqp009.

268 Caroline Haythornthwaite et al., "Challenges for Research and Practice in Distributed, Interdisciplinary Collaboration," in *New Infrastructures for Knowledge Production: Understanding e-Science*, ed. Christine Hine (IGI Global, 2006), 143–66.

269 Petra Sonderegger, "Creating Shared Understanding in Research Across Distance: Distance Collaboration across Cultures in R&D," in *E-Research: Transformation in Scholarly Practice*, ed. Nicolas W. Jankowski (Routledge, 2009).

270 Siemens et al., "More Minds Are Brought to Bear on a Problem."

vocabularies and practices.[271] If historians wish to discuss their digital research with other historians who are not a digital history collaboration, they may now find themselves confronted with a boundary of different practices and vocabularies that they did not experience before. As such, collaborations potentially constitute what I term intradisciplinary boundary construction.

In addition to such disciplinary boundary practices, digital history collaborations interact with institutional boundaries. Here too, institutional boundaries may be crossed, as scholars collaborate across different institutes, such as a collaboration between a history and a computer science department, or become embedded across different departments, e.g., a computer scientist employed at the history department. In contrast, digital history collaborations may lead to institutional boundaries to be constructed, as digital history centres or labs are institutionalised.

Studying Engagement Across Boundaries

In an earlier paper, I have explored these boundary practices quantitatively through an online questionnaire on digital humanities collaborations.[272] I found that most participants in digital humanities collaborations came from the humanities and that most collaborations were led by humanities scholars. In line with these findings, two-thirds of the collaborations described by respondents were embedded in the humanities building of an institute, rather than a computer science building or a library. Finally, I found respondents communicated significantly more often with disciplinary peers outside their digital humanities collaboration than with cross-disciplinary collaborators.

These findings suggest that digital humanities collaborations are predominantly rooted within the humanities, corroborating the characterisation of "the digital humanities as a humanities project" by digital humanities scholar Patrik Svensson.[273] Yet boundary practices can be subtle and are conducted over several years, aspects that are hard to investigate with an online questionnaire. How the dominance of humanities scholars in digital humanities collaborations shapes the trading zones in practice cannot be determined from the results of an online questionnaire. To deepen our understanding of boundary practices of digital history

---

271 Wenger, *Communities of Practice*, 103.
272 Max Kemman, "Boundary Practices of Digital Humanities Collaborations," *DH Benelux Journal* 1 (2019).
273 Svensson, "The Digital Humanities as a Humanities Project."

collaborations in practice, the next section, therefore, describes a qualitative study of digital history trading zones.

The below qualitative study describes several trading zones at one site, the University of Luxembourg. In 2013, the Institute for History at this university appointed a professor for contemporary and digital history, who became a driving force behind many subsequent developments of digital history at the university. As his first PhD candidate, hired in 2014, I had the opportunity to observe how he pushed for digital history and how collaborations were initiated, organised and conducted in practice. As such, I observed how he performed boundary practices with cross-disciplinary collaborators and disciplinary peers.

Four institutional units housed within the humanities building (*Maison des Sciences Humaines*) of the University of Luxembourg are central to this study:

1. the humanities faculty (*Faculté des Sciences Humaines, des Sciences de l'Éducation et des Sciences Sociales* – FHSE),
2. the Institute for History (IHIST, part of the humanities faculty established in 2003),
3. the Luxembourg Centre for Contemporary and Digital History (C²DH, established in 2016),
4. the Digital History Lab and the HiPoPhil Lab (both established in 2015) used by both the C²DH and IHIST.

This case study combined methods of ethnographic observation and oral history interviews.[274] I collected observations on boundary practices as they are performed as well as reflections on how these practices were shaped over time. The below discussion thereby provides a diachronic perspective on engagement, boundary practices and how these change over time. I observed how the labs and centre were established, how historians participated and how conflicts were coordinated. To enrich my observations, I conducted 12 interviews with ten people.[275] I interviewed eight historians on permanent contracts at the institute (five) and the centre (three). I furthermore interviewed two members of the centre's Digital Research Infrastructure unit, which provided technical support to the rest of the centre. By describing these institutional units by their histories, starting from the appointment of the professor for digital history, I aim to render visible the interventions and controversies that led to boundary constructions and boundary crossings.

---

274 Geertz, *The Interpretation of Cultures*; Donald Ritchie, *Doing Oral History* (Oxford University Press, 2014).

275 The interviews were semi-structured and diverged regularly from the questions. All interviews were recorded and manually transcribed and coded in MAXQDA.

The following section describes the establishment of the C²DH, especially focusing on the relations between the centre and the institute. For an overview of important events in the establishment of the C²DH, see Figure 3. In the section thereafter, I describe the establishment and evolution of the two laboratories and how historians from the centre and the institute engaged with the laboratories.

Constructing Collaboration through a Digital History Centre

Before describing the history of the C²DH, it is of interest to briefly discuss what differentiates a "centre" from a "department". The literature on the proliferation of centres provides some insights into why the centre was established at the University of Luxembourg and how this affects the relationship with the institute.

In the history of academic research at universities, departments have become the authorities of disciplines where knowledge is generated and passed on to future generations of researchers. As the scholar of organisation studies Richard Whitley concluded; "[s]cience, therefore, became departmentalized".[276] In other words, disciplinary boundaries were very much the same as institutional boundaries. However, in several disciplines, this departmentalisation of science came under pressure as new problems required interdisciplinary approaches. This demanded new organisational forms, for which the interdisciplinary research centre is one model that has proliferated.[277] Similar to the vision of interdisciplinary research working on real world problems, with results that can be applied in a societal context, these centres are envisioned to form a bridge between academia and society, both to industry and the public.[278] In order to reach this vision, rather than an organisation into disciplines or around chairs of professors as seen in departments, centres tend to be organised according to research topics. This "'matrixing' of personnel" places researchers from different backgrounds around shared research topics.[279] Through this reorganising of scholars, centres lead to increased

---

[276] Richard Whitley, "The Rise and Decline of University Disciplines in the Sciences," in *Problems in Interdisciplinary Studies*, ed. R. Jurkovich and J.H.P. Paelinck (Gower Publishing Company, 1984), 16.

[277] Paul K. Hoch, "New UK Interdisciplinary Research Centres: Reorganization for New Generic Technology," *Technology Analysis & Strategic Management* 2, no. 1 (1990): 39–48, https://doi.org/10.1080/09537329008523993; Robinson, "Digital Humanities: Is Bigger, Better?"

[278] Gibbons, "Introduction"; Sally Wyatt, "Mode 2 in Action : Working Across Sectors to Create a Center for Humanities and Technology," *Scholarly and Research Communication* 6, no. 4 (2015).

[279] Hoch, "New UK Interdisciplinary Research Centres," 40.

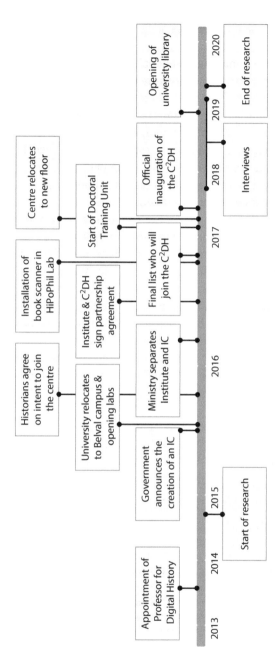

Figure 3: Timeline of notable developments at the University of Luxembourg during my research related to the C²DH.

interdisciplinary collaboration both among members of the centre as with other institutes or corporations.[280]

Centres thus reshaped the traditional organisational structure and cultural practices of research.[281] The new organisational structure demanded new organisational styles in the form of managers.[282] At least in the UK, centres adopted a discourse influenced by business and industry, in order to meet the expectations of societal and economic relevance.[283] The proliferation and success of centres undermined the disciplinary authority of departments, especially with respect to research.[284] The main struggle is, however, with respect to funding; whether the establishment of centres leads to renewed injections of research funding, or a redistribution leading to budget cuts for existing departments.[285]

Within the digital humanities as well, centres have a long history of providing the means to interdisciplinary collaborations among members as well as across institutional boundaries.[286] As such, digital humanities centres have played an important part facilitating the growth of digital humanities as a field. More recently, however, digital humanities centres have been criticised for being an expensive model of scholarship, emphasising the need for continuous funding of work to sustain the organisation. It has consequently been argued that digital humanities centres have served their time as a model for digital humanities work.[287]

In summary, the literature shows not only that the organisation of scholars in a research centre rather than a department leads to different practices, but also

280 Branco L. Ponomariov and P. Craig Boardman, "Influencing Scientists' Collaboration and Productivity Patterns through New Institutions: University Research Centers and Scientific and Technical Human Capital," *Research Policy* 39, no. 5 (2010): 613–24, https://doi.org/10.1016/j.respol.2010.02.013.
281 Julie Thompson Klein, "A Conceptual Vocabulary of Interdisciplinary Science," in *Practicing Interdisciplinarity*, ed. Peter Weingart and Nico Stehr (University of Toronto Press, 2000), 3–24.
282 Hoch, "New UK Interdisciplinary Research Centres."
283 Greg Myers, "Centering: Proposals for an Interdisciplinary Research Center," *Science, Technology, & Human Values* 18, no. 4 (1993): 433–59.
284 Whitley, "The Rise and Decline of University Disciplines in the Sciences."
285 Hoch, "New UK Interdisciplinary Research Centres."
286 Mila Oiva, "The Chili and Honey of Digital Humanities Research:The Facilitation of the Interdisciplinary Transfer of Knowledge in Digital Humanities Centers," *Digital Humanities Quarterly* 14, no. 3 (2020).
287 Andrew Prescott, "Beyond the Digital Humanities Center: The Administrative Landscapes of the Digital Humanities," in *A New Companion to Digital Humanities*, ed. Susan Schreibman, Ray Siemens and John Unsworth (John Wiley & Sons, Ltd., 2015), 459–75, https://doi.org/10.1002/9781118680605.ch32; Robinson, "Digital Humanities: Is Bigger, Better?"; Mark Sample, "On the Death of the Digital Humanities Center," *@samplereality* (blog), March 26, 2010.

that the process of organising scholars into centres is highly political, especially in regard to issues of funding. In the following discussion, I show how this relates to the Luxembourg Centre for Contemporary and Digital History.

Establishment of the C²DH: From Partners to Competitors

One aspect that makes the academic landscape of Luxembourg rather unique is the close relationship between national politics and the university, since there is just one university in the country. The establishment of a centre for contemporary history too started not within the university, but as a political debate. A historian from the institute had been lobbying for a centre for contemporary history for a number of years. At that time, Luxembourg featured several organisations for historical research, namely the Institute for History at the university, but also independent from the university were centres such as the *Centre d'Études et de Recherches Européennes Robert Schuman* and the *Centre Virtuel de la Connaissance sur l'Europe* (CVCE), which both studied European integration and the European Union, the *Centre de Documentation et de Recherche sur la Résistance*, which studied the activities of the Luxembourgish resistance during World War II, and the *Centre de Documentation et de Recherche sur l'Enrôlement forcé*, which studied the Luxembourgish men who were forced to join the German army during World War II. This landscape of historical research institutes was upended following the national elections of 2013, which led to the formation of a new government. For a long time, the Christian CSV (Christian Social People's Party) had been the main party in government, but the 2013 elections led to a government consisting of the liberal DP (Democratic Party), the socialist LSAP (Luxembourg Socialist Workers' Party) and the Greens. The aforementioned historian who had been lobbying was affiliated with the LSAP, and this party subsequently started pushing for the establishment of a centre for contemporary history. This centre should then reinvigorate Luxembourgish contemporary history, as well as cut costs by combining the smaller independent centres into a single larger centre.[288] A recent thesis from a PhD candidate of the Institute for History, who had shown that the Luxembourgish government during World War II was more accommodating to the Germans than was commonly believed, strengthened the argument that more research was needed into contemporary

---

[288] Interviews 3 (December 2017), 5 (January 2018) and 7 (January 2018).

Luxembourgish history.[289] The proposal for a centre for contemporary history was then agreed upon and incorporated in the coalition agreement.

While the parties agreed there should be a centre, they disagreed about how to embed this centre in the existing academic landscape. According to my interviewees, the LSAP wanted to establish this as an independent research centre similar to other countries such as NIOD in the Netherlands or the Leibniz Centre for Contemporary History in Germany, but the DP wanted the centre within the university.[290] At this point, historians from the institute started pushing for the centre to become part of the university, preferably part of the Institute for History. They feared that an independent centre could not guarantee sufficient academic freedom, and argued that the institute already did research on contemporary history, as exemplified by the PhD research on Luxembourgish collaborators in World War II.[291] However, politicians feared that a centre as part of the Institute for History would not be visible enough and that contemporary historical research would end up being overshadowed by research on other historical periods.

The middle ground was to establish a centre within the university, but independent from the faculties. The University of Luxembourg already had an existing structure for this with the interdisciplinary centres (IC). At the time there were two ICs in biomedicine (LCSB – Luxembourg Centre for Systems Biomedicine) and ICT (SnT – Interdisciplinary Centre for Security, Reliability and Trust). These centres operated on the same level as faculties and the directors had the same status as deans. Thus, in June of 2015, the government officially announced the decision to establish an interdisciplinary centre for contemporary history and the university could start the search for a director of the centre to be.[292] Afterwards, several historians were disappointed in the rector of the university. They said he should have pushed more for the centre to be integrated either in the Faculty of Humanities or the Institute for History, and that he too easily accepted the promised funding for a research centre.[293]

---

289 Vincent Artuso, "*La Collaboration Au Luxembourg Durant La Seconde Guerre Mondiale (1940–1945): Accommodation, Adaptation, Assimilation*", Luxemburg-Studien = Études Luxembourgeoises, Band 4 (Frankfurt am Main: Peter Lang Edition, 2013).
290 Interviews 1 (November 2017) and 3.
291 Interviews 4 (January 2018) and 5.
292 "Déclaration du gouvernement sur la situation économique, sociale et financière du pays 2015 (traduction française)", May 5, 2015, https://gouvernement.lu/fr/actualites/toutes_actua lites/discours/2015/05-mai/05-declaration-fr.html; "Résumé des travaux du 5 juin 2015", June 5, 2015, https://gouvernement.lu/fr/actualites/toutes_actualites/communiques/2015/06-juin/05-conseil-gouvernement.html.
293 Interview 3.

As mentioned above, the Institute for History had appointed a professor for contemporary and digital history in 2013. This professor decided to apply for the position of director and was indeed appointed. He was motivated by the rector and the dean of the Faculty of Humanities to do so. Yet some historians attempted to dissuade him from doing so; in one interview this was raised as a possible attempt to form a sort of "historical block" that would be ready to compete with the centre to be.[294] While this strategy did not succeed, it exemplified the first signs of boundary construction.

Note that until now, there had only been plans for a centre for contemporary history. It was this professor for digital history who then pushed to make it a centre for contemporary and digital history. Of interest here is the parallel between argumentation for his initial appointment and his lobbying, which gives insight into the contingencies of how digital history came to be a topic of interest at the university.

In 2013, the professor for modern history was set to retire and a committee was established to hire a replacement. One of the historians from this committee, whom I interviewed, then argued that this was an opportunity to distinguish the history master from existing masters by bringing more attention to digital history. He argued that "there are hundreds of masters of European history, what could be a specific point to distinguish it from other masters is digital history."[295] He pushed within the committee to hire a professor for modern and digital history, which they set out to do. They did not succeed in a candidate for modern and digital history, however, but did find a candidate for contemporary and digital history. At this point the committee had to decide what to give preference, either maintain the period and hire a professor for modern but not digital history or maintain the topic and hire a professor for digital but not modern history. To the disappointment of some historians, who had agreed to include the digital topic with the modern period, the committee decided to give preference to the digital topic and appointed a professor for contemporary and digital history.[296] Later, with the formation of the centre, the professor for digital history followed the same line of argumentation. In the interview he said "there are ten [institutes for contemporary history], we should make a difference, we should be different, and that is why I think it should have 'digital' in the name."[297]

The ministry exemplified an ambivalent relationship to this emphasis on digital history. On the one hand, early announcements, as well as the speech by the

---

294 Interview 4.
295 Interview 1.
296 Interview 1.
297 Interview 4.

minister for higher education at the official inauguration of the centre in May 2017, spoke solely of the institute for contemporary history, *l'Institute d'Histoire du Temps Présent*, or the short-hand IHTP. Yet on the other hand, from the very first announcements, the ministry emphasised innovation of historical research.[298] The centre's strategy was to be guided by digital history and linked to Digital Luxembourg, the government's initiative to coordinate the nation's digital strategy.[299] Furthermore, the first large project of the centre would be an exhibition on World War I that was "not limited to a museum building. It is a digital, interactive and dynamic exhibition. This new project will thus be able to reach a wider audience".[300]

Through arguments of differentiation with existing institutes, a professor of contemporary and digital history who did not meet the original requirement of modern history was appointed and a centre planned for contemporary history became concerned with digital history. Both aspects show that involved historians and politicians shared an understanding of the potential for digital history in Luxembourg, with politicians arguing that "the aim is to seize the opportunity to create a new innovative centre by occupying a niche of competence with socio-economic potential for the Grand Duchy."[301] As a result, the University of Luxembourg founded one of the largest centres related to digital history in the world, consisting of over 100 researchers and support staff.[302]

With the decision to embed the centre inside the university, another debate was how to fit the centre in the existing organisational structure. During the planning phase, historians of the institute conceived of several models for interaction between the institute, the faculty, and the centre. One model was to work with dual affiliations, with the historians in the institute, but affiliated to the centre for interdisciplinary projects. Another model was to define the centre as a digital humanities service centre that would provide expertise and support to the rest of the Faculty of Humanities, as a more auxiliary science.[303] Yet another model was to define four research topics for the centre: digital history, contemporary Luxembourgish history, contemporary European history and longue durée. The

---

298 "Résumé des travaux du 5 juin 2015".

299 "About Us", Digital Luxembourg website, accessed February 15, 2021, https://digital-luxembourg.public.lu/about-us.

300 "Déclaration du gouvernement sur la situation économique, sociale et financière du pays 2015 (traduction française)", quote translated from French. The project itself can be found at "Éischte Weltkrich", accessed May 12, 2021, https://ww1.lu.

301 "Résumé des travaux du 5 juin 2015", quote translated from French.

302 "Self-Evaluation Report", Luxembourg Centre for Contemporary and Digital History, April 2019.

303 Interviews 2 (December 2017), 3 and 7.

longue dureé topic would then consist of the pre-contemporary historians from classical, medieval and modern history.[304] This model was favoured by the historians and at an institute meeting near the end of 2015, the historians voted they would all join the centre to be.[305]

Yet this vote was overruled when the ministry decided this was not the model they favoured. The minister for higher education explicitly told the director of the centre that the professors for classical history and medieval history would not be allowed to join the centre. Boundary construction was performed by a third party, in that the ministry decided the contemporary and non-contemporary historians would not be part of the same institutional unit. In the interviews, historians speculated about the reasoning for this political decision, which significantly affected later relationships between historians. The main reason seemed to be related to why the centre could not be part of the Faculty of Humanities or Institute for History in the first place, namely that the ministry feared non-contemporary historians would overshadow contemporary historians in the centre. A more political reason that was speculated was that these two professors from classical and medieval history were supposedly associated with the CSV, the Christian party that led government before the new government. As written by one historian in an opinion piece in a Luxembourgish newspaper: "the C²DH is seen as the consecration of a certain progressive spirit against an Institute for History associated with a Catholic movement, necessarily conservative, even nationalist."[306] Consequently, the final model was to have two separate institutional units. The Institute for History was to remain within the Humanities faculty, while the centre would become an IC.

The centre organised itself around four research topics; Public History, Contemporary History of Luxembourg, Contemporary History of Europe and Digital History and Historiography. Furthermore, a separate unit for Digital Research Infrastructure was established to facilitate the technical necessities of the four research topics. The centre furthermore employed support staff such as secretaries, financial administrators and communication officers. Apart from the two professors of classical and medieval history, other historians were given the choice to join the centre or remain in the institute. Among these historians, some chose to join the centre as they felt their research was mainly about contemporary history.

---

304 "IC LICHT_profile_proposal_InstitHIST", Institute for History, University of Luxembourg, October 2015.
305 "Protokoll Des Mercredi de l'histoire Vom 14. Oktober 2015", Institute for History, University of Luxembourg, October 20, 2015.
306 "Quelle Dette Pour Quelle Université?", D'Lëtzebuerger Land, July 14, 2017, https://web.ar chive.org/web/20190114192601/http://www.land.lu/page/article/148/333148/FRE/index.html, quote translated from French.

They considered they could improve their research in a setting more focused on contemporary history. Those who chose to remain in the institute did so because they felt that their main research was not about contemporary history, and in some cases because they wanted to remain loyal to the institute. Notice that the reasons were thus not related to digital history. Of the then 34 members of the institute, 14 moved to the centre, including myself.[307]

Having had a choice, this did not mean these scholars felt empowered. Some were disappointed that the ministry reached inside the university, affecting academic freedom. Others were mainly disappointed that two years of debates among themselves for appropriate models were simply overruled, and that they lacked any power to shape the centre. Consequently, some historians from the institute became very critical about the centre's existence, reinforcing the boundaries constructed by the ministry. These criticisms were then reiterated in discussions around where chairs should be embedded. When a professor from the Institute for History retired in 2017, both the centre and institute had the ambition of appointing a successor. As a new centre, with the ambition of becoming a centre of excellence, the rector promised the chair would be succeeded within the centre. In opposition, the institute desired to maintain its research agenda, and the dean of the Faculty of Humanities promised the chair would be succeeded within the institute. Moreover, I described above how the previous professor of modern history came to be replaced by a professor of contemporary history, who then became director of the centre. Historians from the institute consequently argued that his chair should be returned to the institute, as it was originally the chair of modern history.[308]

However, the first position was funded by government during the establishment of the university in 2003 to attract Luxembourgish secondary school teachers to create a critical mass of scholars at the university. The minister of higher education suggested that if a successor was to be appointed, this successor would again be a secondary school teacher, a suggestion heavily critiqued.[309] Yet he did not offer concrete plans for the appointment of a successor. For the second position, the institute was dependent of the rectorate, which was going through a financial crisis and significantly cut research budgets.[310] These struggles thus reached a stalemate without any concrete plans for the future from the ministry or rectorate. This episode demonstrated that while some scholars saw this as a struggle between

---

307 Membres_InstitutHIST_October 2016, November 10, 2016.

308 Interview 1.

309 "Quelle Dette Pour Quelle Université?"

310 "Le C2DH, Victime Collatérale de La Crise à l'Uni", Paperjam, July 7, 2017, https://web.ar chive.org/web/20170708123454/http://paperjam.lu/news/le-c2dh-victime-collaterale-de-la-crise-a-luni.

the centre and the institute, this was caused or at least significantly influenced by a top-down political decision of funding, with historians from neither unit really in power to push for a decision.

Situating the Centre: Interacting through Open Doors

The next phase of boundary practices started when the centre became physically real in office space. Since the University of Luxembourg moved to a new campus in the summer of 2015, all historians all been located on the second floor of the *Maison des Sciences Humaines*, the building accommodating the Faculty of Humanities. In April 2017 the historians who had joined the centre moved to the fourth floor of the same building.[311] The next month, on May 22, 2017, the official inauguration of the centre took place.[312] On this floor, the centre was accommodated in its own wing of the building, which had been empty so far. The constructed boundaries of who was part of the centre and who not thereby became a physical distance as the centre moved to a different floor. Interviewees were divided over whether this increased physical distance led to more positive boundary practices. In general, interviewees corroborated the literature described earlier; with the increased physical distance, it became harder to coordinate, there were fewer informal meetings, a lack of joint coffee breaks and consequently fewer boundary crossings between the institute and the centre.[313] The historians from the centre added this was especially to the regret of historians from the institute, who supposedly felt left behind, having lost many of their colleagues.

The historians from the institute agreed that there was the danger of being seen as the "leftovers", but one interviewee from the institute argued that the increased physical distance improved relations. While "out of sight is out of mind" might in primary instance make collaboration more difficult, this interviewee said it was also healthy not to be continuously confronted with the centre. With the centre's historians gone, the institute could now re-energise the connections among themselves to identify and build a new identity.[314] Just like the centre had, the institute developed a profile based on research topics related to spaces,

---

311 C2DH Move – April 14, 2017, March 16, 2017.
312 Inauguration officielle du Luxembourg Centre for Contemporary and Digital History, May 23, 2017, https://www.c2dh.uni.lu/news/inauguration-officielle-du-luxembourg-centre-contemporary-and-digital-history.
313 Interviews 1, 2, 3, 4, 5 and 7.
314 Interview 2.

material, national identities and power.[315] This could be interpreted as a form of boundary construction, boundary work to shape the institute. Yet this boundary construction would hopefully lead to improved collaborative boundary crossing in the future as the two institutional units would stand on a more equal footing, both with strong identities and ambitions, rather than a power relation between a progressive centre and an institute left behind.

For the centre, the move to a new physical space offered the opportunity to embed its ideals in the architecture. The director envisioned a transparent organisation, defined not by hierarchies but by collaboration. These visions were interpreted architecturally by installing glass corridor walls, several meeting rooms and a large open office for the approximately 20 PhD candidates, including me (see Figure 4). Others in the centre shared an office with one or two others and adopted an "open door policy"; doors were always open for joint discussions and collaboration. This was in contrast to the offices on the second floor, where doors had small windows that most scholars had covered with a poster and PhD candidates shared offices with one or two others.

Over time this architecture became understood not only as a way to showcase ambitions for collaboration, but actually a reflection of individual intentions to collaboration. This caught my attention when some of the PhD candidates criticised

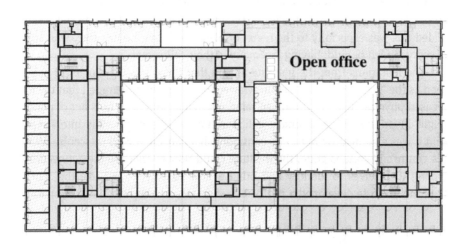

Figure 4: Floorplan of the fourth floor in the Maison des Science Humaine, University of Luxembourg. In blue the area assigned to the C^{2}DH. Exported October 2018.

---

315 "Research", accessed February 17, 2021, https://history.uni.lu/.

the working conditions in the open office space. Some felt they could not concentrate in a space with 20 others, lacked privacy, or were disturbed by additional noise from the hallway due to the open doors. Several PhD candidates entered a process of negotiation with the management of the centre in order to decrease disturbances and improve privacy, for example by closing the doors. However, of interest is that these complaints were simultaneously criticised as conflicting with the collaborative spirit of the centre. The negotiations, therefore, aimed to negotiate the balance between individual working conditions and the collective collaborative spirit. Tim van der Heijden and Andreas Fickers in their analysis of the open office conclude that, ultimately, collaboration did not take place within the open office, but in other spaces within the building.[316] However, they show that the open office facilitated the initiating of collaborations, making it easy to approach potential collaborators before moving to other spaces for further collaboration without disturbing others.

This episode demonstrated the bidirectional relation between physical distance and boundary practices. Maintaining a short physical distance led to boundary crossing, while preferring increased physical distance was interpreted as boundary construction. Subsequent negotiations did not just aim to maintain boundary crossing within the centre, but emphasised the need to shorten the physical distance, and to remove physical barriers such as closed doors.

Maintaining a short physical distance furthermore facilitated cross-disciplinary boundary crossing within the centre. The Digital Research Infrastructure (DRI) unit supported the historical research activities of the centre, consisting of experts coming from engineering, software development, computational linguistics, design and archives. The DRI was arguably positioned between regular IT support and research, providing support for a wide variety of tasks including advanced functionalities in Excel, setting up and maintaining websites, and handling research software licenses.[317] The open door policy of the centre was a significant aspect of the DRI, allowing low-threshold face-to-face communication to coordinate what needed to be provided, and helping historians on their way to work independently afterwards. More towards active research, the DRI investigated how to provide a common digital infrastructure for historical data management. This infrastructure would consist of a graph database including people, organisations, places and time, with heterogeneous semantic relationships. The argument was that these were fundamental units of historical research, allowing a wide range

---

316 Andreas Fickers and Tim van der Heijden, "Inside the Trading Zone: Thinkering in a Digital History Lab," *Digital Humanities Quarterly* 14, no. 3 (2020).
317 Interview 9 (January 2019).

of historical research projects to be supported.[318] Especially for research related to Luxembourg, the ambition was that eventually certain entities such as politicians or organisations might be relevant across multiple research projects, providing cross-project connections. Yet a significant decision by the DRI was to provide individually tailored infrastructures. The DRI aimed to provide combinations of technologies to fit historians' projects, rather than a common generic technology and shaping historians to fit in the provided workflow.

"Infrastructure" was thereby interpreted as providing access to a wide array of infrastructural components that could be fitted by the DRI to fit a historian's project. Historians were not pushed to adopt digital history methodologies. The boundary practices between the centre and institute following the political and physical interventions were, therefore, not reiterated by some digital methodological intervention.

While boundary construction occurred, leading to "us" versus "them" attitudes and interviewees admitted that relations were tense right after the split, they also emphasised this was the past and that they saw opportunities for collaboration. During the summer of 2016 already, the director of the C²DH and the head of the Institute signed an agreement of privileged partnership, formalising their intention to collaborate from the recognition of complementary research agendas and need to share resources.[319] Despite the interventions, several interviewees agreed that the split between the centre and the institute was not an accurate representation of how historians are organised and work.[320] Not all historians from the centre were confident that their research methods would fall within the scope of digital history. Historians from the institute emphasised that they too conducted contemporary and digital history. The opportunity that arose out of this ambiguity was the possibility of boundary crossing. Especially historians who had been at the university before the split were positive that future collaborations would prove fruitful. Historians that joined the university after the split had more difficulty imagining collaboration, mainly due to a lack of awareness of who could be a partner from the other unit.[321]

---

318 Interview 9.
319 Partnership Agreement between the Institute for History (University of Luxembourg, Faculty of Language and Literature, Humanities, Arts and Education) and the Center for Contemporary and Digital History (University of Luxembourg), 2016.
320 Interviews 2, 4, 5, 6 (January 2018) and 7.
321 Interview 6.

Collaborating Units of Historians

Yet, rather than research projects, the most important collaboration was in education. The centre and the institute jointly organised the history bachelor and master and taught courses together. With respect to teaching, both units were satisfied that the increased funding towards the centre meant there were more historians who could teach. Already before the split, the history master included mandatory courses related to digital history, and both the bachelor and master included courses related to all historical periods. One interviewee argued that "with respect to everything regarding education we are simply one group of historians, it is only at the level of research where you have this split."[322] Historians from both units described how they used digital means in their teaching and challenged students to use digital tools for their research papers. There was, however, also some anxiousness about this collaboration. One interviewee from the centre said that historians from the institute were afraid that the centre would make the master completely digital.[323] This fear was not repeated in the interviews with historians from the institute, but one of these historians did express fear that students were drawn more towards contemporary history than earlier periods. He noticed that more master theses were supervised by historians from the centre and covered contemporary history.[324]

The units also collaborated in the training of PhD candidates. In 2015 the Luxembourg National Research Fund (*Fonds National de La Recherche*, FNR) introduced PRIDE (Programme for Research-Intensive Doctoral Education) to fund groups of PhDs rather than individual positions.[325] Professors were forced to jointly request funding. The director of the centre, then still at the institute, was the PI of an application for a doctoral training unit in digital history and hermeneutics, which led to 13 PhD positions and one post-doc who started from March 2017.[326] This grant was a collaboration between the centre, the Institute for History, as well as the institutes for philosophy, linguistics, psychology, geography and computer science. This group of PhDs also acted as boundary crossing; while embedded in the centre (in the aforementioned open office space), they were affiliated to both the centre and the institutes of their supervisors. Explicitly

322 Interview 4.
323 Interview 1.
324 Interview 3.
325 "Programme summary", accessed February 17, 2021, https://www.fnr.lu/funding-instruments/pride/.
326 ""Digital History and Hermeneutics" Doctoral Training Unit", accessed May 12, 2021, https://dhh.uni.lu/about-us/.

envisioned as a trading zone of digital history, the idea was to have all the PhD candidates in one space for interdisciplinary collaborations.[327] From the start, however, the PI had to ensure this actually happened. PhD candidates were given desks at their respective institutes, close to their supervisors. There was thus a competition for physical distance to the PhD candidates. The double affiliations meant PhD candidates were expected to join in on meetings, social events and training of both the centre and their affiliated institutes. Some PhD candidates consequently became confused about which institute they primarily belonged to and supervisors competed for primary affiliation. Over time, these frictions were decreased through discussion, coordination and individual preferences of PhD candidates.

Both aspects of collaboration, training students and PhD candidates, demonstrate how boundary crossing and boundary construction are entwined. The trading zone scheme succeeded insofar as it led to cross-disciplinary collaborations of PhD candidates that co-authored papers. However, a problem was the balance in pursuing a collective cross-disciplinary doctoral programme, while PhD candidates were eventually evaluated on individual disciplinary work.[328] On a small scale, the PhD candidates in a single office thereby exemplified the potential and friction of digital history trading zones.

In conclusion, the C²DH became an interdisciplinary research centre similar to descriptions in the literature. The centre was organised in research teams around topics rather than chairs. These teams met on a regular basis, each headed by a research manager that was also part of the management committee of the centre. Within the centre, English became the working language, in order to sustain an international outlook. This stood in contrast with German and French as working languages in the institute which sustained relationships with German and French academic communities.[329] The centre was established in order to bridge the academic historical work to society and was actively evaluated on societal impact. To meet this requirement, the centre professionalised communication and outreach by installing a communication office, an editorial board for the website that urged all members to write blog posts about events, conferences and research, and by organising regular public events such as debates, lectures, or project presentations. From this, one can see how the centre is an example of the reshaping of organisational structure and cultural practice of research.[330] The centre also became

---

327 "PRIDE Application Form – Digital History and Hermeneutics", 2015.
328 "PRIDE Periodic Report DTU-DHH (Digital History & Hermeneutics)", 2018.
329 On a personal note, this switch to English enabled my integration within the centre to a greater extent than had been the case within the institute, due to my proficiency of these languages.
330 Klein, "A Conceptual Vocabulary of Interdisciplinary Science."

the subject of controversies around funding, leading both to a new injection of funding for the university, as well as a redistribution as scholars moved between the institute and the centre.[331]

Shifting Associations of the Digital History Lab

While centres have proven a successful model to facilitate interdisciplinary collaboration among scholars, another model has been the laboratory. While history professionalised through institutionalisation in departments, other disciplines such as chemistry and physics institutionalised in laboratories, where labs became "badges of scientific credibility and productive utility."[332] Labs did so by association to several concepts that became central to science.

According to the sociologist of science Bruno Latour, the lab as a space is simply a mundane room.[333] What defines the lab is that it allows to investigate phenomena through trial-and-error, where every trial is thoroughly documented. As such, the lab is associated with experimentation. The sociologist of science Karin Knorr Cetina described the lab as a space where "nature" is excluded, kept outside of the lab.[334] She later elaborated this by describing the lab according to three features. First, objects are not taken in whole, but only specific features of interest are considered. Second, objects are not taken in their original location, but incorporated in the laboratory setting. Third, objects are not taken when they naturally occur, but their occurrence is created.[335] As such, the lab is associated with controlled settings.

The diversity of tasks means labs tend to employ a range of personnel such as PhDs, postdocs and lab technicians.[336] The lab is thereby associated with collaboration. Labs provide a safe environment, equipment and services required

331 Hoch, "New UK Interdisciplinary Research Centres."
332 Catherine M. Jackson, "Chemistry as the Defining Science: Discipline and Training in Nineteenth-Century Chemical Laboratories," *Endeavour* 35, no. 2–3 (2011): 61, https://doi.org/10.1016/j.endeavour.2011.05.003.
333 Bruno Latour, "Give Me a Laboratory and I Will Raise the World," in *Science Observed*, ed. Karin Knorr Cetina and Michael Mulkay (SAGE Publications, 1983), 141–70.
334 Karin Knorr Cetina, "The Ethnographic Study of a Scientific Work: Towards a Constructivist Interpretation of Science," in *Science Observed: Perspectives on the Social Study of Science*, ed. Karin Knorr Cetina and Michael Mulkay (SAGE Publications, 1983), 115–40.
335 Karin Knorr Cetina, "The Couch, the Cathedral, and the Laboratory: On the Relationship between Experiment and Laboratory in Science," *Science as Practice and Culture* (1992), 117.
336 Knorr Cetina, *Epistemic Cultures*; Latour and Woolgar, *Laboratory Life*, 197.

to conduct research and provide training.[337] As such, the lab should always be associated with infrastructural space, despite debates on where a lab is located or what activities are performed in a lab.[338] Finally, with the institutionalisation of disciplines in laboratories, the work in labs is what provides the means for the scientific enterprise of hypothesis testing, discovery and falsification. The lab is therefore associated with knowledge production.[339]

Traditionally associated with sciences such as chemistry, physics and biology, the laboratory terminology is regularly imported into the humanities, usually in reference to one or a combination of the features introduced above. For example, libraries have been called the laboratories for the humanities, in order to reference libraries as sites of knowledge production.[340] In contrast, archives have been argued to be more similar to fieldwork rather than labs, where research depends on local conditions, rather than the association of controlled settings.[341] In the context of digital methods, the computer has been called a lab, providing an environment to run tests.[342] Announcing the launch of King's Digital Lab, its director James Smithies wrote of digital tools as similar to laboratory equipment to run experiments.[343] Thus, the computer incorporates the lab's association of experimentation. However, the digital humanities scholar Urszula Pawlicka-Deger argues the humanities lab is essentially a tactical term, in order to incorporate the aforementioned scientific credibility and productive utility of the sciences.[344] In a later article, she furthermore notes that this usage of the laboratory is proving increasingly successful as an alternative to the centre.[345] It is, therefore, of interest that the University of Luxembourg initiated both a centre as

337 Jackson, "Chemistry as the Defining Science."
338 Graeme Gooday, "Placing or Replacing the Laboratory in the History of Science?," *Isis* 99, no. 4 (2008): 783–95, https://doi.org/10.1086/595772; Catherine M. Jackson, "The Laboratory," in *A Companion to the History of Science*, ed. Bernard Lightman (Wiley-Blackwell, 2016), 296–309.
339 Jackson, "The Laboratory."
340 Job Cohen et al., *Duurzame Geesteswetenschappen: Rapport van de Commissie National Plan Toekomst Geesteswetenschappen* (Amsterdam University Press, 2008); Sue Stone, "Humanities Scholars: Information Needs And Uses," *Journal of Documentation* 38, no. 4 (1982): 292–313, https://doi.org/10.1108/eb026734.
341 Eskildsen, "Leopold Ranke's Archival Turn: Location and Evidence in Modern Historiography."
342 Piet Hut and Gerald Jay Sussman, "Advanced Computing for Science," *Scientific American* 257, no. 4 (1987): 136–45; cited in Knorr Cetina, *Epistemic Cultures*.
343 James Smithies, "KDL, Established 2016," King's Digital Lab blog, 21 October, 2016, https://www.kdl.kcl.ac.uk/blog/kdl-launch/.
344 Urszula Pawlicka, "Data, Collaboration, Laboratory: Bringing Concepts from Science into Humanities Practice," *English Studies* 98, no. 5 (July 4, 2017): 526–41, https://doi.org/10.1080/0013838X.2017.1332022.
345 Pawlicka-Deger, "The Laboratory Turn."

well as a lab for digital history, which allows us to explore how these different models are constructed by historians.

Below, I describe the history of two humanities labs at the University of Luxembourg. Through this history, I show how the associations of the labs to the concepts above were not stable but were instead constantly negotiated and shifted.

The HiPoPhil Lab and Digital History Lab: Shifting Associations

As mentioned in the previous section, the University of Luxembourg moved to a new campus in the summer of 2015. In the newly built *Maison des Sciences Humaines* a floor was envisioned for laboratories for the disciplines accommodated in this building. At the previous site, where the historians had been since 2003, the historians had a seminar room with their books and a manual book scanner so that they could lecture students in their own historical library, amid the sources. The historians set out to replicate this seminar room in the new humanities building on the laboratory floor. However, they had to find ways to argue that they too needed a lab. The new campus would get a university library building at the end of 2018.[346] Several interviewees noted that the historians were consequently not allowed to maintain a space for their own library.[347] However, an alternative space to store the books between 2015–2018 was not offered either. The developers furthermore associated labs with experimentation and assumed that historians did not need a lab.

Yet the historians desired to claim space on the laboratory floor to store their books. They followed two strategies to this end. First, to strengthen their position, they made a joint proposal for a lab for historians, but also for philosophers and political scientists, leading to the name HiPoPhil Lab (History, Political science, Philosophy). Second, they had to argue how their use of the room would fall within the scope of a "lab". This is a very literal example of "lab" as a tactical term, while also demonstrating a coercive push towards scientific associations: the historians were not allowed to create their own library, so they associated their library with the concepts of a lab.[348] They did so by emphasising practices of digitisation and creation of databases, requiring scanners and computers with

---

346 "This Is the Day!", Luxembourg Learning Centre, December 9, 2018, https://llc.uni.lu/en/2018/09/12/this-is-the-day/.
347 Interviews 2 and 7.
348 Pawlicka, "Data, Collaboration, Laboratory: Bringing Concepts from Science into Humanities Practice."

specialised software. They also wrote about "sources" rather than "books" to steer clear of further associations of it being a library.[349] They thereby associated the lab with infrastructural space as the site of knowledge production.

The founding of the Digital History Lab is less clear. Most interviewees assumed that the professor for digital history came up with the idea and had lobbied for it. However, this professor said that the lab was already part of the job description, made possible by the hiring committee. In turn, a historian who was part of this committee said that the lab was actually made possible by the historian who had also led the arguments for the HiPoPhil Lab described above. Finally, this historian again said that to his knowledge, the professor for digital history came up with the idea for this lab.[350] Be as it may, the professor for digital history was excited to cultivate this lab. He did not take "lab" to be a tactical term, but envisioned more hands-on practices of history, in association with experimentation, and students working in groups, in association with collaboration. In 2014, this professor and I set out to design the technical specifications of the lab, following these two associations. We first thought of the lab as a computer lab, to provide computational power for digital methods. We then became aware that opposite the lab would be a TIC lab (*Technologies de l'Information et de la Communication*), basically a room filled with computers. We then limited the scope of PCs to just a few for more specialised tasks. Our alternative idea was to explore the lab as a 3D lab, with 3D scanners and a 3D printer, for historians to experiment with the tacit experience of historical objects and their 3D copies. The two labs, sharing a door between them, became more entwined after the opening in 2015. Two 3D scanners were made available in the Digital History Lab and a full-colour 3D printer was set up in a small additional room opposite the HiPoPhil lab. For an overview of the laboratory floor, see Figure 5.

However, despite offering the means for associations to experimentation and collaboration, these were hardly appropriated by historians from either the institute or the centre. In the end, the political scientists and philosophers hardly used the lab. The HiPoPhil Lab was too small for lectures as it could not fit enough students, so it was not used for classes. Finally, the manual book scanner that had been present in the old seminar room was placed in the lab, but the historians and technical support of the university were unable to get it to work after the move. Thus, most historians ultimately used it as a library rather than a lab, mainly associated to infrastructural space. Still, the argument had succeeded in getting the space.

---

349 "Form Template_HiPoPhil_2014_EN", 2014.
350 Interviews 1, 3, 4, 5 and 7.

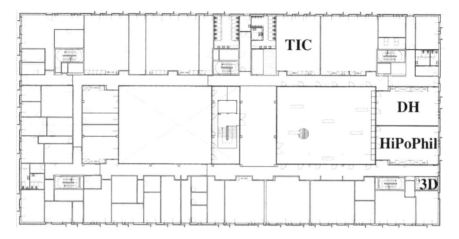

Figure 5: Floorplan of the first floor in the Maison des Science Humaine, University of Luxembourg. The labs described in the text are labelled. Exported October 2018.

The Digital History Lab too became increasingly associated with infrastructural space, set up around a big screen for presentations. It became used for lectures and examinations. Some historians shifted to a tactical usage of the term "lab", with the Digital History Lab simply being closer to their offices than other lecture rooms.[351] With respect to research, the labs became strongly associated with infrastructural space to provide equipment and services related to digitisation. An automated book scanner was installed in the HiPoPhil Lab, with which books could be automatically digitised, processed using optical character recognition (OCR) and stored in a virtual library. The scanner, OCR software and virtual library were maintained by the centre's Digital Research Infrastructure unit. The physical infrastructure of the labs thereby became entwined with the digital infrastructure of the centre. Following requests from historians, more equipment for digitisation was installed for photos, negatives, maps and other sources. Yet a difference between the digital infrastructure of the DRI unit and the physical infrastructures of the labs was in the consequences of acquiring new technology. In contrast with software licences, the acquisition of equipment requires training to be scheduled, space to be reserved to place the equipment and expertise for maintenance.[352] As such, the physicality of lab equipment carried "material implications" that shaped subsequent

---

351 Interviews 1 and 3.
352 Interview 8 (July 2018).

opportunities.[353] That is, to use equipment optimally requires shaping research to include existing equipment, otherwise equipment ends up unused.

The first year, I maintained the lab to a large extent together with IT support from the university, creating inventories of necessary equipment and learning how to use them. At the end of 2016, a full-time coordinator was hired by the C²DH to maintain equipment and provide support for both the labs. The book scanner was a rather expensive machine that could be damaged easily through mistakes, e.g., it contained glass surfaces that would scratch if a user was wearing metal rings or wristbands. The coordinator therefore took it upon himself to operate the machine. The open door policy of the centre was hence not imported to the labs, which required control over access to ensure equipment and the rooms themselves stayed in order.[354] Digitisation of books consequently became an informal service provided through the coordinator and book scanner. Historians could leave a stack of books with a note on his desk, and after two or three weeks they would receive an email with the digitised book files and the stack of books returned on their own desks. Does this make the coordinator similar to a lab technician described in the study of Bruno Latour and Steve Woolgar, thereby importing the association of collaboration?[355] Contrary to those lab technicians, the artefacts handled by the lab coordinator were not used within the lab. That is, historians read books outside of the lab, imported the books into the lab for digitisation, but the digital files were then exported out of the lab for use by historians. The act of digitisation alone was not part of the research. The lab was then arguably not the site of knowledge production. In these cases, which were the majority of digitisation requests, the activities of the lab were arguably insufficient to be associated with collaboration as part of research. The coordinator in this situation was working for rather than with historians, while collaboration should entail a more equal ground of engagement.[356]

The informal process and hidden labour of leaving books with a note on the coordinator's desk had two consequences. First, many historians did not become aware of the time investment going into digitisation. The stack of books and sources to be digitised soon became an almost full-time task, leading to hiring of multiple student workers to support the operation of the automated book

353 Anna Foka et al., "Beyond Humanities qua Digital: Spatial and Material Development for Digital Research Infrastructures in HumlabX," *Digital Scholarship in the Humanities* 33, no. 2 (June 1, 2018): 264–78, https://doi.org/10.1093/llc/fqx008.
354 Interview 8.
355 Latour and Woolgar, *Laboratory Life.*
356 Willard McCarty, "Collaborative Research in the Digital Humanities," in *Collaborative Research in the Digital Humanities*, ed. Marilyn Deegan and Willard McCarty (Ashgate, 2012), 1–10.

scanner. Second, as the coordinator was hired by the centre, his office was on the fourth floor. Historians from the centre consequently utilised his service much more than historians from the institute. One historian from the institute said in the interview that she preferred to scan books herself with the regular office flatbed scanner, which was quicker and right next to her office.[357] Although the physical distance to the lab, located on the first floor, was similar for both the institute and centre, the physical distance to the coordinator became a significant determinant of use. The labs consequently became more aligned with the centre rather than the institute. The historians from the institute were hardly aware of what equipment was present. They maintained their view of the HiPoPhil Lab as a library, and rarely entered the Digital History Lab.

A few scholars, mainly in PhD positions, did try digital experiments within the lab, notably experiments of distant reading. Such projects required a larger number of books to be digitised, for which these scholars received training to learn how to operate the book scanner themselves. Throughout their projects, the lab coordinator assisted where needed, in cooperation with the rest of the Digital Research Infrastructure unit. Such projects were largely conducted from within the HiPoPhil Lab as this provided the book scanner and PCs with OCR software that were powerful enough for subsequent computational analyses such as topic modelling. In these projects then, the labs, especially the HiPoPhil Lab, became associated with experimentation and collaboration.

3D technology did not receive as much interest from historians as we had hoped. Two PhD candidates actively explored 3D scanning, using the available 3D scanners for objects outside of the lab. 3D scanning was thereby arguably associated with controlled settings, in creating a digital representation of phenomena outside the lab that historians could not import physically. For example, one historian scanned Roman tomb stones for close observation in her office. One significant threshold to 3D adoption was that the 3D printer required much more tacit knowledge and time investment than anticipated. The device was promised as a plug-and-play device; loading in the model and simply letting it print. Yet during the 20 hours that it took to print a model, the device demanded close attention, as small mistakes could destroy all the work that had been done. As such, despite several experiments, it did not become an infrastructural component to any historical research. Note that the most significant experiments were with PhD candidates. It was therefore suggested that ideally the material implications of the lab would be incorporated in hiring procedures; to attract PhD candidates who would

---

357 Interview 2.

invest significant time with the lab for their research.[358] Yet during my research at the University of Luxembourg, the Digital History Lab was usually empty, in contrast with a science lab.

In conclusion, both labs ultimately became associated with infrastructural space, especially in the form of equipment and services. The HiPoPhil Lab was always meant as a tactical term, though from the start associated with infrastructural space as well to provide storage and training. It could not provide the space for training but did offer storage and equipment for digitisation as envisioned. Through this equipment for digitisation, the HiPoPhil Lab and Digital History Lab became associated with experimentation and collaboration in a few distant reading projects, at least for the scholars performing those projects. To establish these associations more firmly, efforts were eventually made to build upon these initial experiments in communications and hiring procedures.

Trading Zones Emerging Across Institutional Boundaries

During the four and a half years of my research, the University of Luxembourg significantly changed in practices related to digital history. The above history provides some insights, from my own perspective as well as from the perspectives of several interviewees, into how multiple interventions led to trading zones and boundary practices.

In line with the findings of the online questionnaire, the C²DH can be described as a collaboration consisting of mostly humanities scholars, specifically historians, that was located in multiple offices on a single floor. Participants in this trading zone had regular interactions with other disciplines. Some shared offices or collaborated with computer scientists, (software) engineers, or computational linguists. They also had regular interactions with peers from the historical discipline, among themselves and from the Institute for History, as well as peers at other universities or research institutes. The historians at the centre thus regularly performed boundary crossing, both across disciplinary boundaries within the centre, as across institutional boundaries with historians outside the centre. Furthermore, the status of centre facilitated further cross-institutional collaborations, leading to strategic partnerships with other institutes including the Center for History and New Media at George Mason University. As the centre firmly positioned itself as a place of expertise with respect to digital research and teaching,

---

358 Interview 8.

it acquired the means to influence and help shape the digital strategy of the University of Luxembourg.[359]

Historians from the centre and the institute also performed boundary construction. This boundary construction was often not intended, and occurred through interventions by others, notably politicians and the university's rectorate. Yet historians consequently came to identify themselves with their institutional unit, sceptical of the other unit, separated on different floors in the same building.

While previous research identified group formation at different sites between people with similar backgrounds, the current study demonstrates group formation at a single site, in a single building, between people with similar backgrounds.[360] This boundary construction, however, mainly occurred on a political level, i.e. with respect to attracting new positions and funding. On a scholarly level, historians from both units agreed the split was artificial and that historians would collaborate or even act as a single group with respect to research and teaching. Insofar as there was a split in research, this was between contemporary and non-contemporary history, rather than digital and non-digital history. Although digital history was more explicit at the centre as a topic of interest, the historians at the institute conducted several projects that arguably fell within the scope of digital history.

The historians at the centre did shift practices in three notable ways. First, English became the working language, rather than French and German, both a result of and leading to more internationally diverse hiring. Second, as a centre that was supposed to have societal impact, historians became much more concerned with communication to the public than they had been at the institute. This is not to say that this did not happen at the institute, as several historians there regularly appeared on the radio or in the newspapers, but at the centre this was professionalised more broadly, including a communication office and regular public events. Third, as the centre was organised around research topics rather than the traditional chairs, intended to boost sharing of information, the historians there adopted a more corporate style with a manager per topic and regular team meetings.

Historians did not shift practices towards the few engineers or computer scientists that were present in or collaborated with the centre. Instead, the computational experts of the Digital Research Infrastructure unit arguably shaped their

---

359 Interview with Andreas Fickers, director of the C²DH, March 2020.
360 Armstrong and Cole, "Managing Distances and Differences in Geographically Distributed Work Groups."

practices to fit the conceptions of historical research. Rather than providing a generic infrastructure and shaping historians to work with it, the DRI emphasised the need to provide diverse and loosely coupled infrastructural components to fit the heterogeneous demands of historians. As such, if I were to describe the centre limited to this duality, I would conclude that the centre constituted a connected-asymmetric-homogeneous (subversive) trading zone, with historians in a powerful role and computational experts learning and appropriating historical practices and values through continued interactions. The shifts in practices that historians did exemplify aligned not to computational experts, but to the political goal of the centre. This power relation was not always obvious, and who stated goals not always clear. In that sense, the centre constituted a disconnected-asymmetric-homogeneous (subversive) trading zone, where the historians changed practices through a unidirectional power relation that was not always explicit and involved little engagement with those who ultimately decided the shape of the centre.

In contrast, the presence of a Digital History Lab did not suddenly shape the practices of historians. Some historians adopted technologies and tools that were offered in the labs, yet the majority of historians initially did not engage with the lab apart from occasionally requesting a digital copy of a book. While digital humanities labs have been argued to act as epistemic infrastructures shaping how scholars ask questions, my case study shows this is not by necessity but rather by individual interests.[361] Rather than the labs naturally acquiring associations of experimentation and collaboration, this required efforts in communication and hiring procedures to attract historians to engage with the labs. The presence of labs extended the possibilities of research, yet did not limit possibilities by excluding practices that may not make optimal use of the lab space. The presence of certain tools and technologies did not limit what could be done with the lab space, contrary to the aforementioned material implications of labs, as historians continuously negotiated how the labs would fit their purposes.[362] The labs thereby did not provide much opportunity for cross-disciplinary boundary crossing, nor did the labs give rise to boundary construction between disciplinary or institutional communities. In conclusion, I argue that the labs constituted disconnected-symmetric-heterogeneous (boundary object) trading zones, constantly shifting associations to what it means for a space to be a lab.

---

361 C.f. James W. Malazita, Ezra J. Teboul and Hined Rafeh, "Digital Humanities as Epistemic Cultures: How DH Labs Make Knowledge, Objects, and Subjects," *Digital Humanities Quarterly* 14, no. 3 (2020).
362 C.f. Foka et al., "Beyond Humanities qua Digital."

In conclusion, how disciplinary and institutional boundaries were crossed or constructed depended on who was pushing against existing boundaries and what power they had to do so. While the dimension of engagement shaped interactions between people, this dimension itself was shaped by those who were in the position to decide where scholars would be affiliated or physically placed. The next chapter, therefore, further explores the dimension of power relations.

Power Relations of Negotiation

Coordination

Being part of a collaboration requires participants, both historians and computational experts, to negotiate the goals of the collaboration and the individual tasks of participants. This process is called coordination, defined as "the integration or linking together of different pieces of a project to accomplish a collective task."[363] Coordination is a continuous process, enduring as long as the collaboration does. Throughout the collaboration, participants are in constant negotiation of the project goal(s), while mutually accountable towards one another to fulfil their individual tasks. In the framework of communities of practice, this is the second dimension: the joint enterprise. Through the process of negotiation of a common goal, the pursuit of that common goal and the mutual accountability towards one another in that pursuit, the joint enterprise is what keeps the collaboration together.[364]

Yet a collaboration does not exist in a vacuum, as the previous chapter showed. Negotiations are positioned in a broader system that influences the collaboration, such as the institutes where collaborators are employed, their disciplinary backgrounds, funding structures etc. Furthermore, negotiations are not necessarily level, although this would be the preferred situation, but can be conducted through different power relations. In his exploration of the trading zones of physics, the historian of science Peter Galison discussed three metaphors employed by physicists who feared a loss of control.[365] First, the metaphor of prostitution was used to critique physicists selling out to engineering, focusing on applied rather than fundamental research. Second, the metaphor of handmaidens described the relationship between a boss and a servant, with physicists demanding engineers to perform certain tasks. Third, the metaphor of flies and spiders was used to warn of the danger of physicists following engineers for too long, after which they end up trapped and unable to return.

Control, and specifically who is in control, is an aspect of great significance to the participants of trading zones, leading to desirable or less desirable outcomes. These interactions between participants in trading zones, through coordination and control, are the focus of the current chapter. This chapter thereby

---

363 Cummings and Kiesler, "Collaborative Research Across Disciplinary and Organizational Boundaries," 704.
364 Wenger, *Communities of Practice*, 77–78.
365 Galison, *Image and Logic*, 249, 255, 277–78.

explores the second dimension of trading zones, namely the power relations between (groups of) people.

Studying Power Relations through the Coordination of Individual Incentives

In order to investigate power relations in coordination, I take a bottom-up approach on a micro scale, starting from what drives individual participants' practices in the collaboration. From this bottom-up approach, I consider where participants explicitly or implicitly agree or disagree. To understand how participants negotiate their own practices, goals and tasks and those of others, I investigate their incentives.[366] The goals and incentives of participants in collaborations are not necessarily homogeneous, and the goal of the collaboration as a whole does not necessarily match the individual goals of participants.[367]

In her study of a collaboration between earth scientists and computer scientists, the information scientist Judith Weedman found that the individual incentives of participants significantly impacted the coordination of the collaboration.[368] In this collaboration, she problematised the negotiations required for all participants to agree when the digital system under development was finished. As participants had different incentives, they had different points at which they considered the system to be finished. Depending on one's incentives, a participant may even argue a system is never truly finished.[369] Thus, to better understand these discrepancies and the required coordination, she investigated the individual incentives of participants according to three aspects: 1) reasons for joining the project, 2) individual goals for the project and 3) expected effects of participation after the project has ended. As a short-hand, I refer to these aspects as 1) reasons, 2) goals and 3) expectations.

These three aspects of incentives provide insights at different points of coordination. Reasons show the ambitions of participants before or at the start of the collaboration, before coordination determines what may be feasible or not. Goals may be continuations of the reasons for joining, as participants stick to their

---

366 Judith Weedman, "The Structure of Incentive: Design and Client Roles in Application-Oriented Research," *Science, Technology & Human Values* 23, no. 3 (1998): 315–45, https://doi.org/10.1177/016224399802300303.

367 Karin Knorr Cetina, *The Manufacture of Knowledge: An Essay on the Constructivist and Contextual Nature of Science* (Pergamon Press, 1981), 43.

368 Weedman, "The Structure of Incentive."

369 Susan Brown et al., "Published Yet Never Done: The Tension Between Projection and Completion in Digital Humanities Research," *Digital Humanities Quarterly* 3, no. 2 (2009).

original incentives. Yet through coordination and experiences in the collaboration, additional goals may be added, ambitions might be discarded, or ideas become clearer in the discussion of current practices. Expectations represent not so much what participants desire to achieve during a collaboration, but what participants expect to gain from a participation. Beyond the outcomes of a project, expectations may refer to expected shifts in practices following the sharing of practices in a collaboration. These expectations can thus be continuations of the individual goals or can be alternative paths when individual goals did not come to fruition, or additional expectations added due to positive results. By combining these three aspects, I aim to uncover incentives that stick during the duration of a collaboration, and are thus successfully preserved in negotiations, or incentives that change over time, and are thus shaped by negotiation.

Yet to understand how individual incentives are negotiated, it is necessary to consider pre-existing power mechanisms that render one participant's incentives more likely to survive than another's. I identify two such power mechanisms that position each participant in a specific role in digital history collaborations. First, as part of the hierarchical structure of academia, participants have a position as PhD candidate, postdoc, professor, or otherwise. A participant in the role of professor is in a more powerful position than a participant in the role of PhD candidate or postdoc. As I found in the previous chapter, historians outnumbered computational experts as participants as well as in positions of leadership of collaborations. This imbalance suggests a power relation. Yet historians as envisioned end-users are dependent on computational experts as system designers. In their "ability to implement technological change", computational experts are in a more powerful position than historians who are dependent on this technological change.[370] The second power relation of interest then is disciplinary expertise, which may lead to pushing of technology or a pulling of technology services.

This is not to say that these are the only power relations imaginable. It is impossible to consider all the power mechanisms in a trading zone, for there are far too many.[371] The above two mechanisms, academic position and disciplinary expertise, leave out aspects such as gender, ethnicity, socio-economic status, or the status of institutes or disciplinary communities.[372] Such mechanisms of power

---

370 M. Lynne Markus and Niels Bjorn-Andersen, "Power Over Users: Its Exercise By System Professionals," *Communications of the ACM* 30, no. 6 (1987): 503.

371 Hayward, *De-Facing Power*.

372 For more elaborate discussions of intersectionality in digital humanities, see Roopika Risam, "Beyond the Margins: Intersectionality and the Digital Humanities," *Digital Humanities Quarterly* 9, no. 2 (2015); Barbara Bordalejo and Roopika Risam, *Intersectionality in Digital Humanities* (Arc Humanities Press, 2019).

are important and deserving of study. However, such power mechanisms are not necessarily specific to digital history collaborations as trading zones. Without ignoring these matters then, they fall outside the scope of my analysis. Participants are instead contextualised by their academic position and disciplinary background.

Interviews

To study power relations in trading zones I interviewed participants from a number of case studies, described in the next paragraph. For these case studies, I interviewed as many participants as feasible, to gain insight in the different individual perspectives and incentives for participation in a collaboration. Where possible, interviews were conducted face-to-face by visiting a site and interviewing all present participants. Additional interviews were conducted at later times via Skype. This furthermore provided me insights at different time frames, both during coordination as well as reflections afterwards. I ultimately conducted 28 interviews with 24 participants.

As such, the below analysis considers power relations in reflections and individual incentives, rather than in practice such as may be observed during meetings. In cases where I noticed present disagreements during a visit, I tried to cover this in the interviews. Rather than an ethnographic participant observation, this chapter thereby follows an approach of critical discourse analysis of how collaborators discuss their ambitions, expectations, goals, and frustrations, in order to uncover the power relations underlying these discursive practices.[373]

The majority of interviewees had a background in history, in line with the finding of the previous chapter that digital history collaborations predominantly consist of historians. The incentives uncovered in the interviews might consequently mainly reflect the incentives of historians and should not be seen as an exhaustive list for all collaborators. The uncovered incentives are as such not necessarily generalisable to all digital history collaborations. Instead, my goal is to investigate the negotiation of incentives and tasks, rendering visible the practices of boundary crossing and construction that are arguably generalisable.

Seventeen participants were male and seven were female, where male and female interviewees were distributed over the different positions and disciplinary backgrounds. Four interviewees had the position of "coordinator", an unconventional position in academia. The tasks of a coordinator usually consisted of,

---

373 Michel Foucault, *The History of Sexuality Volume I: An Introduction*, trans. Robert Hurley (Pantheon Books, 1978); Gilbert Weiss and Ruth Wodak, eds., *Critical Discourse Analysis* (London: Palgrave Macmillan UK, 2003), https://doi.org/10.1057/9780230288423.

among other things, bringing collaborators together, communicating between parties, keeping track of practical matters and reporting to the PI of the collaboration. Noteworthy is that three of the four coordinators did not have a PhD title, introducing a possible power relation according to academic hierarchy, to which I return below. For an overview of interviewees see Table 2. All interviews were recorded and manually transcribed and coded in MAXQDA. Coded segments were printed out and manually grouped together to find statements referring to similar concerns. Below I analyse these different concerns and present quotes as examples. Some quotes have been edited slightly for readability. More importantly, the below quotes are translations of statements, since most of the interviews were conducted in Dutch. The quotes included in the analysis below are not thus exact replications of utterances by interviewees.

As can be seen in Table 2, the majority of the interviews was conducted in late 2015. During this first round of interviews, I uncovered rich points deemed of interest for further investigation in later interviews.[374] Furthermore, interviews were conducted through co-construction. Interviewees could fully speak their minds, not only in answering questions but also reflecting on the validity of questions or the need for additional questions.[375] Interviewees could moreover suggest

Table 2: Overview of interviewees by disciplinary background, their position in the collaboration, gender and the period in which interviews took place.

DISCIPLINE	#	ACADEMIC POSITION	#	GENDER	#	PERIOD OF INTERVIEW	#
History	15	Professor	8	Male	17	Late 2015	16
Computational research	4	Postdoc	5	Female	7	Late 2016	1
Software development	3	PhD	4			Early 2017	4
Other humanities	1	Coordinator	4			Early 2018	3
Library	1	Software developer	3			Mid 2018	4
TOTAL	24		24		24		28

---

374 Agar, "Ethnography."
375 Barbara Sherman Heyl, "Ethnographic Interviewing," in *Handbook of Ethnography*, ed. Paul Atkinson et al. (SAGE Publications, 2001), 369–83.

who else to interview. Based on this feedback, I interviewed several scholars outside of the four case studies.

A significant concern developed through co-construction was the balance between contextualisation and confidentiality. When an analysis explicitly mentions which people were interviewed from which collaborations and quotes interviewees by name this gives advantages both in understanding the particularity of case studies and fully exploring the consequences of problems. However, as interviews included disagreements between collaborators, several interviewees preferred to remain anonymous. Therefore, this chapter takes a number of precautions that aim to maximise the analysis of power relations, also in exploring collaboration failures and disagreements, while minimising the identifiable information of interviewees. To contextualise statements of interviewees as part of power mechanisms, I include per statement the academic position of the interviewee and their disciplinary background. All quotes are numbered so that I can refer back to quotes.

Per case study I mention the number of interviewees, the disciplinary backgrounds and positions of interviewees, but not in combination. To anonymise statements, I have furthermore decided to omit several aspects of interviewees. In order not to provide too much information that renders interviewees identifiable, I do not distinguish between different professorships (assistant, associate, or full), but refer to all these interviewees as "professor". I also refer to all interviewees as female, rather than reveal the gender of interviewees.[376] I take this same approach to my description of the case studies in the following section, where I give an abstract description of their goals without rendering them (easily) identifiable. As a result of this approach, rather than exploring power relations per case study, I generalise my discussion of power relations as they relate to digital history trading zones, without explicitly referring to case studies.

This chapter thereby takes a different approach than the previous chapter. The previous chapter was rooted in oral historical and ethnographic research, exploring the contingencies and particularities of emerging trading zones that were, therefore, identifiable. In contrast, this chapter takes inspiration from social scientific research, exploring aspects of trading zones that may be of significance beyond the particular case study.[377]

---

376 The practice of referring to all interviewees as female is inspired by Thomas Franssen et al., "The Drawbacks of Project Funding for Epistemic Innovation: Comparing Institutional Affordances and Constraints of Different Types of Research Funding," *Minerva* 56, no. 1 (March 2018): 11–33, https://doi.org/10.1007/s11024-017-9338-9.

377 Desirée Ciambrone, "Anonymity," in *The SAGE Encyclopedia of Social Science Research Methods*, ed. Michael Lewis-Beck, Alan Bryman and Tim Futing Liao (Sage Publications, Inc., 2004), 18–19, https://doi.org/10.4135/9781412950589.n17; Heather L. Ondercin, "External Validity," in *The*

Case Studies

After a review of digital history collaborations in Belgium, the Netherlands and Luxembourg, I chose four collaborations as case studies; two from Belgium and two from the Netherlands. I chose collaborations that included both historians and computational experts and that were still ongoing. In order to contextualise the interviews, in this section I provide a brief description of the case studies and what each collaboration aimed to achieve. These descriptions are based on the interviews as well as on document analysis of proposals and publications.

Case Study 1: Development of a Large-scale Unstructured Database

The first case study was a four-year project with scholars from multiple universities, where most of the scholars were from history. One research group had digitised material available which laid the basis for the project. Additional data was to be collected and digitised in collaboration with a cultural heritage institute. The project envisioned the development of a system that would combine databases for a bibliography, for unstructured textual data and for structured data (people, places and relations between entities as extracted from the unstructured data). These databases were to be integrated so that historians could jump from structured to unstructured data to find all occurrences of an entity in the texts, or vice versa from the text to find more information about an entity. For example, historians would be able to select a historical person and where this person is mentioned in other texts, as well as gain an overview of related historical persons. The extraction of these entities from the unstructured data was part of the tasks of the computational experts.

The structured database used an existing platform, with some modifications on the level of user interactions and data export. The project hired the developers of the platform to make these modifications. The unstructured database in contrast was built from scratch. A commercial software development company was hired to set up the system and develop required features. Both the developers of the structured database and the developers for the unstructured database were

SAGE Encyclopedia of Social Science Research Methods, ed. Michael Lewis-Beck, Alan Bryman and Tim Futing Liao (Sage Publications, Inc., 2004), 360–62, https://doi.org/10.4135/9781412950589. n318; Peggy Wallace, "Anonymity and Confidentiality," in *Encyclopedia of Case Study Research*, ed. Albert Mills, Gabrielle Durepos and Elden Wiebe (SAGE Publications, Inc., 2010), 22–24, https://doi. org/10.4135/9781412957397.n9.

based in different countries than the historians, so that the technical work was conducted on a large physical distance.

The project included several PhD candidates in history, who were envisioned to use the integrated system for their research. However, while the structured database was successfully implemented and used, the unstructured database posed many challenges and delays. Digitisation of the collections took much longer than anticipated. The digital platform never reached a level of usability where it could facilitate research. Due to these problems, the unstructured database never came to fruition, nor were the databases ultimately integrated in a single system. PhD candidates consequently started entering unstructured data into the structured database instead. This led to questions of whether the structured database needed to be customised to better facilitate unstructured data or whether to continue investments in the envisioned unstructured database. The delay in the unstructured data platform proved especially problematic for the PhD candidates from computational research, who had to resolve to other datasets for their research on unstructured data. The ambition that the work of the PhDs candidates in computational sciences could support the work of the PhD candidates in history was, therefore, abandoned.

I conducted nine interviews with seven participants of this collaboration, spread out over a period of two and a half years. Of these seven participants, five came from history and two from computational research. Three interviewees were professors supervising the research, three were PhD candidates and one was a coordinator. I furthermore had informal discussions with the software developers of the structured database.

Case Study 2: Development of a Structured Database Integrating Data from Multiple Cultural Heritage Institutes

The second case study was a four-year project at a single university. The main collaborators shared an office or had offices in the same hallway, making it a collaboration on a small distance. The collaborators were from different disciplinary backgrounds, about evenly distributed between historians and computational researchers and software developers. Data was collected in collaboration with several cultural heritage institutes. The software developer performed his tasks within the office of the other collaborators. Later in the project this developer was replaced by a software company from another country. During this period the computational researcher on the project spent time at the software company to coordinate development. The collaboration thus emphasised short distances and face-to-face communication throughout the entire project.

The envisioned system integrated the data from the different cultural heritage institutes in a structured database. Some of these datasets were unstructured data and the task of the computational researcher was to extract the entities and entity descriptions so they could be integrated in the structured data. In the first version, software development consisted of creating several visualisations that showed connections between datasets containing an entity, in a way that historians could analyse this information. This system was later replaced by a search interface where historians could search for entities to find in which databases they occurred. As this was a significant shift, the software developer was replaced. The PhD candidate in history was envisioned to use the system for their research. Yet although the system was successfully implemented, it was finalised only late in the project so that the PhD candidate did not end up using the system.

I conducted six interviews with five participants of the collaboration. Three interviewees came from history, one from computational research and one from software development. All interviewees had different roles in the project: one professor supervising the project, one coordinator, one postdoc, one PhD candidate and one software developer.

Case Study 3: Establishing a Digital Humanities Centre

The third case study was an alliance of scholars with the aim to promote digital humanities at their university. During my first round of interviews, the so-called centre consisted of three participants who were located in different buildings of the same university.

A point of interest was the diverging ambitions for the centre, which were connected with the individuals' visions of digital humanities as a whole. While one scholar argued that like digital humanities the centre should disappear within a couple of years, the other envisioned a key role in the development of research infrastructures for the humanities at large. The centre later grew substantially, with affiliates at several humanities research groups from the university and a core of project coordinators and software developers that were located close together. The centre had not yet fully stabilised in form and ambition, but was already actively providing a service role, hosting existing tools and developing new ones.

I conducted four interviews with three participants of the collaboration. All three were in senior positions, including two professors and a coordinator. The three interviewees had different backgrounds in history, literature and the library.

Case Study 4: a Software Team for the Humanities

The fourth case study was a team working to support humanities scholars in their university. Led by a senior scholar with a background in history, the rest of the team consisted of a postdoc and software developers with backgrounds in computer science, artificial intelligence or computational linguistics. All software developers had some affinity with humanities subjects. The team was located in a single office but collaborated with scholars that could be in any other building of the university. Scholars could apply for programming time with a project proposal describing their research project and the requirements for a digital tool to facilitate this research. Programming time was limited to three months part-time of one developer, for which costs would be covered by the university. For larger research projects, more programming time could be requested but this had to be covered financially by the budget of the requesting project. Different from the other case studies, this collaboration developed a wide range of small tools for very specific and predefined research practices. These tools were made to be generic, so that they could be reapplied to other research projects. When the team thought a certain research practice was already covered by existing tools they referred to these tools and rejected the request.

I conducted three interviews with three participants.[378] One interviewee was the leading senior scholar and two were developers.

Other Interviews

To further contextualise the case studies and broaden perspectives, I conducted six additional interviews outside of the case studies where I did not necessarily collect perspectives from multiple participants of a project. From these additional interviewees, five were from history and one from computational research. Three interviewees were professors, and the other three were in postdoc positions or reflected on past participation as a postdoc in a collaboration.

---

378 I conducted a fourth interview, but the recording failed. I have subsequently excluded this interview from analysis.

Incentives

> You have a research idea and you fit that to the call to which you apply. If you get a grant, you try to accomplish your research idea as well as possible. And when you hire researchers, they of course have their own idea and their own line of research they want to work on as well, and they try to fit that into the research project.
>
> (coordinator with background in history – Q1)

As the above quote shows, a project is shaped in multiple stages by the different incentives of participants. To understand the coordination of practices as uncovered in the case studies, in this section I detail the identified incentives of participants. Below, I first describe incentives according to the three factors introduced above: 1) reasons for joining, 2) individual goals and 3) expected effects of participation after the collaboration has ended. By describing the incentives bottom-up, I aim to identify communities of participants with shared incentives. In the next section, I investigate how incentives may conflict with one another.

Reasons for Joining

For the instigators of the collaboration, usually the professor and coordinator, this question is harder to answer. In an online questionnaire on digital humanities collaborations I asked respondents why they had joined their collaboration, to which almost 20% responded that they were the principal investigator (PI).[379] Since they did not join the collaboration, but conceived it, PIs tend to return to the goals as described in the grant proposal as their reason for joining or starting the collaboration. Nevertheless, for both PIs and for researchers employed after a grant, a number of reasons to join can be distilled from the interviews.

One reason, also present in quote Q1, was to acquire funding for research. For example, in one case study, a research group joined the collaboration for the following reasons:

> One reason we joined was to acquire funding for a PhD. Another reason was to implement our already existing research in a larger context, and thereby to jointly collect more data.
>
> (professor in history – Q2)

Not only did this research group join to advance existing research, they looked for additional funding to do so. This reason was mainly shared among the professors and coordinators as collaboration instigators. As many incentives were

---

379 Kemman, "Boundary Practices of Digital Humanities Collaborations."

shared by participants in these two roles, in the rest of this section I refer to them in combination as instigators.

Another reason that is equally pragmatic was to acquire a research position. This reason was especially common among the participants in PhD and postdoc positions. What is of interest is that several interviewees joined a digital history collaboration without necessarily doing so due to an intrinsic interest in digital history. For example, one historian said that "when I applied, I knew little or nothing about digital humanities" (postdoc in history – Q3). Instead, the demand for digital methods came from supervisors:

> Those digital methods were actually determined already by the project. Also, since I have a supervisor who is specialised in [this specific method of] analysis, I tried to, well, it was recommended by her. (PhD candidate in history – Q4)

Several interviewees already had experience with digital practices, either through research projects conducted as an undergraduate or having worked on digital projects in cultural heritage. Yet what interests me here is that these findings counter the idea of digital history coming from the new generation of "digital natives" that intuitively use computers to conduct historical research, despite their more traditional professors. Within these case studies, digital history instead appears to originate from the opposite direction, through professors pushing their PhDs and postdocs to conduct digital methods.

A possible explanation for this is the wave of quantitative history from the 1960s to 1980s and the Dutch wave of alfa-informatics in the 1980s, as mentioned in the introductory chapter. With digital history reintroducing aspects of quantification and informatics, senior scholars who had been educated during those waves were interested in enlarging the scholarly community conducting practices they had been performing individually through the years. Consequently, advancing digital humanities was a reason mainly shared among the instigators.[380] Some interviewees had ambitions with respect to the local university:

> We want to have digital research in our faculty, the faculty [of humanities], here in the university. That is our first goal. But we also want to act as a point for collaboration between the different faculties. (coordinator with background in library science – Q5)

Other interviewees had ambitions on a national level:

---

380 Note that interviewees spoke of "digital humanities" rather than "digital history" specifically, in agreement with my characterisation of digital history as a field overlapping with the field of digital humanities.

> The goal is to advance digital humanities research in Belgium and to experiment with this more broadly. (professor in computational science – Q6)

These ambitions commonly led to the reason of tool development, as an approach to advance digital humanities. This reason was shared among instigators and was the main reason for software developers. By developing tools and technological infrastructures, researchers inside and outside digital history would be facilitated with digital methods:

> It is not the research itself that is the final outcome, but the components that come out that can be provided as a service to the faculty or the broader research community.
> (professor in history – Q7)

This reason then emphasises the digital part of digital history:

> It is of course technology-driven in the sense that without the new technology this project would not have started in the first place. You would not have thought about it then.
> (professor in history – Q8)

In summary, the reasons for joining digital history collaborations were indeed technology-driven, as the above quote shows, to develop tools and advance digital humanities. Furthermore, reasons were related to enable the environment in which to collaborate with funding and a position to work at the university. Notably, historical research does not appear to be a direct reason to join a digital history collaboration, although it does become of importance in the individual goals.

Individual Goals

For the PhD candidates and their supervising professors, an important goal was to finish the thesis, continuing the somewhat pragmatic reason of acquiring a research position mentioned above. One professor said:

> You cannot say 'well, I have software, I will provide that with my thesis, and I will have a PhD in digital history.' [. . .] What the historian must do is write a thesis with five chapters that are of substantial value to the [historical] field [. . .] At the same time she uses digital means in her research. (professor in history – Q9)

As can be seen in the above quote, the historical substance of the thesis was prioritised over the digital history ambitions of the collaboration. Another professor echoed this:

In the last two years of the project we decided, very pragmatically, that ultimately the key outcome for the academics are those PhDs and the research. That is why everyone more or less continued from their own research question, without much further collaboration between the different institutes to work to more of a logistics or practical implementation.

(professor in computational science – Q10)

From these quotes, two characteristics of the PhD thesis become apparent. First, it is disciplinary, rather than interdisciplinary. Second, it is individual, rather than collaborative.[381] As such, the project and the PhD are distinct paths, as explained by one interviewee:

What the PhDs do is that they are part of the digital humanities project, but I think that they are also just writing their PhD, independent of that digital humanities project.

(coordinator with background in history – Q11)

One important rationale for separating a PhD thesis from a collaboration was risk aversion:

If [the project] fails, it cannot be that my thesis also fails. You can to some extent see them separate from one another, as I do. So, there is a sort of secret clause; if [the project] fails, I just graduate with a historical thesis.   (PhD candidate in history – Q12)

Some PhD candidates did try more explicitly to embed their thesis in digital history by making a methodological contribution. This individual goal could be described as advancing digital humanities, like the reason for joining with the same name. This goal was shared by some researchers in PhD or postdoc positions, as well as by instigators. One interviewee said:

[I hope] I can bring the crossroads between classical research and digital humanities into practice fairly concretely [. . .] and bridge the gap with those who are not engaged in digital humanities.   (PhD candidate in history – Q13)

As with the reason to join, advancing digital humanities was related to tool development as a goal. This goal was mainly shared among the instigators of collaborations and software developers. The two goals were related insofar as the tool should demonstrate the utility of digital humanities:

The idea of the project has always been a proof-of-concept, a pilot of sorts or indeed a prototype that can be utilised more broadly.   (coordinator with background in history – Q14)

---

381 These interviewed PhD candidates were in that sense similar to the PhD candidates that I described in my observations of the C²DH in the previous chapter. See also Fickers and van der Heijden, "Inside the Trading Zone."

While the tool was principally developed for the historians in the collaboration, the aim was that the tool could remain useful independent of their research:

> [We are] developing a research environment, very concretely for this project, but it should be duplicatable to other projects. I think that is the most important aspect of what we want to do. (coordinator with background in history – Q15)

The tools under development should, therefore, be applicable beyond the scope of the collaboration in question:

> The challenge is to deliver a product that is useful for historians, but also valid towards [other disciplines]. (professor in history – Q16)

As demonstrators of the utility of digital humanities, another goal of importance was technological research, as can be discerned from the earlier quote Q8 of a project being technology-driven. This goal was shared by the instigators and the computational researchers. For several interviewees, this consisted of analysing the full text of sources to detect entities such as people, places or events and with those entities link sources and datasets:

> My task was to see whether we could distil information from texts. For example, whether we can get events or people or points in time or locations from unstructured texts. [The idea was] to make a sort of event index, or to see here is a certain event in [this] collection, and here is an event in [that] collection, is it about the same yes or no.
> (postdoc in computational science – Q17)

As with tool development, the applicability of the technology was broader than the specific scope of the collaboration. The technology under investigation not only concerned the historical research of the historians of the collaboration, but historical documents in general:

> I am not interested in [the historical field] as such. My field is information extraction and text mining, and I have worked in various fields [of application] in the past [. . .] The particular interest in these documents is that they are of a specific nature. They present particular challenges that you do not find in contemporary data. First, [with contemporary data], some of that is born-digital data, so you do not deal with transcriptions or OCR issues or whatever. Second, there is much more ambiguity and vagueness that is also related to the domain of history. (postdoc in computational science – Q18)

The technological research was, moreover, broader and more ambitious than the specific implementation in the tool under development:

> For me, the success of the project is basically building an interface where all this information is presented in a useful manner, where people can actually perhaps connect primary historical sources to secondary historical sources [. . .] What I am doing might provide additional information to this interface from the original text sources that are not yet structured,

that would be good, but it is not paramount for the success of the project. And it would be good for my personal research objectives, which are not directly connected to digital history objectives of course, but indirectly they are.   (postdoc in computational science – Q19)

This interviewee decoupled the technology from the tool, reducing the tool to a graphical user interface to interact with the data. The interviewee thereby furthermore decoupled the technological research from the goal of advancing digital humanities. However, indirectly they are related, insofar as digital history is understood to concern technological progress in historical practices:

> We also have databases such as [this collection], that is unstructured material. What if you want to link that meaningfully to the structured [data]? That is quite a step [. . .] Are we going to solve this? No. We really are in the prehistory, I would say, of this entire field.
>
> (professor in history – Q20)

The technological research did stand in close relation with the goal using data. This goal connects with most of the other goals, as the sources are what the historian writes her thesis about, what the computational expert writes algorithms for (see quote Q18) and what the tool should make accessible. In quote Q2, the interviewee explained they wanted funding to work with their data. This goal is consequently shared by all participants of collaborations. For the historians, how they investigate sources was fundamental to their research and PhD thesis:

> The project should not take an encyclopaedic approach. It is not just about storing information, but about aggregating a lot of information and asking new questions of it.
>
> (PhD candidate in history – Q21)

For some interviewees, the data was crucial for the goal of advancing digital humanities:

> [Digital humanities is about bringing] together corpora of sources, both texts as well as structured data. Not just within one's own institute, one's own university, research group, but far beyond, also internationally. Such collaborations have been announced many times in the past, but it is now that we finally have the means to do so.   (professor in history – Q22)

The data was usually provided by cultural heritage institutes, which were not formally participating in collaborations in most cases. The relation to these institutes differed between interviewees. In one collaboration, the coordinator took on the role of representing the cultural heritage institutes:

> One of my roles is to represent the parties that act as data providers, and my point of view in all discussions is thus very data-driven, while our PhD candidate is very research-driven. She just wants information she can use for her research, and from the start we have debated how to bring those two together.   (coordinator with background in history – Q23)

Yet the work of cultural heritage institutes was also diminished by some as too limited:

> The thing with archives is that they archive, they are not engaged with what researchers want to do with it for their research.   (coordinator with background in history – Q24)

As such, participants argued to be more ambitious than the practices of cultural heritage institutes in unlocking the affordances of digitised data. The collaborations under investigation thereby indeed considered themselves as a balancing of the digital history duality with the digital, in computational research and tool development, and the historical, in historical research. Beyond this balance, the above quotes show how non-academic partners are included only in a role of service to the collaboration. Beyond the trading zone of historians and computational experts, these collaborations showcase a power asymmetry between academic partners as collaborators and cultural partners as passive data providers. These cultural heritage institutes consequently could not coordinate their goals and expected effects of providing the data.[382]

Expected Effects of Participation

Finally, participants coordinated activities and practices to fulfil what they expected to gain from collaboration. Following from the goal to finish the thesis, one expectation was the completion of PhDs. This expectation was similarly shared by PhD candidates and their supervising professors:

> We have [several] PhDs now in a postdoc programme [. . .] That is a nice result from this project, that we have given our PhDs the opportunity to grow, to take further steps in their career.   (professor in history – Q25)

One professor contrasted the importance of this incentive with that of tool development:

> We are occupied with acquiring and managing projects rather than that we are doing research ourselves. With acquiring a project, it is also really the goal that the doctorates are defended and that publications come out. What is more or less a mismatch is that just

---

382 I can only touch the surface of this power asymmetry, since an in-depth exploration is beyond the scope of this book. For critiques of this power asymmetry see Reto Speck and Petra Links, "The Missing Voice: Archivists and Infrastructures for Humanities Research," *International Journal of Humanities and Arts Computing* 7, no. 1–2 (2013): 128–46, https://doi.org/10.3366/ijhac.2013.0085; Cook, "The Archive(s) Is a Foreign Country: Historians, Archivists, and the Changing Archival Landscape."

implementing solid solutions based on technologies that have already proven their worth is
perhaps not sufficiently innovative or original to get publications.

(professor in computational science – Q26)

This quote furthermore indicates that incentives were shaped by the expectations
for future funding. This expectation, shared mainly by instigators, not only concerned future funding as an expectation in itself, but also the anticipation of what
needed to be delivered from the current collaboration to qualify for future funding:

> We more or less realised what we promised to realise. The doctorates are there, the publica-
> tions are there. We will eventually also open up our dataset [. . .] I think that [the funder]
> will be satisfied.   (professor in history – Q27)

Another interviewee instead emphasised the tool as necessary for future funding:

> One of the goals we have now set for ourselves is to bring our system to the attention of
> researchers and institutes related to the same type of research. That way we can try to get
> continued funding with them.   (coordinator with background in history – Q28)

This argument aligns with another expectation, that of tool usage. This expectation was mainly shared among the historians of a collaboration, in roles of instigators, PhD, or postdoc. Although this is related to the earlier reason and goal
of tool development, the participants are not the same. While tool development
was associated with those on the providing side of the tool, the instigators and
the software developers, tool usage was associated with those who received the
tool to conduct research. Eventually, the historians were tasked with using the
tool to investigate or demonstrate its utility:

> Essentially, I am the guinea pig that has to show that one can do research with the inter-
> face and with the integrated data.   (PhD candidate in history – Q29)

Yet what I find significant is that this expectation is far more modest than the
ambitions earlier in the collaboration. Rather than using the tool for research, it
was limited to testing with a smaller case study:

> *Interviewer*: Her role is limited to a use case considering how this works, what she can
> learn from it and how she can provide feedback to what you are developing?
>
> *Interviewee:* Yes, and that is not meant to denigrate her role, but that is different from what
> we had envisioned from the start.   (coordinator with background in history – Q30)

In some cases, the system was not sufficiently finished to even conduct a test with
a historical case study. A question might be what the collaboration had successfully achieved to support acquisition of future funding and continue in the field of
digital history. However, rather than disappointment in failing to deliver a system,

interviewees emphasised the success of the collaboration in the expected development of know-how. Insofar as collaborations did not entirely achieve their goals, this was pointed out to be an inherent risk of innovative research. In quote Q20 the research was described as a "prehistory"; experimental work conducted before a technology becomes entirely usable. Another interviewee argued:

> In hindsight it was a bit too ambitious. But really, I am convinced that we are doing pioneering work. (professor in history – Q31)

This expectation, shared by instigators, refers to the development of expertise in running interdisciplinary collaborations and learning from successes as well as failures. Know-how covered multiple facets of digital history, such as the technological approaches:

> Ultimately a production-ready version does not have to come out of [the project], that is not the goal. This is more a technology project aimed at the know-how that is developed. [This is also useful for] the companies that continue to work toward a productive system, that they can use parts in a new product. (professor in history – Q32)

Know-how also covered project management as an inherent aspect of digital humanities:[383]

> Another thing is the learning process really. How do you conduct digital humanities? How do you bring these parties together, what do you run into? Everything that on a methodological organisational side succeeds or fails has to be put on paper. (professor in history – Q33)

Finally, development of know-how covered working with the data:

> In historical research, of course, the by-catch is always at least as important as the envisioned goal. By making the texts available we ran into problems that exist elsewhere too and that have not yet been solved in the field. (professor in history – Q34)

The last quote furthermore points to the expectation of a transformed dataset. Independent of specific tools or methods, collaborations provided a new dataset by having linked or enriched existing datasets. This expectation was related to the goal of using data, but while that goal was shared by all participants, here it was mainly shared among the instigators. The transformed dataset was an explicit

---

[383] For more on project management as an inherent aspect of digital humanities, see Anna Maria Neubert, "Navigating Disciplinary Differences in (Digital) Research Projects Through Project Management," in *Digital Methods in the Humanities*, ed. Silke Schwandt (transcript Verlag, 2020), 59–86, https://doi.org/10.14361/9783839454190-003; Lynne Siemens, "Project Management and the Digital Humanist," in *Doing Digital Humanities: Practice, Training, Research*, ed. Constance Crompton, Richard J. Lane and Raymond George Siemens, 1st edition (New York, NY: Routledge, 2016), 343–57.

deliverable of collaborations, usable for others: "our data [. . .] is very complete, so it can be used as a ground truth set for future research" (professor in history – Q35). While the delivered tool may or may not receive continued development, historians could use the existing facilities to keep expanding their dataset:

> [The platform] is still in progress, there is not really an end to it. We can keep on adding data for years to come. (professor in history – Q36)

The dataset was as such a fairly stable deliverable, enabling future research.

Finally, most participants shared the expectation of methodological innovation, whether or not the tool would be usable for the historical research. For some, it referred to facilitating new methods:

> Can the researcher do more than they could before? I find that very important. I find it pleasing when I can look back and think I have done something new in this project for myself and really learned something. (software developer – Q37)

In several cases, the increased ability of the researcher referred to the ability of examining more source material:

> I have consulted a larger dataset than [another researcher] ever could, simply because I had digital accessibility of sources [. . .] So I think I took an older method into the 21st century. (PhD candidate in history – Q38)

In summary, expected effects were both individual, such as completing one's PhD thesis, but also extended to the research community more widely, bringing methodological innovation or a dataset for others to build upon.

Grouping Incentives

From the interviews I have identified 15 different reasons, goals and expectations that shaped practices at different points of collaborations. When connecting these reasons, goals and expectations, several underlying incentives emerge. For example, the reason to acquire a research position, the goal to finish the thesis and the expectation of completion of PhD are arguably continuations of the same incentive: that one wants to conduct and complete research. Grouping incentives as such, I distinguish six categories of incentives: 1) funding, 2) digital history/humanities (DH), 3) data, 4) tool development, 5) historical research and 6) computational research (see Table 3).

These incentives are intuitive for digital history. If the goal had just been to uncover these incentives, I may not have needed to go through the different reasons, goals and expectations. Yet it is to be expected that not all incentives can

Table 3: Grouping of incentives. Phrasing of incentives shortened to fit the table.

INCENTIVE	REASONS FOR JOINING	INDIVIDUAL GOALS	EXPECTED EFFECTS OF PARTICIPATION
FUNDING	*Acquire funding* (instigators)		*Future funding* (instigators)
DH	*Advancing DH* (instigators)	*Advancing DH* (instigators, PhD candidates, postdocs)	*Methodological innovation* (all) *Development of know-how* (instigators)
DATA		*Using data* (all)	*Transformed dataset* (instigators, computational researchers)
TOOL	*Tool development* (instigators, software developers)	*Tool development* (instigators, software developers)	*Tool usage* (historians)
RESEARCH (HISTORICAL AND COMPUTATIONAL)	*Acquire position* (PhD candidates, postdocs)	*Finish the thesis* (PhD candidates, professors) *Technological research* (instigators, computational researchers)	*Completion of PhD research* (PhD candidates, professors)

be pursued equally. A collaboration ultimately has to prioritise incentives and decide whether the challenges of one can be handled by decreasing attention to another. By taking this bottom-up approach, it is possible to describe who in the collaboration is related to which incentives.

For the first four incentives, funding, DH, data and tool development, the main participants are the professors in history leading the collaborations and the coordinators. Together, these two types of participants formed the collaboration instigators. The incentive tool development was also held by the software developers. However, in these case studies the software developers were hired and did not actively try to shape the collaboration. It can thus be argued that these four incentives were all held by the same community of practice, in the sense that this was a community of like-minded participants that aimed to align the practices of the collaboration to their incentives. I call this community the collaboration instigators. When interviewees spoke of "the project", it was commonly in reference to these four incentives. The instigators thereby aligned the project with their individual incentives.

For the final incentives related to research, two communities become apparent. The first community is related to historical research, with the main participants the PhD candidates and postdocs and their supervising professors in history, who also led the collaboration. I refer to this community of practice as the historians. Note that this community did not include the coordinator. Although most coordinators had a background in history, the coordinator was not responsible for the historical research. As such, in some cases the coordinator would oppose historians in their incentives to shape the collaboration toward the historical research. This is exemplified by quote Q23, where the coordinator explicitly took on a data-driven position against the research-driven position of the PhD candidate in history.

The other type community is related to computational research, where the main participants were the computational researchers and the instigators. I call this community the technologists, since they emphasised the technological aspects of the collaboration. Note that this community not only included computational researchers, but also the historians in senior positions and coordinators that desired to advance digital history through the development of technology, as exemplified by quote Q8.

In summary, three communities emerge through the identification of communities holding similar incentives: collaboration instigators, historians and technologists (see Figure 6). Of significance is that while some collaboration participants align with a single community, others are part of multiple communities. Notably, the professor in history leading the collaboration is part of all three and is the bridge between all the different incentives.

Crossing Boundaries

In several interviews, professors emphasised the need to have coordinators in the collaboration to "get everyone on the same page". Yet the above analysis of incentives showed that coordinators did so by emphasising the incentives of the

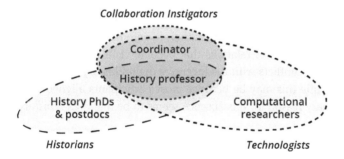

Figure 6: Communities of practice holding similar incentives.

collaboration instigators, such as tool development and data transformation. Furthermore, while coordinators had more time to keep an eye on progress, they did not usually have the power to decide which direction to take. For that coordinators were dependent on the professor in history. As such, the academic hierarchy power mechanism affected the practices of coordinators:

> In a certain hierarchy, she was lower in the sense that she was not a PhD nor a professor. She was just someone hired to do the job. She could not say [to the professor] I need this, and [to the PhD candidate] I need this.   (postdoc in computational science – Q39)

Yet even for the professors this could prove difficult, especially in collaborations with multiple professors from multiple institutes:

> It is quite difficult to do, because she is not the boss of [the other professors]. There was no project leader telling everyone what to do.   (postdoc in computational science – Q40)

In such collaborations, which occurred when collaborations occurred between different research groups or institutes, the professors experienced symmetric power with respect to their academic positions.

The professors arguably took on the role of what Étienne Wenger called the "broker" between multiple communities of practice, or what Jennifer Edmond called the "digital humanities intermediary".[384] That is, they coordinated and introduced practices or incentives from one community of practice into another. This is a significant new role for the professor in history, and one I return to later in the final chapter.

To further understand how incentives were negotiated between these communities, in the next section I investigate situations of conflicting incentives.

Conflicting Incentives

I distinguish six different incentives held by participants of the collaborations. Each of these incentives may oppose one another. In this section, I highlight situations where one incentive conflicted with another, to gain insight into the process of coordination and the power relations that become visible through these conflicts. Interestingly, no conflicts with the incentive digital history became apparent in this study. While this may be because most participants aligned with this incentive, the primary reason for this absence seems to be that digital history

---

384 Wenger, *Communities of Practice*, 108–10; Edmond, "The Role of the Professional Intermediary in Expanding the Humanities Computing Base."

as an incentive was approached through other incentives such as tool development or data. These incentives that needed to be conducted first then led to conflicts within the collaborations as described below.

Historical Research & Computational Research

The first conflict is perhaps the most intuitive in the context of digital history: the opposition between the digital and the history. For the historians the historical research took priority over the computational research. This was especially clear with the goal to finish the thesis, where historians considered their thesis independent of the technology under development. Historians thereby detached their research from the technological research:

> It is usually [them] that ask me to reflect on what they have created or what I think of a certain plan they have, rather than the other way around, because I can usually work fine without their input.   (PhD candidate in history – Q41)

To the extent that the two incentives were connected, historians saw the technology in a facilitating role:

> Everything that happens ultimately has the goal that I can do better research [. . .] The programming work I see as a sort of facilitating matter.   (PhD candidate in history – Q42)

Moreover, when the computational experts required input from the historians, the latter did not see this as part of their research:

> She does not really realise that the problem she is modelling and the way that she tries to structure the information actually consists of a vital part of research as well. She does not see this as research. She still sees that the main output of her research is the historical research.   (postdoc in computational science – Q43)

Yet if the collaboration would entirely prioritise the historical over the computational research, this would entail the use of readily available technology:

> If you want to make a tool that a historian will trust for their own research, then most people use methods that are well-defined [. . .] or very basic things that are robust. These things work and are well-tried. Now if you want to go a step further [. . .] there is a higher risk and a higher uncertainty about the results. That is why I am not sure whether this tool will be readily usable.   (postdoc in computational science – Q44)

As it was not satisfactory for collaborations to lack technological innovations, the computational research did not always succumb to the desires from the historians. At several times, the technology was prioritised over the requirements for historical research. For example, in one case a historian tried to limit the scope of the technology to the scope of her historical research. The technologists did not follow this line, as they considered this an unsustainable route:

> Did you think of the consequences for the future [. . .] You cannot just take parts out [. . .] That would be a decision that no longer allows you to do other things in the future.
>
> (professor in history – Q45)

For the historians it could consequently become increasingly difficult to continue negotiation with the technologists:

> When there is a functionality available, I can do something with it and we can take the next step as far as I am concerned. Yet for her it often seems more of a discussion on a philosophical level. Sometimes that surpasses me. The back-end remains something I feel I cannot do much with. (PhD candidate in history – Q46)

What is of interest in this conflict is the extent to which historians were implied to not properly understand the technology, and how that configures the conflict. Attempts by historians to shape the practices of technological research were consequently hampered due to a lack of expertise of what this incentive entailed. In the opposite direction, historians would detach the historical research from the technological research, so that only they could shape their own practices of historical research.

Historical Research & Tool Development

The second conflict, between the tool development and the historical research, is probably as intuitive to digital history as the first. This conflict was partially caused by promises made in the grant application:

> The promise you make to [the funder] is that you say, 'we will do historical research and that is input for the tool development, and what I can do with the tool is input for my historical research.' But in our case, it turned out that does not really work in practice. [The PhD] has almost finished her thesis, and there is very little that she discovered by actually using [our tool]. (coordinator with background in history – Q47)

The second aspect, where the historians could use the tool for their research, proved difficult under time constraints and delays in development. Consequently, historians would again detach their research from the tool development:

> Each historian works individually on their own little island, that practice is hard to change. We still notice that the PhDs affiliated with the project also prefer to set up their own little data collection, on their own hard drive, rather than sharing everything. And there is a reason why they do that. The infrastructure [. . .] is far from where we are supposed to be.
>
> (professor in history – Q48)

Another problem that emerged was that some participants lacked interest in the technological goals of a collaboration and how those come to fruition. For example, one interviewee argued that how a tool functions is not of concern to historians:

> We did not say how it should work technically, because in principle for us the technical side should not be relevant to the end-user, as long as the tool works.
> (coordinator with background in history – Q49)

Yet how tools work on a technical level and whether they work well for historians cannot be considered strictly independent. In several cases the tool development was not intentionally prioritised over historical research, yet the way historical research could be conducted was shaped by decisions made with respect to the tool. For example, the data model of a tool required historians to provide their data in a certain way:

> The data design of the structured environment is fairly complex, it includes a lot of objects and sub-objects and object descriptors. We had to put all our data in the proper format.
> (professor in history – Q50)

Historians tried to shape tool development by providing functional requirements. Yet the communication and coordination of those functionalities proved more complex than anticipated:

> We thought [the software developers] were experienced and knew what we meant. We did not consider that our requests could be interpreted otherwise.
> (coordinator with background in history – Q51)

In this case, a mismatch occurred between how historians described a functionality and how developers interpreted that functionality in code. As the developers had technically satisfied the requirement, it was contractually difficult for the historians to further shape the system. Further adjustments required additional budgeting, which was lacking. Another dependency that was not anticipated by historians was the time required to develop functionalities:

> There is absolutely a disconnect between how we want to use the tools and the time that is needed to develop that. We do not have a good handle on how long any given request takes to translate into code.
> (postdoc in history – Q52)

Once a tool was created and made available to historians, yet another dependency was the performance of the tool. In one collaboration, the tool was hosted by the computational researchers. Yet the server was used by multiple research projects. When another project ran their experiments, the historians' tool crashed or operated so slowly it was deemed unusable. According to the coordinator of this collaboration, after the historians complained they wanted better support, the computational researchers simply replied with "no, that server is for multiple experiments, you are just one of the experiments" (coordinator with background in history – Q53). The PI of this project underscored the historians' dependency on the expertise of computational researchers:

> You are very dependent on what the computational researchers as experts, which they are, say and argue should be in the project proposal [. . .] In hindsight I think they should have said more about the really practical things, such as computation capacity, server space, the stability of software, how that is managed. You need money for that too. We did not have budget for that in the project, as idiotic as that seems now.   (professor in history – Q54)

Finally, even when a tool was delivered and performed well, the practice of continued development conflicted with the expectations of historians that the same action should lead to the same results:

> A very sleek and finished looking tool makes you think as a user that it is finished. But we know that it is constantly being tinkered with under the hood. The collections and the number of [sources] that we are dealing with are constantly changing.
> (postdoc in history – Q55)

In this conflict of incentives, it is of interest that again the extent to which historians' lack of understanding computational practices shaped the conflict. Ignorance of how long development takes, how a tool is hosted, or how a feature request is interpreted and how those factors affect performance and usability led to tools that did not meet the expectations of historians. As such, the historians were dependent on the computational researchers and software developers to bring about usable systems. Here too, historians consequently detached the historical research from the tool development, so that the historical research was not shaped too much by the tool. Historians especially tried to secure their research from failing when the tool did not meet expectations or arrived too late. As such, this detachment should be seen as a risk aversion strategy.

Computational Research & Tool Development

That there is a conflict of incentives between the tool development and the technological research may be less obvious of digital history. One might expect that these two incentives refer to the same aspect of the collaboration, namely the overall development of a digital method for the historians, the "digital" in digital history. Yet in quote Q19 the computational researcher separated the incentives. Where the technological research is innovative and carries risk of failure, the tool should be stable and usable, as argued in quote Q44. For the historians this detachment could prove problematic, as this meant that the computational researchers prioritised their own research agenda over the project's goal of facilitating historical research with a tool.

This conflict of incentives is, therefore, perhaps the most fundamental to digital history collaborations. The detachment of tool development from technological research means that the vision of historical researchers and computational researchers collaborating toward a common goal might not work out as hoped:

> The usual clash at risk is that I want something and that [the computational researcher] says 'I can do that with one hand tied behind my back. At an academic department in computer science that is not interesting for me. That is not innovative'.
> (coordinator with background in history – Q56)

To counter problems arising from this detachment, and to ensure that the tool development would commence, tasks were separated between computational researchers and software developers. While the computational researchers would provide input for tool development, the responsibility to deliver a working tool lay primarily with the software developers. Furthermore, other tasks related to the tool were delegated to IT personnel in the university or the university library:

> You need someone in-house who can maintain the server, because the programmer you asked for that usually does not have the skills or the desire to, or their time is too valuable [. . .] It took a while before we found the right person here in the university who would do that as part of their job.   (coordinator with background in history – Q57)

In this conflict of incentives, computational researchers detached the technology from the tool in order to focus on their research and publications, rather than maintaining a stable tool. Consequently, the digital history collaborations in my investigations distributed non-research tasks to partners such as software developers, IT personnel, or librarians. This detachment too can be seen as a risk aversion strategy, to secure the goal of the collaboration to provide a tool. In case the technological research succeeds on time, it can be implemented in the tool. If the research however fails or is delayed, the tool can still be delivered without the innovative technology. In this case, as exemplified in quote Q19, the tool is reduced to an interface to the data, which brings me to the next conflict of incentives.

Data & Tool Development

In the grouping of incentives, I identify both data and tool development as belonging to the same participants of a collaboration, namely the collaboration instigators. Moreover, I found that the tool was essentially seen as a gateway to the data (see quotes Q19 and Q29). There should not be a conflict of incentives. However, integrating the data in the tool proved to be complicated. A major stumbling block was the processing of large amounts of data. This took more time than anticipated, introducing delays. One collaboration consequently significantly adjusted their goals. Originally, the collaboration was to investigate a transnational history, but instead they could only work with data relating to a single nation:

> It started with these grand ambitions, with sources from all different countries. They never materialised, mostly because of copyright problems, but also because of the actual amount of time it takes to get them into the right format to even go into our database. [. . .] Now the project is about Dutch history instead, because those [sources] have already been digitised. (postdoc in history – Q58)

When collaborations succeeded in importing data in the tool a consideration was how the tool transformed the data, as certain aspects of the data would be emphasised or hidden. A common issue was the role of optical character recognition (OCR), which is never perfect and can thereby obscure some sources from view.[385] For example, when some sources are not machine-readable, but others are, only the latter sources will be usable in the tools under development.

Another issue for collaborations that connected multiple datasets was how to treat parts of a dataset that were not connected to another dataset. In one case, this led to a system where items that were not in multiple datasets could no longer be retrieved:

> When you searched you would only find [items] that were in two or three or more databases. If you would add information at a later time, you could no longer access the largest database to extract information, because those links had not been made.
> (coordinator with background in history – Q59)

In this situation, the collaboration had to coordinate whether to emphasise the objects or the links between objects, with significant consequences for how historians could use the system for their research. Eventually, they had to rebuild the system entirely to emphasise the objects themselves, rather than the relations between objects.

In short, while data and tool development were not opposed as incentives, the integration of the data and implementation of the tool affected one another,

---

385 Optical character recognition (OCR) is an essential step in transforming historical sources into machine-readable data. The performance of OCR thereby shapes the validity of historical research using computational means. For critical discussions see Jarlbrink and Snickars, "Cultural Heritage as Digital Noise"; David A. Smith and Ryan Cordell, "A Research Agenda for Historical and Multilingual Optical Character Recognition" (NUlab, Northeastern University, 2018).

introducing unintended trade-offs. First and foremost, the integration of data proved much more time consuming than anticipated, leaving less time for tool development, or significantly altering the tool. Second, decisions made in the tool could emphasise or obscure data unintentionally, leading to the next conflict.

Data & Historical Research

The relevance and quality of the data was the key issue for the historians. Even if the tool would work as envisioned, the historians could not conduct proper research without data of interest:

> You remain dependent on the substance and quality of the data that is provided by the project partners. Even with a magnificent system, with everything visualised, it is quite possible that the relevant information is simply not in the data.   (PhD candidate in history – Q60)

Furthermore, interviewees discussed cases where data fit the tool under development rather well. Yet in these cases they were critical of how this introduced a bias, as the tool emphasised the data that worked well with the tool, rather than the data that did not:

> The Leeuwarden newspaper has been OCRed and digitised very well, for several hundreds of years. A lot of studies consequently refer to the Leeuwarden newspaper and not to other newspapers. The risk is that for the next ten years there is a bias for Leeuwarden in historical studies.   (postdoc in history – Q61)

Historians thus remained well aware of the limitations of certain datasets. Some feared that historical research would be biased in ways that do not correspond to the true importance of historical events or objects, like the Leeuwarden newspaper.[386] Yet by conducting historical research as part of a collaboration that is supposed to work on certain data, historians were expected to do research with these datasets. One interviewee was especially critical of their data, saying "nobody would ever choose these sources if they had a choice" (postdoc in history – Q62). Instigators, therefore, had to coordinate the balance between the historical

---

386 For discussions about biases in historical research following digital availability, see Ian Milligan, "Illusionary Order: Online Databases, Optical Character Recognition, and Canadian History, 1997–2010," *Canadian Historical Review* 94, no. 4 (2013): 540–69, https://doi.org/10.3138/chr.694; Kobie van Krieken, "Using Digital Archives in Quantitative Discourse Studies: Methodological Reflections," *Tijdschrift Voor Tijdschriftstudies* 38 (2015): 43–50, https://doi.org/10.18352/ts.343; Thomas Smits, "TS Tools: Problems and Possibilities of Digital Newspaper and Periodical Archives," *Tijdschrift Voor Mediageschiedenis* 139 (2014): 139–46.

research and the work on the dataset, so that data deemed not of interest by historians would not be discarded too hastily.

Historians also extended their research beyond the data worked on by the collaboration. For the instigators, this could be unsatisfying, as it meant historians built their "own little data collection" (quote Q48). Yet in the role of supervising a PhD, professors acknowledged the necessity of using data that may not be digitised yet:

> She also works in the paper archives [. . .] like all of us historians. I too have worked in the archives, doing the diligent manual work. (professor in history – Q63)

What this quote furthermore exemplifies is that even for historians with a digital focus, working with material sources in archives remains part of the expected historical process.[387] This expectation to work with data that was not yet digitally available led to requests for functionality to add one's own data into a tool. In one collaboration, historians emphasised the need for the data model and tool to allow working with incomplete data and the ability to add data later on:

> We as PhD candidates in history were looking for an environment where, before you have a [complete dataset], you can already start enriching the available data.
> (PhD candidate in history – Q64)

The historians in PhD and postdoc positions were tasked to work with the data, yet saw their research in a wider context than the collaboration. Ultimately, historians took a question-driven approach, cherry-picking relevant data from the datasets and acquiring additional data from other sources. In contrast, instigators took a data-driven position to ensure the datasets were still used, as exemplified by quote Q23.

Data & Computational Research

Data also proved a stumbling block for computational research. Computational researchers were accustomed to starting a research project with a fairly clearly defined dataset that fit the proposed research method. In digital history collaborations, this was not the case:

> [The cultural heritage institute] said 'yes we have data'. As it turned out they had a nice shelf with handwritten books. (postdoc in computational science – Q65)

---

387 See also Gerben Zaagsma's argument that historical scholarship in the digital age is "hybrid" by nature, combining digital and traditional methods. "On Digital History."

In another collaboration, the data was available in digital form, but still not immediately suitable for computational approaches:

> When you investigate the dataset, row by row [. . .] you discover that those datasets contain big errors or that entire columns are wrong. Sometimes you have to leave data out because it is only comprehensible to the person who created the dataset.
>
> (coordinator with background in history – Q66)

In one case, the computational researcher ultimately resorted to readily available datasets, rather than the dataset that was worked on in the collaboration. Because the computational researcher was then no longer working on the same dataset as the historians, the historical and computational research drifted apart. In the eyes of some historians, the computational research then lost its purpose and value:

> [They] did not collaborate with the historians working on the project. There was no real research question, no real feedback to a historical research question.
>
> (professor in history – Q67)

While the "ambiguity and vagueness" (quote Q18) made digital history interesting for computational researchers, it also introduced risks. The data may end up being inadequate for the collaboration to implement the envisioned technology, at least not without intensive additional work. As a result, some computational researchers detached their research from the collaboration goals to work with a specific dataset, and acquired data that facilitated their research better.

Funding

Finally, an important influence on the collaboration is the funding. I identify funding as an incentive especially for collaboration instigators. In the expectations I found that instigators tried to shape the project to meet the funders' demands both for the current and future grants. It can thus be argued that funders shaped collaborations from the outside. One interviewee mentioned that funding was what necessitated collaborations in the first place. With funders increasingly requiring interdisciplinary collaborations in teams, historians see themselves pushed toward such collaborations, whether they want to or not:

> You now forge unorthodox alliances because the knife is on the throat. You have to be able to look beyond borders to keep along.   (professor in history – Q68)

Following such requirements from funding organisations, another historian expected that they could only acquire funding by focusing on digital history:

> I do not think I would ever get a grant as a philosopher of history. If I ever want to get a grant for anything, my only option is to do that on digitisation. (professor in history – Q69)

Digital history collaborations are expensive, however, reinforcing the need to keep applying for funding:

> You are continuously short on money, so you have to continuously apply for grants to go further.   (professor in history – Q70)

Digital history is expensive for several reasons. A common reason is that the collaborative aspect is expensive, requiring personnel to conduct the proposed research. Another expense is the investment in experimenting with unstable technology. While one could object to this practice and argue that historians should wait for technology to stabilise before historians invest in a technology's application, one interviewee argued this is a good thing:

> I have seen how much money just drained away, because the technology was followed while it was still undergoing so much maturation. At the same time, I do not criticise that, because that means that demands have been made of it, and that the development is known.
> (professor in history – Q71)

Thus, this historian argued that by engaging with the technology during its maturation, historians can try to influence the technology to fit their needs and better steer the development to align with their demands. Historians are moreover better able to understand how a technology came to be and how it works. While this may require significant investments, the end result is that the technology is hopefully better suited for historical research than if historians had not participated during its development.

Apart from enabling historians through grants, funders simultaneously limited what can be done with a grant. While funders promote collaboration and the development of digital systems, historians criticised the lack of adequate funding for software development:

> There is very little money available for software development, while this kind of project really run[s] on good people with high work rates [. . .] The best programmers are at private companies, who pay a lot more. And [the funder] does not really consider that.
> (coordinator with background in history – Q72)

Funders furthermore did not always consider sustainability, instead limiting the scope of grants to innovative research. Collaborations consequently did not have a clear picture of how they could continue work on the system that was developed, since the national funder did not provide grants for sustained development:

> [The PI] would like to continue this course, but the tricky thing is, and everybody is con-
> fronted by that with [the funder], that they do not fund continuation projects, only new
> innovative things.   (coordinator with background in history – Q73)

Finally, funders limited the outcomes of coordination. That is, through coordination and the experiences of the collaboration, scholars might discover that
their initial idea could be improved. Yet funders did not allow too much devia-
tion from the initial proposal:

> If I would write the project proposal now, I would do a number of things entirely differ-
> ently. But the proposal has already been written and [the funder] only allows minimal de-
> viations, so you sort of have to do it the way you wrote it.
>   (coordinator with background in history – Q74)

While funders enabled digital history collaborations, they simultaneously confined what could be done in these collaborations, limiting the decisions that
could be made through coordination. Since collaborators anticipated the need
for future funding requests, they furthermore had to ensure the current collaboration was satisfactory to funders to sustain a good track record. Funders were
not part of the collaboration and were not actively part in the meeting between
historians and computational experts. However, from the outside they are important actors that affect the field of action of digital history collaborations for
both participating historians and computational experts.

    In the next section, I conclude this chapter to consider how the different
actors discussed in this chapter, both within and outside the collaborations, negotiate power relations.

Power Asymmetries of Digital History Trading Zones

In this chapter, I investigate how power relations affect the negotiation of practices in digital history trading zones. As introduced in the second chapter, I consider two dynamics of power relations. First, the extent to which participants in a
trading zone constrain or enable the actions of other participants. Second, the extent to which participants in a trading zone are able to define their own boundaries of action. Power relations in trading zones are thereby defined as the extent
to which some participants are less able to shape their own field of action, and
where one party is able to shape the field of action of the other party to a greater
extent than vice versa. By analysing how the different communities of practice
within these collaborations coordinated conflicting incentives, different practices
of shaping fields of action become visible.

Shaping One's Own Field of Action

For the first dynamic of power relations, the ability of participants to shape their own field of action, I observed that historians detached their objectives from the objectives of the collaboration instigators and the technologists. This is a significant activity that goes beyond a mere disagreement of incentives. Historians did not only prioritise their historical research over the tool development and technological research, which may be expected. I moreover find that historians conducted their research parallel to and independent of the outcomes of the tool and technology, as exemplified by quote Q41. Historians did not require the technology nor the tool under development to be able to conduct their research. Furthermore, when historians used the dataset worked on by the collaboration, they took a question-driven approach, cherry-picking data deemed of interest to their research, and acquiring additional data from other sources (e.g., see quotes Q23 and Q60). As such, historians shaped their field of action to fit their conceptions of what makes good historical research, in order to be able to finish their research. This historical research must conform to the disciplinary values of history, and should be conducted individually, especially in the case of a PhD.

Yet not only historians shaped their fields of action as such. Computational researchers also detached their computational research from the objectives of the collaboration instigators, and thereby indirectly from the historians. Computational researchers stressed their work was research, which may or may not result in a usable technology. Consequently, they argued that the tool development should not depend on the technology (quote Q19). Furthermore, they argued if tools should be readily usable, the collaboration could better implement stable technologies rather than technologies under investigation (quote Q44). As such, computational researchers shaped their fields of action to remain research according to their disciplinary values, rather than software development or maintenance (e.g., see quote Q56).

Both detachments can be seen as risk aversion strategies, since failure or delay of the technological research should not lead to a failure of the tool development. Failure or delay of the tool development should likewise not lead to a failure of the historical research (see quote Q12). It is for this reason that the professor in history, part of all three communities holding incentives, allowed this detachment to take place. Participants were thus fairly successful in shaping their own field of action according to their communities' incentives.

Shaping the Other's Field of Action

Participants of collaborations also tried to shape the fields of action of their collaborators and vice versa, the second dynamic of power relations. Historians in PhD and postdoc positions saw their fields of action shaped by their supervisors, the professors in history. Having applied to a research position, their supervisors recommended methodological approaches that fit the goals of the collaboration. Supervisors in the role of collaboration instigators recommended the PhDs candidates in history to use digital methods determined by the collaboration (quote Q4) and asked not to set up one's "own little data collection" (quote Q48). Yet as part of the detachment of historical research from the tool and technology, supervisors recommended that PhD candidates in history ultimately needed to produce a historical thesis (quote Q9) and the disciplinary value of working not just with digital data, but also with "paper archives" (quote Q63).

Even though historians detached their historical research from the tool development and computational research, they communicated their requirements in the hopes of steering development. Historians thereby tried to shape the fields of action of the collaboration instigators and the technologists. Furthermore, in response to the detachment of computational researchers from the tool development, collaborations hired software developers or contacted IT personnel for sustaining tools. By relying on a commercial or supporting party, collaboration instigators hoped that they could shape the software development without being confronted with opposing incentives, as seen in quote Q56. However, these attempts at shaping were ineffective. Instigators did not adequately anticipate the interpretation of feature requests (quote Q51), the time required for implementation (quote Q52), nor the costs of sustained performance (quote Q54). In all these cases, the historians received a tool that did not facilitate their research as envisioned.

As such, the envisioned power relation of historians influencing the work of software developers and computational researchers was overturned. Historians had insufficient insight in the fields of action they tried to shape. Historians lacked knowledge of the practices of software developers and computational researchers to effectively shape those practices. This lack of expertise in the practices of collaborators has been called knowledge asymmetry.[388] The division of tasks in a collaboration is related to the division of knowledge, but this introduces

---

388 Anurag Sharma, "Professional as Agent: Knowledge Asymmetry in Agency Exchange," *Academy of Management Review* 22, no. 3 (1997): 758–98, https://doi.org/10.5465/AMR.1997.9708210725.

the problem that one participant may not be able to evaluate the contributions of another participant. As a direct result of cross-disciplinary interactions, where participants have limited insight into other collaborators' disciplinary knowledge, I call this "interdisciplinary ignorance". Lacking knowledge of how computational experts performed their tasks, historians were unable to shape the field of action of computational experts, putting the latter in a more powerful position. Knowledge asymmetry consequently led to power asymmetry.

An additional problem for the historians was that this did not hold true in the other direction. Historians as end-users were dependent on software developers and computational researchers as system designers.[389] In cases where the software developers lacked understanding of historical practices, e.g., by misinterpreting feature requests (quote Q51), this meant that the results were not to the satisfaction of the historians. The existing dependency of historians on computational experts put historians in a less powerful position. Knowledge asymmetry reinforced this power relation, as historians could not adequately shape the fields of action of the computational experts. It could be argued that this is why collaboration instigators emphasised the development of know-how, so that in future collaborations knowledge asymmetry and resulting power asymmetry may be decreased significantly. I return to this matter in the next chapter.

Finally, in the attempted shaping of the fields of action of collaborators, it becomes visible how engagement configured power relations. In the previous chapter, I noted that humanities scholars tend to outnumber computational experts in collaborations suggesting a possible power relation. Yet in the current chapter, I find disciplinary diversity led to conflicts of incentives, such as between the historical and the computational research. However, a majority of historians as participants did not guarantee a power relation to the advantage of the historians. I find existing power mechanisms such as the dependence of historians on the computational experts and the power balance between professors supervising the research groups granted computational researchers the autonomy to detach research objectives when needed. Furthermore, knowledge asymmetry put computational experts in a more powerful position. Moreover, I noted in the previous chapter that collaborations tend to be conducted on a large physical distance. With increased physical distance, it was easier for participants to detach their objectives and more difficult to hold collaborators accountable. With irregular communication it was more difficult for collaborators to remain cognizant of the practices of collaborators, limiting the ability to shape the fields of action of collaborators. Distance thereby reinforced knowledge asymmetry. In

---

389 Markus and Bjorn-Andersen, "Power Over Users: Its Exercise By System Professionals."

short, with increasingly distant engagement, coordination became increasingly difficult, especially to the disadvantage of the historians.

External Shaping

Finally, not only did participants within a collaboration coordinate practices with one another; they saw their practices influenced by external parties. The most significant external party shaping the field of action of the collaboration was the funder. Funders published calls for grants to which the collaboration must fit their research ideas, pushing for collaboration and innovation (e.g., quotes Q1, Q68, Q73). Yet perhaps most significantly, by working with a grant, collaborations were tied to specific time frames.[390] Collaborations struggled to conduct historical research with a tool that needed to be built from scratch in the same time period, as exemplified by quote Q47. In the first two case studies, the collaboration lasted four years, just as the PhD positions. In these four years, the collaboration had to 1) enrich the dataset to be fed into the tool, 2) investigate the technology to be implemented in the tool, 3) develop the tool, and 4) the historians should use all these things to conduct their research. Yet this did not work in practice. In the conflicts described above, delays in data, in computational research and in tool development rendered the promise that historians would use it for fundamental research unattainable. Furthermore, since funders preferred to fund innovations rather than continued work, it was difficult to do a follow-up project in which historians would use the tool developed in the preceding project, as exemplified in quote Q73. This time frame arguably stimulated the detachments of historians and computational researchers, as they anticipated that delays could ultimately lead to failure, which should be prevented at all costs.

Another external party shaping the field of action of the collaboration was arguably the cultural heritage institute as data provider. Data providers both enabled as well as confined practices by providing data in a certain shape. The power relation here was unintended, yet still present. Collaborations were confronted with incomplete datasets, data in incompatible formats, datasets with many mistakes, or datasets that still needed to be digitised (e.g., quotes Q65 and Q66). These complexities shaped what a collaboration could achieve in the time frame and tools were changed significantly to accommodate the available data. Here too, knowledge asymmetry played a role in the sense that researchers lacked insight in the

---

390 See also Franssen et al., "The Drawbacks of Project Funding for Epistemic Innovation."

quality and form of data until they received it. Furthermore, funding played a role as cultural heritage institutes joined collaborations as "partners" rather than "collaborators". Consequently, the digitisation of sources or the rectifying of data were regularly tasks for which a budget was not available. Even when collaborations were aware of the need to digitise additional material, they were not adequately prepared for incomplete data. The expectation of the transformed dataset was less an ambition than a necessity, and significantly altered the design and planning of collaborations.

Trading Zones Resulting from Power Relations

The interactions between the communities of collaboration instigators, historians and technologists, as well as with funders and data providers, thereby exemplified a range of different types of trading zones. The detachment by historians and computational researchers arguably led to disconnected trading zones by moving towards individual pursuits rather than mutual engagement. Insofar as this strategy enabled researchers to shape their own practices, these trading zones could be characterised as disconnected-symmetric-heterogeneous (boundary object) trading zones. That is, collaborators no longer actively engaged with one another to exchange, trade or push practices across disciplinary boundaries. The collaboration itself thereby functioned as a boundary object, with participants subscribing to the general purpose of a collaboration, while individually shaping goals according to their incentives.

In contrast, knowledge asymmetry led to asymmetric-homogeneous (subversive) trading zones, both connected or disconnected. That is, with or without engagement, historians saw their practices pushed and shaped by what computational experts provided. In these cases, two strategies emerged. First, in the case of connected subversive trading zones, participants aimed to develop know-how in order to decrease knowledge asymmetry. The aim was to develop a connected-symmetric-heterogenous (interactional expertise) trading zone where the historical and computational communities could engage with one another through a broker who could coordinate in-between with adequate know-how of both sides. Second, in the case of disconnected subversive trading zones, collaboration instigators decided to work with software developers or IT personnel in a service role, rather than computational experts as equal partners. This led to a disconnected-asymmetric-heterogeneous (enforced) trading zone, without mutual sharing of practices and the ability to more simply demand certain services. Finally, being external to collaborations, funders and data providers shaped the practices of a collaboration without the ability for reverse shaping of funders and data providers.

However, the lack of continuous negotiation allowed collaborations to recontextualise demands or datasets. Collaborations reimagined how to interpret the boundaries set by funders and data providers, thereby arguably shaping their own practices. During the collaboration, the grant requirements and datasets thereby constituted boundary objects as part of disconnected-symmetric-heterogeneous (boundary object) trading zones.

Resistance

The philosopher Michel Foucault argued that power relations lead to resistance.[391] When a person sees their field of action being shaped by another party, they will respond. When this person sees the shaping as not in their own best interest, certain forms of resistance may occur. In the digital history collaborations that I have investigated, resistance was performed in the detachment of incentives. Historical research was detached and retracted to the community of historians, hardly bridging disciplinary boundaries anymore. Likewise, computational research was detached and retracted to the disciplinary communities of computational researchers. This detachment served as a risk aversion strategy, to sever dependencies that may lead to one's own research failing.

However, I also interpret this detachment as a strategy to protect disciplinary practices. For the historians, the important goal was to publish historical papers or a historical thesis, in order to advance their careers in the historical disciplinary culture. Likewise, for the computational researchers, the important goal was to publish papers that would help advance their careers in their computational disciplinary cultures. Detachment of incentives served to protect oneself from entering too far into another disciplinary culture, similar to the metaphor of the fly caught in the spider's web. Ultimately, the PhD candidate needed to write an individual and disciplinary thesis, not a collaborative interdisciplinary digital history thesis, as exemplified by quote Q9 and others.

In cases where the shaping by another was seen as advantageous to oneself, a scholar might instead choose to succumb. When the professor in history shaped the field of action of the PhD candidate in history, the response was not resistance. The response was instead enculturation, where the PhD candidate learned the practices of the historical discipline, their perceived own disciplinary community, through their supervisor.[392] A question may be whether some

---

391 Foucault, "The Subject and Power."
392 Brown, Collins and Duguid, "Situated Cognition and the Culture of Learning."

historians then choose to learn of other disciplinary practices, such as software development and computational research, in order to position themselves more strongly in digital history as a career opportunity (e.g., see quote Q69), or in order to decrease knowledge asymmetry. In the next and final chapter, I explore the dimension of changing practices and the extent to which historians indeed shift towards computational cultures.

Changing Practices

Practices of Historians

In considering historical scholarship, I have focused on what it is that historians do. I have thereby taken a social perspective of historical scholarship, analysing how historians construct their research through practices that render them recognisable and legitimate as historians. This stands in contrast with an epistemic perspective of historical scholarship consisting of what makes particular research questions historical questions or certain knowledge contributions to historiography. I thereby follow what has been called the "practice turn" in studies of scholarship and science.[393] While this so-called turn originated in studies of natural sciences and laboratory experiments, the conceptualisation of science as a set of mutually recognised practices rather than a highly specific type of knowledge renders this lens useful for studying historical scholarship as well.[394]

What practices then make a historian recognisable as practicing historical scholarship? In some cases, such practices may concern seemingly quaint details that strongly signify the presence of lack of historical practices, for example in the use of footnotes.[395] A full review of all such historical practices is beyond the scope of this book, but in the literature several fundamental practices become apparent.

Historical scholarship arguably fundamentally centralises practices surrounding the primary sources that are analysed. It is for this reason that the history of historical research is commonly traced back to Leopold van Ranke (1795–1886) who set ambitions for historical scholarship as the rigorous study of archival source material.[396] A first fundamental practice of historians then is archival research, as repeated by the professor in history in quote Q63 in the previous

---

[393] Andrew Pickering, ed., *Science as Practice and Culture* (The University of Chicago Press, 1991); Theodore R. Schatzki, Karin Knorr-Cetina and Eike von Savigny, eds., *The Practice Turn in Contemporary Theory* (New York: Routledge, 2001).

[394] Hans-Jörg Rheinberger, "Culture and Nature in the Prism of Knowledge," *History of Humanities* 1, no. 1 (2016): 155–81, https://doi.org/10.1086/685064.

[395] Anthony Grafton, *The Footnote: A Curious History* (Cambridge, Mass: Harvard University Press, 1999).

[396] Iggers, "The Professionalization of Historical Studies and the Guiding Assumptions of Modern Historical Thought"; Iggers, "The Crisis of the Rankean Paradigm in the Nineteenth Century."

chapter.[397] Wilhelm Dilthey (1833–1911) furthermore argued that a historian should interpret a document by placing it in its historical context and try to read it through a historical viewpoint, rather than seeing sources as direct reflections of the past. A second fundamental practice of historians then is hermeneutics. Finally, following the arguments of Von Ranke, Dilthey and Johann Gustav Droysen (1808–1884), a third fundamental practice is source criticism.[398] Source criticism consists of the analysis of sources through external criticism, verification of the authenticity of a source and internal criticism, interpretation of what was written and why.[399] The philosopher Hans-Georg Gadamer summarised the fundamental practice of hermeneutical interpretation of sources as follows:

> [I]n Dilthey's grounding of the human sciences hermeneutics is more than a means. It is the universal medium of the historical consciousness, for which there no longer exists any knowledge of truth other than the understanding of expression and, through expression, life. Everything in history is intelligible, for everything is text. "Life and history make sense like the letters of a word." Thus Dilthey ultimately conceives inquiring into the historical past as deciphering and not as historical experience.[400]

In studying the practices of digital history, a matter of concern becomes to what extent these practices of deciphering the past through sources are transformed or perhaps even replaced. With respect to archival research, historians such as Lara Putnam and Julia Laite show how the vastly improved accessibility and findability of source material alters the questions that can be asked and answered, since sources can easily be collected from multiple archives across the globe.[401] Historians such as Gerben Zaagsma and Helle Strandgaard Jensen as well as digital library experts such as Trevor Owens and Thomas Padilla argue that this change in archival research demands changing practices of source criticism, especially with regard to external source criticism in reflecting on the politics

---

397 Eskildsen, "Leopold Ranke's Archival Turn: Location and Evidence in Modern Historiography"; Kasper Risbjerg Eskildsen, "Inventing the Archive," *History of the Human Sciences* 26, no. 4 (2013): 8–26, https://doi.org/10.1177/0952695113496094.
398 Philipp Müller, "Understanding History: Hermeneutics and Source-Criticism in Historical Scholarship," in *Reading Primary Sources: The Interpretation of Texts from Nineteenth- and Twentieth-Century History*, ed. Miriam Dobson and Benjamin Ziemann (Routledge, 2009), 21–36; Fickers, "Update Für Die Hermeneutik."
399 John Tosh, *The Pursuit of History: Aims, Methods and New Directions in the Study of History*, 6th ed. (Routledge, 2015).
400 Gadamer, *Truth and Method*, 243, emphasis in original.
401 Putnam, "The Transnational and the Text-Searchable: Digitized Sources and the Shadows They Cast"; Laite, "The Emmet's Inch."

of digitisation, adding questions such as why a source was digitised.[402] Internal criticism moreover demands new practices as well, insofar as the ability to understand the importance of a document is hindered due to the loss of materiality, where size, smell, fingerprints or other damages might indicate the importance or use of a document.[403] In addition, the historian Mats Fridlund writes of digital resource criticism as the critical reflection on the tools and software used to consult digital sources.[404] Finally, the historian Andreas Fickers argues that such changes in (digital) source criticism demand a new digital hermeneutics to reflect on how a source can be interpreted when it is consulted via a user interface or is aggregated and analysed as data.[405]

As I argued in Chapter 2, such descriptions of changing practices arguably present digital history as disconnected-asymmetric-homogeneous (subversive) trading zones. That is, historians are presented as passive users of technology, engaging with tools and systems designed by others without the means or control to change those technologies. It is the technologies that are presented as shaping historical practices, insofar as digital objects, OCR or user interfaces enable and confine how historians can conduct their scholarship. In this book, however, I look at the digital history that is produced when historians engage with computational experts during the development of technologies. In this final chapter, I consider the extent to which practices of historians engaged in cross-disciplinary collaborations change. This chapter thereby explores the third and final dimension of trading zones, namely that of changing practices.

---

402 Helle Strandgaard Jensen, "Digital Archival Literacy for (All) Historians," *Media History* (2020), 1–15, https://doi.org/10.1080/13688804.2020.1779047; Zaagsma, "On Digital History"; Trevor Owens and Thomas Padilla, "Digital Sources and Digital Archives: Historical Evidence in the Digital Age," *International Journal of Digital Humanities* (2020), https://doi.org/10.1007/s42803-020-00028-7; see also Thylstrup, *The Politics of Mass Digitization*.

403 See also the exploration by the digital humanist Alan Liu on how digital media affects our sense of history: *Friending the Past: The Sense of History in the Digital Age* (Chicago ; London: The University of Chicago Press, 2018).

404 Mats Fridlund, "Digital History 1.5: A Middle Way between Normal and Paradigmatic Digital Historical Research," in *Digital Histories: Emergent Approaches within the New Digital History*, ed. Mats Fridlund, Mila Oiva and Petri Paju (Helsinki University Press, 2020), 69–87, https://doi.org/10.33134/HUP-5-4.

405 Fickers, "Update Für Die Hermeneutik."

Changing and Exchanging Practices in Trading Zones

The studies described in the previous two chapters provide insight into the changing practices of historians in digital history collaborations. In Chapter 3, I described how the University of Luxembourg institutionalised digital history through the establishment of the Centre for Contemporary and Digital History (C²DH) and the Digital History Lab. I found that some historians indeed exemplified changing practices where they adopted computational technologies for their scholarship. For example, a few scholars, mainly in PhD positions, tried digital experiments of distant reading in the Digital History Lab, digitising collections and using the available computers for their experiments. Two PhD candidates explored 3D scanning, using the available 3D scanners for objects outside of the lab. Yet the Digital History Lab required efforts in communication and hiring procedures to attract historians to engage with the facilities.

Likewise, as part of the C²DH, several historians adopted digital methods or conducted digital experiments such as publishing digital collections on websites or distant reading documents or born-digital sources (notably using LDA topic modelling).[406] A Digital Research Infrastructure (DRI) unit was established to support such digital projects. Yet a significant decision by the DRI unit was to provide tools tailored to each project, rather than a standardised infrastructure on which historical projects could or should be implemented. Historians were moreover not pushed to adopt digital methods.

In Chapter 4, I described several case studies of digital history collaborations in which historians collaborated with cross-disciplinary partners from computational disciplines. Within these collaborations, incentives emerged that were indeed new for historians, notably incentives around tool development, tool usage and the production of a transformed dataset. Research included tasks and practices not towards the production of a monograph or article, but towards the development of digital tools and datasets for adoption in the historical community.

---

406 For more elaborate discussions of the potential of LDA topic modelling for historical research, see René Brauer and Mats Fridlund, "Historicizing Topic Models. A Distant Reading of Topic Modeling Texts within Historical Studies," in *Cultural Research in the Context of "Digital Humanities": Proceedings of International Conference 3–5 October 2013, St Petersburg*, ed. L.V. Nikiforova and N.V. Nikiforova (2013), 152–63; Jo Guldi, "Critical Search: A Procedure for Guided Reading in Large-Scale Textual Corpora," *Journal of Cultural Analytics* (2018), https://doi.org/10.22148/16.030; Simon Hengchen, "When Does It Mean: Detecting Semantic Change in Historical Texts" (PhD thesis, Universitè Libre de Bruxelles, 2017); Glenn Roe, Clovis Gladstone and Robert Morrissey, "Discourses and Disciplines in the Enlightenment: Topic Modeling the French Encyclopédie," *Frontiers in Digital Humanities* 2 (2016), https://doi.org/10.3389/fdigh.2015.00008.

The use of tools was an incentive to demonstrate the utility of the developed tools, as well as the promise of digital history. Yet not all historians in the collaborations subscribed to these incentives. Rather, these incentives were largely limited to the coordinator and the professor in history as PI of the collaboration. Other historians instead exemplified detachment, detaching their historical research from the collaboration to ensure that their work could continue and remain recognisable as contributing to historical scholarship.

I furthermore found several changes in practices that were, however, arguably not the result of engagement with computational experts. The boundaries between the C^2DH and the Institute for History were significantly influenced by political and institutional interventions, rather than practices of digital history. While the historians in the centre did change their practices and formed a group identity, this was not necessarily in the direction of computational practices.

Similarly, the collaborations in Chapter 4 were shaped by external parties in ways not necessarily in the direction of computational practices. Funders shaped the practices of collaboration instigators by setting boundaries of what should be delivered in order to remain eligible for future funding. Perhaps even more significantly, funders set deadlines for when collaboration results needed to be delivered, imposing limitations on the time historians could spend on acquiring additional sources or the further development of digital tools. Cultural heritage institutes, in the role of external data providers, shaped collaborations through limitations of what could be done with data and the time required to transform data to suitable forms for the technologies under development.

Such examples of changing practices could be interpreted as constituting disconnected-asymmetric-homogeneous (subversive) trading zones, in the sense that historians did not continuously engage with funders or data providers to negotiate what needed to be done. Yet this lack of continuous engagement enabled collaborations to recontextualise and reimagine demands or datasets, thereby remaining in control to shape their own practices. I argue that the professors in history as PIs of the collaborations therefore pushed the trading zones towards disconnected-symmetric-heterogeneous (boundary object) trading zones, in the sense that requirements and datasets could mean different things to different communities of people. Rather than align all collaborators around a singular understanding, the project and dataset were used as boundary objects to enable engagement were needed.

In Chapter 4 I furthermore identified connected-asymmetric-homogeneous (subversive) trading zones, where historians engaged and negotiated with computational experts yet remained unable to ensure the tools and systems met historical requirements. Historians were dependent on computational experts for the development of technologies that would facilitate historical research. Yet they lacked knowledge of how computational experts conducted their work and were consequently unable to shape the practices of computational experts. In these cases, professors in history as PIs emphasised the need to develop know-how to ensure better control in future collaborations. I argue that they thereby aimed to steer these trading zones towards connected-symmetric-heterogeneous (interactional expertise) trading zones where historians would possess the knowledge to ensure they could protect their historical practices in mutual negotiation with computational experts.

In short, professors in history actively pushed toward trading zones of interactional expertise and boundary objects, as represented in Figure 7. The resulting trading zones correspond to the characterisation of digital humanities by Patrik Svensson as a heterogeneous space of collaborative (symmetric) negotiation.[407] Yet my findings expand Svensson's characterisation in two notable ways.

First, that digital history largely consists of symmetric-heterogeneous trading zones is not by nature. What the professors in history across the different

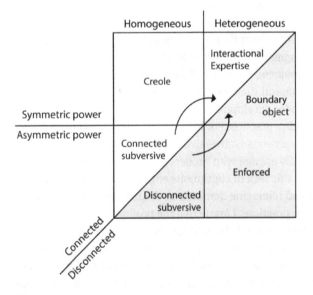

Figure 7: Pushing asymmetric-homogeneous (subversive) trading zones into symmetric-heterogeneous (fractioned) trading zones. Note that in this process trading zones are not necessarily pushed from connected to disconnected or vice versa.

---

407 Svensson, "The Digital Humanities as a Humanities Project."

digital history trading zones shared was their mutual objective to actively push collaborations towards symmetric-heterogeneous trading zones. Their goal was to enable collaboration between historians and computational experts without demanding historians become homogeneous with computational experts. Instead, they ensured that their historical collaborators would remain in control of their own research. They allowed their historical collaborators to detach the historical work from the goals of the collaborations when and where necessary. Digital history collaborations did not organically grow into symmetric-heterogeneous trading zones but were the product of deliberate design and continuous negotiation.

Second, Svensson arguably characterises digital humanities more specifically as disconnected-symmetric-heterogeneous trading zones when he identifies "the digital" as the boundary object around which these trading zones emerge. Yet my findings demonstrate that perhaps even more important are the connected-symmetric-heterogeneous trading zones of interactional expertise. It is this development of interactional expertise, or "know-how" as my interviewees called it, that enabled and sustained the digital history trading zones.

Interactional Expertise and Brokerage

Throughout this book I describe multiple examples of scholars engaging in cross-boundary practices, developing know-how and adopting practices not originating from historical scholarship. In Chapter 3, I describe the professor of digital history and director of the centre, who initiated and managed cross-disciplinary collaborations as well as political negotiations. In Chapter 4, I discuss the role of professors in history connecting the incentives in collaborations between collaboration instigators, historians and technologists, and enabling collaborations by receiving grants from funders. Bridging practices and incentives between distinct communities, these professors acted as what Étienne Wenger calls "brokers". Brokers are actors that are able to introduce aspects of one community of practice into another, connecting the two communities and enabling coordination. Brokers do so by "processes of translation, coordination, and alignment between perspectives", acts that are exemplified by the professors in history that I describe in the previous chapters.[408]

---

408 Wenger, *Communities of Practice*, 109.

To better understand what brokerage entails, the sociologists Katherine Stovel and Lynette Shaw in their review of this practice describe two dimensions.[409] First, bias refers to the extent to which a broker is closer to one community than the other. For example, a broker might know more individuals from one community than the other or have better knowledge of their individual research projects. A broker might have a background in history and thereby have more affinity with other historians, even when not conducting historical research within a collaboration themselves. Leaders of digital history collaborations tended to come from history. The bias of brokers was thus towards history. Yet this bias did not necessarily mean that brokers prioritised historical incentives and practices over computational ones.

The second dimension is cohesion, referring to the extent to which one or both sides are cohesive groups or loose individuals. Cohesion is linked to group identity, where a cohesive community could be more likely to reject a broker as not part of their group. Some historians described in the previous preferred to collaborate with individual software developers rather than computer scientists, as this made it easier to set the agenda of development. Computer scientists formed a cohesive group sharing incentives and practices, and as such they could secure and protect their practices during negotiations. Software developers instead were hired on an individual basis and were much more dependent on the requirements posed by the collaboration instigators. In Chapter 3, it was institutionalisation that shaped cohesion. While historians and computational researchers together formed a group in the Luxembourg Centre for Contemporary and Digital History (C^{2}DH), historians from the Institute for History formed another group. Brokerage between historians and computational researchers within the centre or brokerage between historians of the two units proved fairly fruitful, since in both cases there was a shared group identity, respectively institutional and disciplinary. Brokerage between the historians of the institute and computational researchers of the centre was, however, much more difficult.

Furthermore, Stovel and Shaw describe an incentive for brokerage in the ability to gain profits or power by being central to interactions between separate communities. The interacting communities are dependent on the broker, so that the broker can exploit their central position. The broker moreover has an information advantage with respect to the separate communities, being able to act on or emphasise the information that is to their advantage. It could be argued that the brokers in my investigations had an advantage for funding applications, being

---

409 Katherine Stovel and Lynette Shaw, "Brokerage," *Annual Review of Sociology* 38, no. 1 (2012): 139–58, https://doi.org/10.1146/annurev-soc-081309-150054.

able to draw upon a network of collaborators and synthesise perspectives. However, within a collaboration, I found brokers were mainly dependent on their collaborators to fulfil their tasks (e.g., quote Q40 in the previous chapter). This indicates that brokers did not gain a power advantage as a result of their brokering within the collaboration.

The exploitation of brokerage is related to the role the broker takes in the connection. Stovel and Shaw distinguish between brokers as intermediaries or as catalysts. As intermediary, all information between the historians and computational experts has to pass through the broker, providing a power advantage. This is the model that is invoked with Jennifer Edmond's concept of "digital humanities intermediary", who should be someone "at an early point in the value chain who has a broad knowledge of computing and research and a *mandate* to disseminate this information".[410] In contrast, as catalyst, the broker only makes the connection by introducing the historians and computational experts, after which the broker is no longer required or mainly serves to solve problems of interactions. This is the model argued by the software developer Tracey Berg-Fulton and her collaborators, who write that the catalyst in digital art history collaborations "serves as the collaborative glue, creating the critical, translational linkages needed between all of these skill-sets, ensuring that communication and progress are systematically made".[411] Here too, the catalyst requires some power mechanism to make final decisions when historians and computational experts disagree and to keep the collaboration aligned towards a common goal. The need for a power advantage explains why the professors in history were more likely to serve as broker rather than the envisioned collaboration coordinators who were regularly in junior or non-research positions. This suggests that a power advantage is a precondition for rather than a result of cross-disciplinary brokerage. Since brokers may opt to act as intermediary or catalyst depending on local contexts, I employ the broader term digital history broker.

A difficulty of brokerage is that brokers need to preserve the balance of not becoming full members of any one community nor be rejected.[412] Despite their bias towards history, brokers would not always align with the historians in a collaboration, sometimes prioritising technological over historical goals. Instead, brokers

---

410 Edmond, "The Role of the Professional Intermediary in Expanding the Humanities Computing Base," 373, emphasis mine.
411 Tracey Berg-Fulton et al., "A Role-Based Model for Successful Collaboration in Digital Art History," *International Journal for Digital Art History*, no. 3 (2018): 159, https://doi.org/10.11588/dah.2018.3.34297.
412 Wenger, *Communities of Practice*, 110.

embodied the vision of digital history as "dual citizenship" or "in-betweenness".[413] From this position, brokers recognise the "existence of a problem space shared by a technological and a historical question".[414] In other words, digital history brokers are able to recognise both the historical and the technological research problems to draw connections and possible synergies between them.[415]

Besides social connections to collaborators from both history and computational domains, digital history brokers need to have an understanding of the practices and discourses of both sides. In the trading zones model, these brokers are called interactional experts: "in order to broker trades, interactional experts will have to understand not only the content of another domain but also its perspective – the way it frames the problem".[416] Digital history brokers are, therefore, those who can recognise a common research problem by considering it from both the historical and the computational perspectives. The ability to act as broker consequently depends on a scholar possessing interactional expertise.

Harry Collins and Robert Evans, who coined the term, distinguish three levels of expertise: no expertise, interactional expertise and contributory expertise.[417] Contributory expertise is what one holds in their own discipline, enabling them to contribute to research, publish and apply for jobs. When PhD candidates in history learned from professors in history how to do research, they learned how to write a historical thesis that contributes to the historiography and learned how to act as historians. Interactional expertise is instead defined as being able to interact interestingly with contributory experts. As such, interactional expertise is proposed to be the ability to participate in the language of one community, but not

---

413 Svensson, "The Digital Humanities as a Humanities Project"; Patrik Svensson, "Envisioning the Digital Humanities," *Digital Humanities Quarterly* 6, no. 1 (2012).

414 Berg-Fulton et al., "A Role-Based Model for Successful Collaboration in Digital Art History," 159.

415 An interesting avenue for future research that I did not investigate is whether digital history brokers are able to solve the paradox of digital history. This paradox is a classic problem of the chicken or the egg, asking what comes first; digital history research questions using future methods or digital history methods facilitating future questions? Historians need to come up with the research questions that benefit from computational approaches, while computational experts need to develop the computational approaches to facilitate those research questions; see Boonstra, Breure and Doorn, "Past, Present and Future of Historical Information Science."

416 Michael Gorman and Jim Spohrer, "Service Science: A New Expertise for Managing Sociotechnical Systems," in *Trading Zones and Interactional Expertise: Creating New Kinds of Collaboration*, ed. Michael Gorman (MIT Press, 2010), 84.

417 Harry Collins and Robert Evans, "The Third Wave of Science Studies: Studies of Expertise and Experience," *Social Studies of Science* 32, no. 2 (2002): 235–96, https://doi.org/10.1177/0306312702032002003.

their practices. For example, a professor in history might be able to discuss with a computational expert the nature of an algorithm, without the ability to write code themselves. Interactional experts to that end develop an inter-language, a language between languages.

In the previous chapter I described that brokers were actively learning in digital history collaborations, developing know-how. Through the interactions between historians and technologists, brokers learned how to understand the technology, the data and how to conduct project management. This development of know-how was even seen as a key outcome of digital history collaborations. In cases where knowledge asymmetry led to power asymmetry, the development of interactional expertise was emphasised to improve brokerage in future collaborations, in order to restore symmetric power relations.

The importance of the concept of interactional expertise becomes clear when Harry Collins and his collaborators write that:

> Could it be that the growth of [creole trading zones] is the unusual case? It may be that, when examined closely, what appear to be integrated networks of scientists are really conglomerations of small groups bound together by rich interactional expertises. [. . .] The interactional expertise trading zone seems so widespread that it might be argued that this, rather than the [creole trading zone] model, it is the norm for new interdisciplinary work.[418]

When analysing interdisciplinary work such as digital history, we might therefore expect to find networks of interactional experts, rather than a homogeneous community of practice. Pidgins or jargons as inter-languages employed by interactional experts may thus prove to be the norm for interdisciplinary collaborations, rather than creole as trading zone. The inter-language of interactional expertise is developed through social interactions and enculturation within another community, thereby coming to understand both explicit linguistic and tacit knowledge of a discipline. A broker consequently possesses the discursive proficiency to translate between the two communities.[419] It is, therefore, argued that interdisciplinary collaborations require an interactional expert to enable translation and coordination.[420]

An important difference, however, is in the individual nature of interactional expertise. Every broker might develop their own inter-language as required during the collaboration to ensure interactions between the historians, technologists

---

418 Collins, Evans and Gorman, "Trading Zones and Interactional Expertise," 661–62.
419 Robert Evans and Harry Collins, "Interactional Expertise and the Imitation Game," in *Trading Zones and Interactional Expertise: Creating New Kinds of Collaboration*, ed. Michael Gorman (MIT Press, 2010), 53–70.
420 Collins and Evans, "The Third Wave of Science Studies."

and collaboration instigators remain fruitful and interesting. There is thus not necessarily a collective inter-language of digital history, since brokers come from different backgrounds and encounter different problems. Furthermore, with a collective inter-language there would no longer be a necessity to translate back into one's discipline, since the inter-language acts as a new discipline by itself.[421] If digital history or digital humanities (DH) more broadly would indeed constitute a discipline in itself, members of this discipline would no longer need to translate back into other disciplines such as English or history. Instead, members of the DH discipline could develop contributory expertise to publish in DH journals, contribute to DH debates and apply for DH jobs.

I find participants instead emphasised the need to maintain ties to their disciplinary cultures of origin and communicated more often with disciplinary peers than with cross-disciplinary collaborators. The role of a digital history broker was thereby context dependent. While in one situation a broker might stand in-between two communities of practice, emphasising matters not related to traditionally historical interests, in another situation the broker might instead act like a traditional historian. While historians as part of collaborations might indeed contribute to DH journals and conferences, they still emphasised the need to make contributions to the historical discipline (e.g., quote Q9 from the previous chapter).

The historians in digital history collaborations were not supposed to unlearn practices from history. A lack of contribution to the historiography was deemed a research failure. Historians were, however, incentivised to engage with computational experts and learn how computational approaches might aid historical research. I argue that brokers thereby actively prevented the formation of connected-symmetric-homogeneous (creole) trading zones, where there is no longer a difference in contributory expertise between what once were historians and computational experts. At the very least, brokers did not push towards such trading zones. Instead, brokers emphasised the need for digital history to provide benefit to historical scholarship.

Infrastructuring

Throughout this book, I encountered digital history collaborations involved in the development of infrastructures promising to support and innovate historical scholarship. As I argued in the introductory chapter, the design of digital infrastructures

---

421 Galison, *Image and Logic*.

directly influences what questions can be asked, what analyses can be conducted and what historical knowledge can be generated. Digital research infrastructures therefore demand deep engagement between historians and computational experts to ensure they can adequately facilitate historical research.

In Chapter 3 I analysed interviews with two experts in infrastructural roles at the C^2DH, supporting historians by providing digital as well as physical infrastructures. For both experts, their role was negotiated with historians to contextualise the digital and physical infrastructures in historical practices. In Chapter 4, I analysed interviews with historians collaborating towards the development of systems and technologies without users but envisioned to be applicable beyond the scope of the project (e.g., quotes Q15 and Q16). In all cases, efforts towards infrastructures were met with some form of resistance: boundary construction between the centre and the institute, historians not appropriating infrastructures or transforming these into something else than envisioned, and detachment by historians and computational experts in order to preserve their individual objectives within collaborations.

The development of infrastructures thus concerned as much technological feasibility as social readiness for appropriation and embedding in practices. In the introductory chapter, I described this as the two-sided uncertainty of digital history: historians are uncertain how they as historians should use digital methods and computational experts are uncertain how digital methods should work with historical datasets. In order to capture practices related to both sides of this uncertainty, the term "infrastructuring" has been used by scholars building on the works of Susan Leigh Star and her collaborators. They argue that infrastructures are defined not by their technological aspects but by their appropriation in communities of practice.[422] Infrastructuring has been defined as follows:

> [I]nfrastructuring can be seen as an ongoing process and should not be seen as being delimited to a design project phase in the development of a freestanding system. Infrastructuring entangles and intertwines potentially controversial "a priori infrastructure activities" (like selection, design, development, deployment, and enactment), with "everyday design activities in actual use" (like mediation, interpretation and articulation), as well as "design in use" (like adaptation, appropriation, tailoring, re-design and maintenance).[423]

---

422 Susan Leigh Star and Geoffrey C. Bowker, "How to Infrastructure," in *Handbook of New Media: Social Shaping and Social Consequences of ICTs*, ed. Leah A. Lievrouw and Sonia Livingstone (SAGE Publications, 2006), 230–46; Star and Ruhleder, "Steps Toward an Ecology of Infrastructure."
423 Erling Björgvinsson, Pelle Ehn and Per-Anders Hillgren, "Participatory Design and 'Democratizing Innovation,'" in *Proceedings of the 11th Biennial Participatory Design Conference*

Infrastructuring thereby concerns both the activities before an infrastructure is implemented, as well as the ongoing work during appropriation and renegotiation of practices. As such, the boundaries between infrastructure designers and users are crossed to negotiate and contextualise technologies in work practices.[424] The act of designing is, therefore, no longer limited to the practices of infrastructure developers, but is performed through interactions between historians as users, computational experts and technology.[425] Infrastructures are thereby no longer conceptualised as static entities that intervene in the practices of scholars, the frame commonly used in references to cyberinfrastructures.[426] Instead, infrastructures are ever-changing socio-technical systems, forever under development and maintenance.[427] This seems especially true for digital infrastructures, which are much more malleable than physical infrastructures, following the "permanent extendibility" of software.[428]

When infrastructures are truly successful, they become invisible to the people who use them.[429] For example, much of the work of archivists and librarians or the organisational structures of archives and libraries overall remains invisible to historians.[430] Historians do not need to relearn how to use an archive or library every time they enter one, but learn the conventions of how to use these infrastructures as part of their disciplinary community of practice.[431] In contrast,

---

on – PDC '10 (New York, New York, USA: ACM Press, 2010), 43, https://doi.org/10.1145/1900441.1900448.

424 Lucy Suchman, "Located Accountabilities in Technology Production," *Scandinavian Journal of Information Systems* 14, no. 2 (2002): 91–105.

425 Helena Karasti, Volkmar Pipek and Geoffrey C. Bowker, "An Afterword to 'Infrastructuring and Collaborative Design,'" *Computer Supported Cooperative Work* 27, no. 2 (2018): 267–89, https://doi.org/10.1007/s10606-017-9305-x.

426 Daniel E. Atkins et al., "Revolutionizing Science and Engineering Through Cyberinfrastructure: Report of the National Science Foundation Blue-Ribbon Advisory Panel on Cyberinfrastructure" (National Science Foundation, 2003); Paul N. Courant et al., "Our Cultural Commonwealth: The Report of the American Council of Learned Societies Commision on Cyberinfrastructure for the Humanities and Social Sciences" (American Council of Learned Societies, 2006).

427 Karasti and Blomberg, "Studying Infrastructuring Ethnographically."

428 Volkmar Pipek and Volker Wulf, "Infrastructuring: Toward an Integrated Perspective on the Design and Use of Information Technology," *Journal of the Association for Information Systems* 10, no. 5 (2009): 447–73, https://doi.org/10.17705/1jais.00195; Manovich, *Software Takes Command*, 337.

429 Star and Ruhleder, "Steps Toward an Ecology of Infrastructure."

430 Sammie L. Morris and Shirley K. Rose, "Invisible Hands: Recognizing Archivists' Work to Make Records Accessible," in *Working in the Archives: Practical Research Methods for Rhetoric and Composition*, ed. Alexis E. Ramsay et al. (Southern Illinois University Press, 2010), 51–78.

431 Arlette Farge, *The Allure of the Archives*, trans. Thomas Scott-Railton and Natalie Zemon Davis (1989; repr., Yale University Press, 2013).

I do not assume that these digital infrastructures are already in place, invisibly supporting the practices of historians, appropriated as a disciplinary practice. Infrastructures can take decades to form.[432] The work in this book should thus not be seen as an ethnography of infrastructure.[433] Instead, by employing this concept, I wish to bring to light the work done on infrastructures in the making, before appropriation by users, as well as during contextualisation of experimental systems.[434] That is, before digital infrastructures finally become invisible to historians.

Infrastructuring aims to resolve the infrastructural tensions that emerge when historians experiment with interventions in historical practice by means of digital technologies.[435] Such tensions arise because infrastructures have distributional consequences; they improve or emphasise certain practices, aspects or even people, while obscuring or demoting others. In this book, I have described several controversies that can be understood as infrastructural tensions. With respect to the distributional consequences of infrastructures, the historians Petri Paju, Mila Oiva and Mats Fridlund warn that digital history may lead to uneven competition between history departments, resulting in "more divisions among historians".[436] Indeed, Chapter 3 showed how investments in a new research unit related to digital history affects the sustainability of existing research institutes. Professors moving from the institute to the centre were not replaced, leaving the institute in a weaker position than before. When a new professorship was in discussion, the two research units found themselves in competition for resources to attract people in senior positions.

One way in which digital history brokers have acquired investments is by aligning with political agendas related to economic growth. The centre was in part guided by alignment with Digital Luxembourg, the government's initiative to coordinate the nation's digital strategy. Such alignment can also be found in the European Commission report on the digital strategy for cultural heritage, which included how digitisation provides both cultural and economic benefits

---

432 Karasti, Pipek and Bowker, "An Afterword to 'Infrastructuring and Collaborative Design.'"
433 C.f. Susan Leigh Star, "The Ethnography of Infrastructure," *American Behavioral Scientist* 43, no. 3 (1999): 377–91, https://doi.org/10.1177/00027649921955326.
434 Laura J. Neumann and Susan Leigh Star, "Making Infrastructure : The Dream of a Common Language," in *Proceedings of the Participatory Design Conference* (Cambridge, USA, 1996), 231–40; Suchman, "Located Accountabilities in Technology Production."
435 Steven J. Jackson et al., "Understanding Infrastructure: History, Heuristics and Cyberinfrastructure Policy," *First Monday* (2007), https://doi.org/10.5210/fm.v12i6.1904.
436 Petri Paju, Mila Oiva and Mats Fridlund, "Digital and Distant Histories: Emergent Approaches within the New Digital History," in *Digital Histories: Emergent Approaches within the New Digital History*, ed. Mats Fridlund, Mila Oiva and Petri Paju (Helsinki University Press, 2020), 15, https://doi.org/10.33134/HUP-5-1.

as key themes.[437] The then European Commissioner for Digital Agenda, Neelie Kroes, received this report saying "[b]ringing our museums' and libraries' collections online not only shows Europe's rich history and culture but can also usher in new benefits for education, for innovation and for generating new economic activities".[438] Likewise, the European Time Machine project proposal for the European FET Flagship grant up to one billion euro described the economic opportunity of cultural heritage as "rather than being a cost, cultural heritage investment will actually be an important economic driver across industries".[439] A recent DARIAH position paper on cultural heritage data instead aligned their arguments for digital cultural heritage with political incentives such as increased investments in Artificial Intelligence and the demand for digital literacy.[440]

Such alignments, however, may lead to resistance from peers who see such acts as neoliberal, rendering digital history an economic rather than scholarly enterprise. Brokers thus have to balance their arguments towards policymakers, in order to attract funds, as well as towards their peers, to remain recognisable as historical scholarship. Furthermore, brokers have to defend how redistribution of funding from traditional historical scholarship to digital history benefits the historical community.

Another distributional consequence is that emerging infrastructures render some research practices easier, while other practices become harder or even impossible. Following from the previous tension, Chapter 3 showed that a strong research centre related to contemporary history led to concerns that students would more often choose a contemporary historical topic for their theses. In Chapter 4, a fundamental concern around digital infrastructures was how some sources become very accessible and easily findable, while other disappear from view. Historians raised concerns that uneven quality of OCR between sources might bias historians to analyse those sources, while others are never found. Historians should at least be aware of such biases to critically reflect on their own research practice. This problem becomes especially urgent when using

---

437 Elisabeth Niggemann, Jacques De Decker and Maurice Levy, "The New Renaissance: Report of the 'Comité Des Sages'" (Luxembourg: European Commission, 2011).

438 "Digital Agenda: "Comité des Sages" calls for a "New Renaissance" by bringing Europe's cultural heritage online", European Commission Press Release, January 10, 2011, https://ec.europa.eu/commission/presscorner/detail/en/IP_11_17.

439 "Unleashing Big Data of the Past – Europe Builds a Time Machine", Time Machine, March 1, 2019, https://www.timemachine.eu/unleashing-big-data-of-the-past-europe-builds-a-time-machine/.

440 Toma Tasovac, Sally Chambers and Erzsébet Tóth-Czifra, "Cultural Heritage Data from a Humanities Research Perspective: A DARIAH Position Paper" (2020).

infrastructures developed by enterprises, such as the Google Books corpus and the Google Ngram Viewer described in Chapter 1.

The above distributional consequence is at least in part caused by another infrastructural tension of digital history, namely that the promise of digital history is largely confined by the limitations of the available data. The uneven quality of OCR is not simply a technological limitation, solved by improving a set of algorithms. Very often, the quality of the source material itself, whether it was printed on expensive high-quality paper or on cheap low-quality paper, confines the possibilities of OCR. At the same time, important and well-preserved sources may not be fit for methods of mass-digitisation, thereby staying behind in prioritisation of large-scale datasets.[441] The analytical power of digital history is thereby limited by a set of dependencies that run down to the actual physical material of sources. Furthermore, while more recent sources may in principle be more easily available technologically, copyright and privacy laws limit what periods can be sufficiently facilitated using digital infrastructures. For example, while web archives as born-digital data are not limited by issues of OCR, websites contain copyrighted or privacy-sensitive material that render many sources inaccessible for historical analysis.[442] For brokers it therefore remains important to recognise how digital research infrastructures may complement physical research infrastructures, rather than replace them.

Another tension to the potential of digital history is the limited sustainability of systems as they require continuous funding and attention.[443] While this issue is beyond the scope of this book, it was noted in quote Q73 by the history coordinator who found it difficult to attract funding for continuous development and maintenance, rather than innovations. This problem is however not specific to digital history, insofar as digital research infrastructures from other disciplines have likewise been confronted with limitations to sustainability.[444] Yet digital history brokers may provide synergies between their knowledge of digital

441 Prescott and Hughes, "Why Do We Digitize?"

442 Milligan, *History in the Age of Abundance?*

443 For a more elaborate discussion of sustainability see Christine Barats, Valérie Schafer and Andreas Fickers, "Fading Away . . . The Challenge of Sustainability in Digital Studies," *Digital Humanities Quarterly* 14, no. 3 (2020); James Smithies et al., "Managing 100 Digital Humanities Projects: Digital Scholarship and Archiving in King's Digital Lab," *Digital Humanities Quarterly* 13, no. 1 (2019).

444 European Commission. Directorate General for Research and Innovation, *Sustainable European Research Infrastructures: A Call for Action* (LU: Publications Office, 2017), https://data.europa.eu/doi/10.2777/76269; Giorgio Rossi et al., "Supporting the Transformative Impact of Research Infrastructures on European Research" (European Commission, 2020).

research infrastructure and of historical research infrastructures such as archives and libraries which have proven sustainable for the last centuries.

Finally, a tension that may arise during infrastructuring is when people are confronted with double binds. A double bind occurs when people are given two conflicting messages simultaneously.[445] This is perhaps most apparent in my discussion of PhD candidates, who despite being part of a cross-disciplinary collaboration were evaluated on individual disciplinary works. Another double bind is arguably found in project funding for digital history, where projects should develop innovative technologies as well as conduct historical research, without space to take one step after another.

This final tension of double binds may be most fundamental to infrastructuring, since it concerns the question of how to evaluate cross-disciplinary collaborative works according to disciplinary values of what constitutes valid research, particularly in a discipline that has traditionally emphasised solitary scholarship. Susan Leigh Star and Karen Ruhleder provide two recommendations for addressing double binds.[446] First, the development of a shared understanding of both communities building and appropriating infrastructures. I suggest that this is what digital history brokers do when they develop interactional expertise in the context of digital history. Second, the development of institutional mechanisms for education and legitimisation of appropriate skills. Multiple professors actively sought to include digital methods in the university curriculum:

> If you consider this department, we are investing in a lecturer of digital humanities to be part of faculty staff. In the first year we will introduce digital humanities in the bachelor. We already have a minor of digital humanities in our faculty, which is very successful. The research master is next, we will introduce aspects of digital humanities there as well. All of that is new, those are developments of the last year or two. And that won't disappear soon. That means that you are educating a new generation of students who already have that link [with digital methods] by nature. (professor in history, Q75)

Yet substantially including digital methods in the curriculum proved difficult. The above statement was made in an interview in 2015. When I interviewed this professor again in 2020, he disappointedly admitted that they had not been able to embed digital history in the curriculum. A problem was that introducing a new subject would mean removing other subjects, which was met with resistance since other lecturers did not want to cancel their own courses. Another problem was that many lecturers simply did not want to learn digital methods themselves in order to be able to teach digital methods in their courses. This

---

445 Star and Ruhleder, "Steps Toward an Ecology of Infrastructure."
446 Star and Ruhleder.

was the critique by another professor in history when trying to embed digital history in the curriculum:

> We should invest much more in the level of faculty, in training the trainers. We need this generation of people who can use digital tools, or at least are not afraid of learning to play with them. We need people who do not say that this is no longer for their generation, but a matter for future generations. We have colleagues who will be here for another ten, twenty years who already have that mentality. I find it hard to accept that.
>
> (professor in history, Q76)

Beyond education, legitimisation was developed by creating institutional mechanisms to recognise and evaluate contributions of digital history. Yet in contrast with the local negotiation in trading zones, institutional and political tensions such as legitimisation "resist local resolution".[447] Instead, they are negotiated broader, in the wider complex of (historical) scholarship including peer review systems, hiring committees, publishers and funders.[448] To this end, several reports have provided recommendations for improving evaluation and recognition of digital history scholarship. One significant attempt has been the Guidelines for the Professional Evaluation of Digital Scholarship in History by the American History Association committee chaired by Edward Ayers.[449] The committee argued that departments should recognise the opportunities of the digital environment and develop expertise and methods to evaluate digital scholarship. At the same time, they argued that historians pursuing digital scholarship should engage their non-digitally inclined peers by explaining or demonstrating how their research contributes to historical scholarship.

In line with this final recommendation, another significant attempt was the report by the Arguing with Digital History working group convened by the Roy Rosenzweig Center for History and New Media.[450] This working group recommended that digital historical scholarship should be based in historical argumentation, and that vice versa the historical community should learn how to recognise arguments in their new digital forms. For example, the working group noted that in publishing a digital collection "historians construct an argument by making choices about which metadata schema to employ, which categories of information

---

447 Star and Ruhleder, 126.

448 Julie Thompson Klein and Holly J. Falk-Krzesinski, "Interdisciplinary and Collaborative Work: Framing Promotion and Tenure Practices and Policies," *Research Policy* 46, no. 6 (2017): 1055–61, https://doi.org/10.1016/j.respol.2017.03.001.

449 Edward L Ayers et al., "Guidelines for the Professional Evaluation of Digital Scholarship in History" (American Historical Association, 2015).

450 Arguing with Digital History working group, "Digital History and Argument" (Roy Rosenzweig Center for History and New Media, 2017).

to include, which controlled vocabularies to deploy, and even the language and word choices used to describe the item".[451] The task for a digital history broker may then be to ensure that even technical matters such as metadata schemas are decided by historical argumentation and that this consideration is described in recognisable historical form.

Note that both recommendations indeed point to the necessity of interactional expertise trading zones, consisting of historians who can negotiate and coordinate digital methods and tools while remaining embedded in their historical communities. Yet the practice of infrastructuring itself does not fit within such recommendations, since it does not lead to historical arguments that fit within the frame of peer review. Furthermore, brokering occurs across the boundaries of communities of practice, thereby not fitting traditional forms of assessment.[452] The infrastructural work in digital history and digital humanities more broadly has consequently been criticised for lacking intellectual contributions to scholarship.[453] For example, the digital humanist Willard McCarty has criticised the focus on infrastructure as to "surrender the discipline to servitude".[454] He fears that developing infrastructures for the research agendas of historical scholarship (or other humanities subjects in the wider digital humanities) renders the digital humanities unable to develop a research agenda of its own. In this context it is important to note that McCarty speaks of the digital humanities as a discipline in itself. This entails that the digital humanities (or digital history) should constitute a connected-symmetric-homogeneous (creole) trading zone, as I showed in chapter 2. Yet digital history brokers pushed towards symmetric-heterogeneous (fractioned) trading zones, thereby not defining digital history as a discipline with its own research agenda. In that sense, the agenda of the historical discipline is the agenda for digital history.

The digital humanist Jennifer Edmond notes that the success of digital humanities thus far has been in implementing research infrastructures that have reached large audiences.[455] She agrees, however, that focusing on infrastructure carries a risk, namely that digital humanities scholars become preoccupied

---

451 Arguing with Digital History working group, 5.

452 Wenger, *Communities of Practice*, 110.

453 Sheila Anderson, "What Are Research Infrastructures?," *International Journal of Humanities and Arts Computing* 7, no. 1–2 (2013): 4–23, https://doi.org/10.3366/ijhac.2013.0078; Willard McCarty, "The Residue of Uniqueness," *Historical Social Research/Historische Sozialforschung* 37, no. 3 (2012): 24–45.

454 McCarty, "The Residue of Uniqueness," 37.

455 Jennifer Edmond, "Collaboration and Infrastructure," in *A New Companion to Digital Humanities*, ed. Susan Schreibman, Ray Siemens and John Unsworth (Wiley-Blackwell, 2016), 54–65.

with infrastructure as a goal in itself rather than as a means towards research. In contrast with McCarty, the risk identified by Edmond is not that the agenda of digital humanities is set by scholars from other fields, but that the agenda is filled entirely by operational matters of maintenance and continuous development.

The digital humanist Martin Paul Eve notes that one strategy for escaping the problem of disciplinary evaluation misunderstanding digital histories contributions is the establishment of specific departments.[456] The C²DH could be seen as an example of such a specific institute where procedures are developed to hire and promote scholars based on their digital works. Institutional units such as the C²DH and King's Digital Lab furthermore provide the means and resources to manage both infrastructures as well as conduct scholarship.[457] The C²DH furthermore promotes digital history works beyond its own premises in launching and sustaining a journal for digital history.[458] Eve warns however that "the banishment of DH to its own departmental area is a problematic move".[459] Digital history confined to its own institutional space risks developing infrastructures without anyone who will use them for their own disciplinary purposes. Yet this is arguably what digital history brokers prevent by pushing digital history trading zones towards symmetric-heterogeneous trading zones to ensure that research infrastructures remain relevant to historical scholarship.

However, a limitation of such debates about legitimisation of digital history practices and work on infrastructures is that they present these issues in the context of digital history and digital humanities. Following the argument from Susan Leigh Star and Karen Ruhleder that infrastructural tensions "resist local resolution", digital history brokers should look beyond such community boundaries. Arguably, none of the infrastructural tensions discussed above is exclusive to digital history and it would be hubris to assume that the digital history community can resolve these tensions by itself. Improving the recognition and evaluation of practices and activities not directly leading to disciplinary contributions in the form of publications is a topic increasingly discussed in science policy. Multiple reports discuss the importance of methods of evaluation that take into account contributions to collaborations, interdisciplinary practices, as

---

456 Martin Paul Eve, "Violins in the Subway: Scarcity Correlations, Evaluative Cultures, and Disciplinary Authority in the Digital Humanities," in *Digital Technology and the Practices of Humanities Research*, ed. Jennifer Edmond (Open Book Publishers, 2020), 105–22, https://doi.org/10.11647/obp.0192.05.

457 Smithies et al., "Managing 100 Digital Humanities Projects."

458 "Journal of Digital History", accessed May 12, 2021, https://journalofdigitalhistory.org/.

459 Eve, "5. Violins in the Subway," 29.

well as societal impact.[460] Beyond the digital humanities, the evaluation of brokering in scholarship has received much attention in literature.[461]

To address infrastructural tensions thus requires local solutions to engage with and diffuse to national or even global communities of practice and programs. By acquiring interactional expertise, digital history brokers are able to develop local approaches to the methodological and epistemological tensions introduced by the interactions between computational practices and historical scholarship. Yet by implementing these approaches in education and developing guidelines for legitimisation, brokers are at the forefront to integrate local approaches in the global community of practice. Once these infrastructural tensions are resolved or mitigated, infrastructures can be properly appropriated:

> An infrastructure occurs when the tension between local and global is resolved. That is, an infrastructure occurs when local practices are afforded by a larger-scale technology, which can then be used in a natural, ready-to-hand fashion.[462]

When a digital history broker then succeeds in mitigating infrastructural tensions, infrastructures no longer demand continuous efforts of infrastructuring. It is at this point that the connected-symmetric-heterogeneous (interactional expertise) trading zones of digital history depending on these brokers can shift towards disconnected-symmetric-heterogeneous (boundary object) trading zones (see Figure 8). In these trading zones, it is the infrastructures themselves that function as boundary objects, robust enough to remain recognisable across different trading zones and sites of scholarship, while plastic enough to adapt to the heterogeneous needs of historians. The information scientists Geoffrey Bowker and Susan Leigh Star hereto introduced the concept of boundary infrastructures as systems of boundary objects that are appropriated across communities at a

---

460 Ingrid Bauer et al., "Next Generation Metrics" (2020), https://doi.org/10.5281/ZENODO. 3874801. In the Netherlands, a position paper authored by the institutional representatives of universities, funders and scholarly institutes argued for more diverse evaluation methods, see VSNU et al., "Ruimte voor ieders talent: naar een nieuwe balans in het erkennen en waarderen van wetenschappers" (2019).
461 E.g. Simon Maag et al., "Indicators for Measuring the Contributions of Individual Knowledge Brokers," *Environmental Science & Policy* 89 (2018): 1–9, https://doi.org/10.1016/j.envsci. 2018.06.002; Julie Thompson Klein, "Evaluation of Interdisciplinary and Transdisciplinary Research: A Literature Review," *American Journal of Preventive Medicine* 35, no. 2 (2008): S116–23, https://doi.org/10.1016/j.amepre.2008.05.010; Daniel Stokols et al., "The Ecology of Team Science," *American Journal of Preventive Medicine* 35, no. 2 (August 2008): S96–115, https://doi.org/ 10.1016/j.amepre.2008.05.003; Daniel Stokols et al., "Evaluating Transdisciplinary Science," *Nicotine & Tobacco Research* 5, no. Suppl_1 (2003): S21–39.
462 Star and Ruhleder, "Steps Toward an Ecology of Infrastructure," 114.

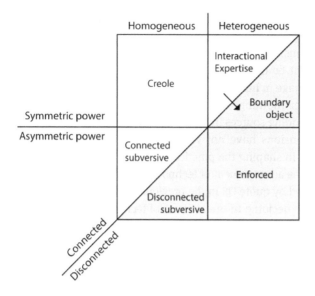

Figure 8: Resolving infrastructural tensions by scaling local solutions for symmetric-heterogeneous digital history to globally accessible infrastructures of boundary objects. Digital history brokers thereby push trading zones from connected to disconnected in order to scale beyond the locally negotiated collaboration.

larger scale.[463] Boundary infrastructures offer the structure to enable the full range of necessary tools necessary for research, while still providing sufficient flexibility for local variations of practices. They argue that this concept thereby explicitly recognises the heterogeneity and ambiguity of practices conducted by varying communities of practice. Digital history research infrastructures should then provide sufficient structure to enable recognisable historical research for differing communities of practice, while offering sufficient flexibility to move between more traditional and more digital methods and between close and distant reading.

Practices of Digital History Brokering

Digital history brokers thereby exemplify significant shifts in practices. Brokers conduct project management; coordinate practices from archival and library domains such as data collection, transformation and description; learn about the

---

463 Geoffrey C. Bowker and Susan Leigh Star, *Sorting Things out: Classification and Its Consequences*, Inside Technology (Cambridge, Mass: MIT Press, 1999), 285–318.

potential and limitations of computational technologies and where to apply these; employ inter-languages to translate between the different collaborating communities; and finally transform historical questions into infrastructural problems. This final aspect might be the most significant shift for historians, which requires them not just to engage in hermeneutics of sources found through archival research, but to consider the range of possible practices, hermeneutical or otherwise, enabled by embedding sources in digital infrastructures.

Since infrastructural tensions have not yet been resolved, digital history brokers might prove central in shaping the practices of future historians through infrastructuring. Insofar as the advancement of technology prompts digital history collaborations, as exemplified by quote Q8 in the previous chapter, digital history brokers play a central role in deciding future avenues of technology for historical research. Brokers thereby not only developed interactional expertise to collaborate with computational experts. They furthermore developed political proficiency to negotiate the socio-economic potential of digital history strategies with politics, university administrators and funding agencies.

The development of technology consists of a continuous variation and selection of decisions and interpretations; a developing technology can therefore take many directions, but stabilises in form and utility through negotiation. Once a technology stabilises, surrounding problems disappear, its characteristics become assumed as essential and the meaning of the technology is shared by the community.[464] By brokering the negotiation of this shared meaning, digital history brokers are "seeding ideas and work practices" to be enabled by future infrastructures.[465] Yet brokers do this while remaining aligned with the values of historical scholarship. They thus aim to enable future methods of historical scholarship, without altering what it means to be a historian.

In conclusion, digital history brokers transform their own practices, so that other historians do not have to but can employ digitised sources and digital methodology through infrastructures in a fashion that naturally fits into their practices as historians. It is for this reason that digital history does not occupy a singular position between the digital and the historical, for this position is continuously negotiated on the level of institutes, collaborations and individuals. Notably, by engaging with computational practices while simultaneously protecting

---

464 Trevor J. Pinch and Wiebe E. Bijker, "The Social Construction of Facts and Artefacts: Or How the Sociology of Science and the Sociology of Technology Might Benefit Each Other," *Social Studies of Science* 14, no. 3 (1984): 399–441, https://doi.org/10.1177/030631284014003004.
465 Paul N. Edwards et al., "Understanding Infrastructure: Dynamics, Tensions, and Design. Report of a Workshop on "History and Theory of Infrastructures: Lessons for New Scientific Infrastructures"" (2007), 19.

historical practices, digital history brokers continuously move along this dimension to meet what is demanded at that place and point in time. The result of these activities are the boundary infrastructures, which likewise do not occupy a single position between the digital and the historical but offer sufficient flexibility for historians to move across this spectrum.

Towards the Digital History Future

It is without question that the digital turn has affected and will continue to affect historical practices, even if perhaps not necessarily transforming the disciplinary culture. The infrastructures for historical scholarship are now both physical and digital, encompassing increasingly digitised and born-digital sources. Historians are therefore indeed increasingly using computers for historical research, answering the challenges that have been raised for as long as there have been computers. Yet historians do so in diverging ways, and adoption of computers does not entail that all historians become programmers, as was argued by Emmanuel Le Roy Ladurie.

Instead, I argue that recognising the boundary practices of historians in trading zones that incorporate strategies along the dimensions of engagement, power relations and changing practices raises awareness of a number of issues. First, not all historians engage equally, but some will be more active in engagement and adoption of practices than others. Second, all historians aim to preserve control over their own fields of actions, otherwise disconnecting engagement. Third, sharing of practices can be shallow, or historians may indeed strive to become computational experts themselves. My findings suggest that connected-symmetric-heterogeneous (interactional expertise) trading zones are the most fruitful in negotiating practices. The value of digital history brokers is that they enable the negotiation of computational practices on behalf of their disciplinary peers. The historical community is thereby able to import and adapt methods and tools without losing its disciplinary values. When infrastructural tensions are resolved, these trading zones may become disconnected-symmetric-heterogeneous trading zones of boundary infrastructures.

Just as infrastructures are no longer fully analogue or digital, neither should historians be fully analogue or digital. Rather than a dichotomy of practices, I see the historical community of practice evolving towards a spectrum of analogue to digital. The methods and tools that are being negotiated towards historical values will then be available for use as needed; distant reading supplementing rather than displacing close reading. It is then that computational methods can become infrastructural, aiding historical research, learned as part of membership and embedded among the spectrum of practices available to historians.

Acknowledgments

I would like to thank many people, more than could or should be written out, but I would like to express special gratitude to a number of people who significantly impacted this book.

Andreas Fickers offered supervision and mentorship and educated me how historians think. While guiding me along a scholarly path that would prove fruitful, at the same time he allowed me the freedom to develop my own ideas. Benoît Majerus and Pelle Snickers critically discussed my work in progress, but always with constructive and kind comments. Valérie Schafer, Tim Hitchcock, Susan Legêne and Christoph Schommer joined my PhD thesis defence committee and engaged with my arguments, pointing me to further improvements for the work on this book after the PhD thesis. My colleagues at the Centre for Contemporary and Digital History, at the Institute for History, and others at the University of Luxembourg allowed me to learn how historians work in practice and took ample time for discussions to develop my thinking. In particular (but in no particular order), I enjoyed the jokes, discussions with and feedback from Anita Lucchesi, Sytze van Herck, Tim van der Heijden, Gerben Zaagsma, Lars Wieneke, Frédéric Clavert, Estelle Bunout, Marten Düring, Brigitte Melchior-Dolenc, Pit Peporte, Sonja Kmec, Andrea Binsfeld, Joëlle Weis, Lucas Duane and Christoph Purschke. During the *Practicing Critical Interdisciplinarity* course, Ariane König and Jerome Ravetz provided a platform for presenting my work and sharpening my understanding of interdisciplinarity. Before I started my PhD research, Martijn Kleppe, Henri Beunders, Stef Scagliola and Franciska de Jong at Erasmus University Rotterdam introduced me to the subjects of digital humanities and digital history. They provided me a sandbox where I could try out methods and questions until I found a topic that was engaging enough to spend four years on a single question. Besides discussions at work, I enjoyed countless discussions on Twitter which gave inspiration, welcome distractions and feedback on ideas that fit 140–280 characters. I particularly enjoyed (again in no particular order) the discussions with and feedback from Ted Underwood, Simon Hengchen, Scott Weingart, Michael Piotrowski, Cerstin Mahlow, Ian Milligan, Mirko Tobias Schäfer, Martin Grandjean, James Baker, Thomas Franssen, Melodee Beals, Joris van Zundert, Marieke van Erp, Annemieke Romein, Chiel van den Akker and Melvin Wevers.

Since this book concerns the infrastructures of research, I would also like to thank the people who have been infrastructural to me being a PhD candidate at the University of Luxembourg, enabling my research in sometimes invisible ways: the cleaners of the *Maison des Sciences Humaines*, the caterers that provided my infamous sandwiches and the IT & Media Centre staff that maintained

Open Access. © 2021 Max Kemman, published by De Gruyter. [(cc) BY-NC-ND] This work is licensed under the Creative Commons Attribution-NonCommercial-NoDerivatives 4.0 International License.
https://doi.org/10.1515/9783110682106-006

devices and helped out with technical problems such as the 3D printer, which never truly worked. I also thank the respondents of my online questionnaire and the interviewees who kindly took the time to participate. I could not have written this book without their participation.

On a personal level, I am deeply grateful to my wife Lindi, who supported me throughout this venture and joined me for a stay in Luxembourg and Belgium. I would probably not have ended up pursuing a PhD in Luxembourg without her, nor would I have finished this book without her support and patience through the years. Our children Felix, Rowas and Tilly provided welcome distractions to stop writing for a minute and enjoy a snowball fight or a walk in the sun. I thank my parents, Peter and Jojanne, for always supporting me. My friends, Jesse, Timon, Jeroen and Michaël provided friendship on a distance by inviting me to join in our bi-weekly meetings through FaceTime while I was in another country. Although my Wallonian internet connection was not always up for it, I am glad I could join in and stay connected. Finally, I would like to thank the Lord, for blessing me with my amazing family, friends and colleagues.

Bibliography

Agar, Michael. "An Ethnography By Any Other Name . . .." *Forum Qualitative Sozialforschung /
Forum: Qualitative Social Research* 7, no. 4 (2006). https://doi.org/10.17169/fqs-7.4.177.

Agar, Michael. "Ethnography." In *Culture and Language Use*, edited by Gunter Senft, Jan-Ola
Östman and Jef Verschueren, 110–20. John Benjamins Publishing Company, 2009.

Aiden, Erez and Jean-Baptiste Michel. *Uncharted: Big Data as a Lens on Human Culture.*
Riverhead Books, 2013.

Amit, Vered. "Introduction." In *Constructing the Field: Ethnographic Fieldwork in the
Contemporary World*, edited by Vered Amit, 1–18. Routledge, 2000.

Anderson, Ian G. "Are You Being Served? Historians and the Search for Primary Sources."
Archivaria 58 (2004): 81–129.

Anderson, Sheila. "What Are Research Infrastructures?" *International Journal of Humanities
and Arts Computing* 7, no. 1–2 (2013): 4–23. https://doi.org/10.3366/ijhac.2013.0078.

Antonijević, Smiljana. *Amongst Digital Humanists: An Ethnographic Study of Digital
Knowledge Production.* Pre-Print. Basingstoke New York, NY: Palgrave Macmillan, 2015.

Arguing with Digital History working group. "Digital History and Argument." Roy Rosenzweig
Center for History and New Media, 2017.

Armstrong, David J. and Paul Cole. "Managing Distances and Differences in Geographically
Distributed Work Groups." In *Distributed Work*, edited by Pamela Hinds and Sara Kiesler,
167–86. MIT Press, 2002.

Atkins, Daniel E., Kelvin K. Droegemeier, Stuart I. Feldman, Hector Garcia Molina, Michael L
Klein, David G. Messerschmitt, Paul Messina, Jeremiah P. Ostriker and Margaret H. Wright.
"Revolutionizing Science and Engineering Through Cyberinfrastructure: Report of the
National Science Foundation Blue-Ribbon Advisory Panel on Cyberinfrastructure."
National Science Foundation, 2003.

Ayers, Edward L. "The Pasts and Futures of Digital History." *History News* 56, no. 3 (2001): 5–9.

Ayers, Edward L, David Bell, Peter Bol, Timothy Burke, Seth Denbo, James Gregory, Claire
Potter, Janice Reiff and Kathryn Tomasek. "Guidelines for the Professional Evaluation of
Digital Scholarship in History." American Historical Association, 2015.

Barata, Kimberly. "Archives in the Digital Age." *Journal of the Society of Archivists* 25, no. 1
(2004): 63–70. https://doi.org/10.1080/0037981042000199151.

Barats, Christine, Valérie Schafer and Andreas Fickers. "Fading Away . . . The Challenge of
Sustainability in Digital Studies." *Digital Humanities Quarterly* 14, no. 3 (2020).

Baron, Jaimie. *The Archive Effect: Found Footage and the Audiovisual Experience of History.*
Routledge, 2014.

Bauer, Ingrid, David Bohmert, Alexandra Czernecka, Thomas Eichenberger, Juan
Garbajosa, Horia Iovu, Yvonne Kinnaird, et al. "Next Generation Metrics," 2020.
https://doi.org/10.5281/ZENODO.3874801.

Becher, Tony. "Towards a Definition of Disciplinary Cultures." *Studies in Higher Education* 6,
no. 2 (1981): 109–22. https://doi.org/10.1080/03075078112331379362.

Becher, Tony, and Sharon Parry. "The Endurance of the Disciplines." In *Governing Knowledge*,
edited by Ivar Bleiklie and Mary Henkel, 9:133–44.Springer, 2005. https://doi.org/10.1007/
1-4020-3504-7_9.

Becher, Tony, and Paul R. Trowler. *Academic Tribes and Territories: Intellectual Enquire and the Culture of Disciplines*. 2nd ed. The Society for Research into Higher Education & Open University Press, 2001.

Berg-Fulton, Tracey, Alison Langmead, Thomas Lombardi and David Newbury. "A Role-Based Model for Successful Collaboration in Digital Art History." *International Journal for Digital Art History*, no. 3 (2018). https://doi.org/10.11588/dah.2018.3.34297.

Berners-Lee, Tim, and Daniel Connolly. "Hypertext Markup Language (HTML) A Representation of Textual Information and MetaInformation for Retrieval and Interchange." w3.org. W3, 1993.

Berners-Lee, Tim, and Mark Fischetti. *Weaving the Web: The Original Design and Ultimate Destiny of the World Wide Web by Its Inventor*. Harper San Francisco, 1999.

Bernstein, Ethan S., and Stephen Turban. "The Impact of the 'Open' Workspace on Human Collaboration." *Philosophical Transactions of the Royal Society B: Biological Sciences* 373, no. 20170239 (2018). https://doi.org/10.1098/rstb.2017.0239.

Bingham, Adrian. "'The Digitization of Newspaper Archives: Opportunities and Challenges for Historians.'" *Twentieth Century British History* 21, no. 2 (2010): 225–31. https://doi.org/10.1093/tcbh/hwq007.

Bischoff, Frank M., and Kiran Klaus Patel. "Was Auf Dem Spiel Steht. Über Den Preis Des Schweigens Zwischen Geschichtswissenschaft Und Archiven Im Digitalen Zeitalter." *Zeithistorische Forschungen – Studies in Contemporary History* 17, no. 1 (2020): 145–56.

Björgvinsson, Erling, Pelle Ehn and Per-Anders Hillgren. "Participatory Design and 'Democratizing Innovation.'" In *Proceedings of the 11th Biennial Participatory Design Conference on – PDC '10*, 41–50. New York, New York, USA: ACM Press, 2010. https://doi.org/10.1145/1900441.1900448.

Blair, Ann. *Too Much to Know: Managing Scholarly Information before the Modern Age*. New Haven, Conn: Yale University Press, 2010.

Bloch, Marc. *The Historian's Craft*. Translated by Peter Putnam. Repr. Manchester: Manchester Univ. Press, 2004.

Bod, Rens. *De Vergeten Wetenschappen: Een Geschiedenis van de Humaniora*. Prometheus, 2010.

Boonstra, Onno, Leen Breure and Peter Doorn. "Past, Present and Future of Historical Information Science." *Historical Social Research / Historische Sozialforschung* 29, no. 2 (2004): 4–132.

Bordalejo, Barbara, and Roopika Risam. *Intersectionality in Digital Humanities*. Arc Humanities Press, 2019.

Borgman, Christine L. *Big Data, Little Data, No Data*. MIT Press, 2015.

Borgman, Christine L. "The Digital Future Is Now: A Call to Action for the Humanities." *DHQ: Digital Humanities Quarterly* 3, no. 4 (2009).

Borgman, Christine L. "What Are Digital Libraries? Competing Visions." *Information Processing and Management* 35, no. 3 (1999): 227–43. https://doi.org/10.1016/S0306-4573(98)00059-4.

Bowker, Geoffrey C. "The History of Information Infrastructures: The Case of the International Classification of Diseases." *Information Processing and Management* 32, no. 1 (1996): 49–61. https://doi.org/10.1016/0306-4573(95)00049-M.

Bowker, Geoffrey C., and Susan Leigh Star. *Sorting Things out: Classification and Its Consequences*. Inside Technology. Cambridge, Mass: MIT Press, 1999.

Boyce, Peter, Donald W. King, Carol Montgomery and Carol Tenopir. "How Electronic Journals Are Changing Patterns of Use." *The Serials Librarian* 46, no. 1–2 (2004): 121–41. https://doi.org/10.1300/J123v46n01_14.

Brauer, René, and Mats Fridlund. "Historicizing Topic Models. A Distant Reading of Topic Modeling Texts within Historical Studies." In *Cultural Research in the Context of "Digital Humanities": Proceedings of International Conference 3-5 October 2013, St Petersburg*, edited by L.V. Nikiforova and N.V. Nikiforova, 152–63, 2013.

Breisach, Ernst. *Historiography: Ancient, Medieval & Modern*. 2nd ed. Chicago: University of Chicago Press, 1994.

Brier, Stephen. "Confessions of a Premature Digital Humanist." *The Journal of Interactive Technology & Pedgagoy*, no. 11 (2017).

Brown, John Seely, Allan Collins and Paul Duguid. "Situated Cognition and the Culture of Learning." *Educational Researcher* 18, no. 1 (1989): 32–42. https://doi.org/10.3102/0013189X018001032.

Brown, Susan, Patricia Clements, Isobel Grundy, Stan Ruecker, Jeffery Antoniuk and Sharon Balazs. "Published Yet Never Done: The Tension Between Projection and Completion in Digital Humanities Research." *Digital Humanities Quarterly* 3, no. 2 (2009).

Brügger, Niels, and Niels Ole Finnemann. "The Web and Digital Humanities: Theoretical and Methodological Concerns." *Journal of Broadcasting & Electronic Media* 57, no. 1 (2013): 66–80. https://doi.org/10.1080/08838151.2012.761699.

Burdick, Anne, Johanna Drucker, Peter Lunenfeld, Todd Resner and Jeffrey Schnapp. *Digital_Humanities*. MIT Press, 2012.

Bush, Vannevar. "As We May Think." *The Atlantic Monthly* 176, no. 1 (1945): 101–8.

Buurma, Rachel Sagner, and Laura Heffernan. "Search and Replace: Josephine Miles and the Origins of Distant Reading." *Modernism/Modernity* 3, no. 1 (2018).

Cady, Susan A. "The Electronic Revolution in Libraries: Microfilm Déjà Vu?" *College & Research Libraries* 51, no. 4 (1990): 374–86.

Centivany, Alissa. "The Dark History of HathiTrust." *Proceedings of the 50th Hawaii International Conference on System Sciences*, 2017, 2357–66.

Champion, Erik M. "Digital Humanities Is Text Heavy, Visualization Light, and Simulation Poor." *Digital Scholarship in the Humanities*, 2016. https://doi.org/10.1093/llc/fqw053.

Choi, Bernard C.K., and Anita W.P. Pak. "Multidisciplinarity, Interdisciplinarity and Transdisciplinarity in Health Research, Services, Education and Policy: 1. Definitions, Objectives, and Evidence of Effectiveness." *Clinical and Investigative Medicine* 29, no. 6 (2006): 351–64.

Ciambrone, Desirée. "Anonymity." In *The SAGE Encyclopedia of Social Science Research Methods*, edited by Michael Lewis-Beck, Alan Bryman and Tim Futing Liao, 18–19. Sage Publications, Inc., 2004. https://doi.org/10.4135/9781412950589.n17.

Cohen, Daniel J., Michael Frisch, Patrick Gallagher, Steven Mintz, Kirsten Sword, Amy Murrell Taylor, William G. Thomas and William J. Turkel. "Interchange: The Promise of Digital History." *The Journal of American History* 95, no. 2 (2008): 452–91.

Cohen, Job, Annemarie Bos, Godelieve Laureys, Sijbolt Noorda, Frits van Oostrom and Paul Schnabel. *Duurzame Geesteswetenschappen: Rapport van de Commissie National Plan Toekomst Geesteswetenschappen*. Amsterdam University Press, 2008.

Collins, Harry, and Robert Evans. "The Third Wave of Science Studies: Studies of Expertise and Experience." *Social Studies of Science* 32, no. 2 (2002): 235–96. https://doi.org/10.1177/0306312702032002003.

Collins, Harry, Robert Evans and Michael Gorman. "Trading Zones and Interactional Expertise." *Studies in History and Philosophy of Science* 38, no. 4 (2007): 657–66. https://doi.org/10.1016/j.shpsa.2007.09.003.

Collins, Harry, Robert Evans and Michael Gorman. "Trading Zones Revisited." In *The Third Wave in Science and Technology Studies,* edited by David S. Caudill, Shannon N. Conley, Michael Gorman and Martin Weinel, 275–81. Cham: Springer International Publishing, 2019. https://doi.org/10.1007/978-3-030-14335-0_15.

Cook, Terry. "Easy To Byte, Harder To Chew: The Second Generation of Electronic Records Archives." *Archivaria* 33 (1991): 202–16.

Cook, Terry. "The Archive(s) Is a Foreign Country: Historians, Archivists, and the Changing Archival Landscape." *The American Archivist* 74, no. 2 (2011): 600–632. https://doi.org/10.17723/aarc.74.2.xm04573740262424.

Cook, Terry. "What Is Past Is Prologue: A History of Archival Ideas Since 1898, and the Future Paradigm Shift." *Archivaria,* no. 43 (1997): 17–63.

Courant, Paul N., Sarah E. Fraser, Michael F Goodchild, Margaret Hedstrom, Charles Henry, Peter B. Kaufman, Jerome Mcgann, Roy Rosenzweig, John Unsworth and Bruce Zuckerman. "Our Cultural Commonwealth: The Report of the American Council of Learned Societies Commision on Cyberinfrastructure for the Humanities and Social Sciences." American Council of Learned Societies, 2006.

Cummings, Jonathon N., and Sara Kiesler. "Collaborative Research Across Disciplinary and Organizational Boundaries." *Social Studies of Science* 35, no. 5 (2005): 703–22. https://doi.org/10.1177/0306312705055535.

Darnton, Robert. *The Case for Books: Past, Present, and Future.* New York: PublicAffairs, 2009.

Day, Ronald E. *Indexing It All: The Subject in the Age of Documentation, Information, and Data.* History and Foundations of Information Science. Cambridge, Massachusetts: MIT Press, 2014.

De Jonge Akademie. "Grensverleggend: Kansen En Belemmeringen Voor Interdisciplinair Onderzoek." KNAW, 2015.

Deegan, Marilyn, and Kathryn Sutherland. *Transferred Illusions: Digital Technology and the Forms of Print.* Ashgate, 2009.

Derrida, Jacques. "Archive Fever: A Freudian Impression." *Diacritics* 25, no. 2 (1995): 9–63.

Drucker, Johanna. "Humanities Approaches to Graphical Display." *Digital Humanities Quarterly* 5, no. 1 (2011): 1–21.

Duguid, Paul. "'The Art of Knowing': Social and Tacit Dimensions of Knowledge and the Limits of the Community of Practice." *The Information Society* 21, no. 2 (2005): 109–18. https://doi.org/10.1080/01972240590925311.

Düring, Marten. "The Potential of Agent-Based Modelling for Historical Research." In *Complexity and the Human Experience: Modeling Complexity in the Humanities and Sociol Sciences,* edited by Paul A. Youngman and Mirsad Hadzikadic, 121–37. Pan Stanford Publishing, 2014.

Earhart, Amy E. "Digital Humanities Within a Global Context: Creating Borderlands of Localized Expression." *Fudan Journal of the Humanities and Social Sciences* 11, no. 3 (2018): 357–69. https://doi.org/10.1007/s40647-018-0224-0.

Edmond, Jennifer. "Collaboration and Infrastructure." In *A New Companion to Digital Humanities,* edited by Susan Schreibman, Ray Siemens and John Unsworth, 54–65. Wiley-Blackwell, 2016.

Edmond, Jennifer. "The Role of the Professional Intermediary in Expanding the Humanities Computing Base." *Literary and Linguistic Computing* 20, no. 3 (2005): 367–80. https://doi.org/10.1093/llc/fqi036.

Edmond, Jennifer, Frank Fischer, Laurent Romary and Toma Tasovac. "Springing the Floor for a Different Kind of Dance – Building DARIAH as a Twenty-First-Century Research Infrastructure for the Arts and Humanities." In *Digital Technology and the Practices of Humanities Research*, edited by Jennifer Edmond, 207–34. Open Book Publishers, 2020. https://doi.org/10.11647/obp.0192.09.

Edwards, Paul N., Steven J. Jackson, Geoffrey C. Bowker and Cory P. Knobel. "Understanding Infrastructure: Dynamics, Tensions, and Design. Report of a Workshop on 'History and Theory of Infrastructures: Lessons for New Scientific Infrastructures,'" 2007.

Ende, Jan van den, and Wilfred Dolfsma. "Technology-Push, Demand-Pull and the Shaping of Technological Paradigms – Patterns in the Development of Computing Technology." *Journal of Evolutionary Economics* 15, no. 1 (2005): 83–99. https://doi.org/10.1007/s00191-004-0220-1.

Eskildsen, Kasper Risbjerg. "Inventing the Archive." *History of the Human Sciences* 26, no. 4 (2013): 8–26. https://doi.org/10.1177/0952695113496094.

Eskildsen, Kasper Risbjerg. "Leopold Ranke's Archival Turn: Location and Evidence in Modern Historiography." *Modern Intellectual History* 5, no. 3 (2008): 425–53. https://doi.org/10.1017/S1479244308001753.

European Commission. Directorate General for Research and Innovation. *Sustainable European Research Infrastructures: A Call for Action*. LU: Publications Office, 2017. https://data.europa.eu/doi/10.2777/76269.

Evans, Robert, and Harry Collins. "Interactional Expertise and the Imitation Game." In *Trading Zones and Interactional Expertise: Creating New Kinds of Collaboration*, edited by Michael Gorman, 53–70. MIT Press, 2010.

Eve, Martin Paul. "Violins in the Subway: Scarcity Correlations, Evaluative Cultures, and Disciplinary Authority in the Digital Humanities." In *Digital Technology and the Practices of Humanities Research*, edited by Jennifer Edmond, 105–22. Open Book Publishers, 2020. https://doi.org/10.11647/obp.0192.05.

Farge, Arlette. *The Allure of the Archives*. Translated by Thomas Scott-Railton and Natalie Zemon Davis. 1989. Reprint, Yale University Press, 2013.

Fickers, Andreas. "Towards A New Digital Historicism? Doing History In The Age Of Abundance." *VIEW Journal of European Television History and Culture* 1, no. 1 (2012): 19–26.

Fickers, Andreas. "Update Für Die Hermeneutik. Geschichtswissenschaft Auf Dem Weg Zur Digitalen Forensik?" *Zeithistorische Forschungen – Studies in Contemporary History* 17, no. 1 (2020): 157–68.

Fickers, Andreas. "Veins Filled with the Diluted Sap of Rationality: A Critical Reply to Rens Bod." *BMGN – Low Countries Historical Review* 128, no. 4 (2013): 155–63.

Fickers, Andreas, and Tim van der Heijden. "Inside the Trading Zone: Thinkering in a Digital History Lab." *Digital Humanities Quarterly* 14, no. 3 (2020).

Fogel, Robert W., and Stanley L. Engerman. *Time on the Cross: The Economics of American Negro Slavery*. 1974. Reprint, New York; London: W.W. Norton, 1995.

Foka, Anna, Anna Misharina, Viktor Arvidsson and Stefan Gelfgren. "Beyond Humanities qua Digital: Spatial and Material Development for Digital Research Infrastructures in HumlabX." *Digital Scholarship in the Humanities* 33, no. 2 (June 1, 2018): 264–78. https://doi.org/10.1093/llc/fqx008.

Fokkens, Antske, Serge ter Braake, Niels Ockeloen, Piek Vossen, Susan Legêne and Guus Schreiber. "BiographyNet: Methodological Issues When NLP Supports Historical

Research." In *Proceedings of the Ninth International Conference on Language Resources and Evaluation (LREC'14)*, edited by Nicoletta Calzolari, Khalid Choukri, Thierry Declerck, Hrafn Loftsson, Bente Maegaard, Joseph Mariani, Asuncion Moreno, Jan Odijk and Stelios Piperidis, 3728–35. Reykjavik, Iceland: European Language Resources Association (ELRA), 2014.

Foster, Clifton D. "Microfilming Activities of the Historical Records Survey, 1935–42." *The American Archivist* 48, no. 1 (1985): 45–55.

Foucault, Michel. *The Archaeology of Knowledge And the Discourse on Language*. Translated by A.M. Sheridan Smith. Pantheon Books, 1972.

Foucault, Michel. *The History of Sexuality Volume I: An Introduction*. Translated by Robert Hurley. Pantheon Books, 1978.

Foucault, Michel. "The Subject and Power." *Critical Inquiry* 8, no. 4 (1982): 777–95. https://doi.org/10.1086/448181.

Franssen, Thomas, Wout Scholten, Laurens K. Hessels and Sarah de Rijcke. "The Drawbacks of Project Funding for Epistemic Innovation: Comparing Institutional Affordances and Constraints of Different Types of Research Funding." *Minerva* 56, no. 1 (March 2018): 11–33. https://doi.org/10.1007/s11024-017-9338-9.

Franzosi, Roberto. "A Third Road to the Past? Historical Scholarship in the Age of Big Data." *Historical Methods: A Journal of Quantitative and Interdisciplinary History* 50, no. 4 (2017): 227–44. https://doi.org/10.1080/01615440.2017.1361879.

Fridlund, Mats. "Digital History 1.5: A Middle Way between Normal and Paradigmatic Digital Historical Research." In *Digital Histories: Emergent Approaches within the New Digital History*, edited by Mats Fridlund, Mila Oiva and Petri Paju, 69–87. Helsinki University Press, 2020. https://doi.org/10.33134/HUP-5-4.

Gadamer, Hans-Georg. *Truth and Method*. 1960. Reprint, Bloomsbury Academic, 2014.

Galison, Peter. "Computer Simulations and the Trading Zone." In *The Disunity of Science: Boundaries, Contexts, And Power*, edited by Peter Galison and David J. Stump, 118–57. Stanford University Press, 1996.

Galison, Peter. *Image and Logic: A Material Culture of Microphysics*. The University of Chicago Press, 1997.

Galison, Peter. "Limits of Localism: The Scale of Sight." In *What Reason Promises*, edited by Wendy Doniger, Peter Galison and Susan Neiman, 155–70. Berlin, Boston: De Gruyter, 2016. https://doi.org/10.1515/9783110455113-020.

Galison, Peter. "Trading with the Enemy." In *Trading Zones and Interactional Expertise: Creating New Kinds of Collaboration*, edited by Michael E. Gorman, 25–52. MIT Press, 2010.

Gavin, Michael. "Agent-Based Modeling and Historical Simulation." *DHQ: Digital Humanities Quarterly* 8, no. 4 (2014).

Geertz, Clifford. *The Interpretation of Cultures: Selected Essays*. Basic Books, Inc., 1973.

Gibbons, Michael. "Introduction." In *The New Production of Knowledge: The Dynamics of Science and Research in Contemporary Societies*, edited by Zaheer Baber, Michael Gibbons, Camille Limoges, Helga Nowotny, Simon Schwartzman, Peter Scott and Martin Trow, 24:1–19. SAGE Publications, 1994. https://doi.org/10.2307/2076669.

Gieryn, Thomas F. "Boundary-Work and the Demarcation of Science from Non-Science: Strains and Interests in Professional Ideologies of Scientists." *American Sociological Review* 48, no. 6 (1983): 781–95. https://doi.org/10.2307/2095325.

Gooday, Graeme. "Placing or Replacing the Laboratory in the History of Science?" *Isis* 99, no. 4 (2008): 783–95. https://doi.org/10.1086/595772.

Gorman, Michael, and Jim Spohrer. "Service Science: A New Expertise for Managing Sociotechnical Systems." In *Trading Zones and Interactional Expertise: Creating New Kinds of Collaboration*, edited by Michael Gorman, 75–106. MIT Press, 2010.

Grafton, Anthony. *The Footnote: A Curious History*. Cambridge, Mass: Harvard University Press, 1999.

Graham, Shawn, Ian Milligan and Scott Weingart. *Exploring Big Historical Data: The Historian's Macroscope*. Imperial College Press, 2015.

Green, Harriett E. "Facilitating Communities of Practice in Digital Humanities: Librarian Collaborations for Research and Training in Text Encoding." *The Library Quarterly* 84, no. 2 (2014): 219–34. https://doi.org/10.1086/675332.

Guldi, Jo. "Critical Search: A Procedure for Guided Reading in Large-Scale Textual Corpora." *Journal of Cultural Analytics*, 2018. https://doi.org/10.22148/16.030.

Guldi, Jo. "The History of Walking and the Digital Turn: Stride and Lounge in London, 1808 – 1851." *The Journal of Modern History* 84, no. 1 (2012): 116–44.

Guldi, Jo, and David Armitage. *The History Manifesto*. Online. Cambridge: Cambridge University Press, 2014. https://doi.org/10.1017/9781139923880.

Ham, F. Gerald. *Selecting and Appraising Archives and Manuscripts*. The Society of American Archivists, 1993.

Hart, David. "On the Origins of Google." National Science Foundation, 2004.

Haythornthwaite, Caroline, Karen J. Lunsford, Geoffrey C. Bowker and Bertram C. Bruce. "Challenges for Research and Practice in Distributed, Interdisciplinary Collaboration." In *New Infrastructures for Knowledge Production: Understanding e-Science*, edited by Christine Hine, 143–66. IGI Global, 2006.

Hayward, Clarissa Rile. *De-Facing Power*. Contemporary Political Theory. Cambridge: Cambridge University Press, 2000.

Hedstrom, Margaret. "Archives, Memory, and Interfaces with the Past." *Archival Science* 2, no. 1 (2002): 21–43. https://doi.org/10.1007/BF02435629.

Hengchen, Simon. "When Does It Mean: Detecting Semantic Change in Historical Texts." PhD thesis, Universitè Libre de Bruxelles, 2017.

Hey, Tony, Stewart Tansley and Kristin Tolle, eds. *The Fourth Paradigm: Data-Intensive Scientific Discovery*. 2nd ed. Microsoft Research, 2009.

Heyl, Barbara Sherman. "Ethnographic Interviewing." In *Handbook of Ethnography*, edited by Paul Atkinson, Amanda Coffey, Sara Delamont, John Lofland and Lyn Lofland, 369–83. SAGE Publications, 2001.

Hitchcock, Tim. "Big Data, Small Data and Meaning." Historyonics, 2014.

Hitchcock, Tim. "Confronting the Digital: Or How Academic History Writing Lost the Plot." *Cultural and Social History* 10, no. 1 (2013): 9–23. https://doi.org/10.2752/147800413X13515292098070.

Hoch, Paul K. "New UK Interdisciplinary Research Centres: Reorganization for New Generic Technology." *Technology Analysis & Strategic Management* 2, no. 1 (1990): 39–48. https://doi.org/10.1080/09537329008523993.

Hockey, Susan. "The History of Humanities Computing." In *A Companion to Digital Humanities*, edited by Susan Schreibman, Ray Siemens and John Unsworth, Online., 3–19. Blackwell, 2004.

Hudson, Pat, and Mina Ishizu. *History by Numbers: An Introduction to Quantitative Approaches*. Second edition. Bloomsbury Academic, 2017.

Hunt, Lynn. "French History in the Last Twenty Years: The Rise and Fall of the Annales Paradigm." *Journal of Contemporary History* 21, no. 2 (1986): 209–24. https://doi.org/ 10.1177/002200948602100205.

Hunter, Andrea. "Digital Humanities as Third Culture." *MedieKultur: Journal of Media and Communication Research* 30, no. 57 (2014): 18–33.

Hut, Piet, and Gerald Jay Sussman. "Advanced Computing for Science." *Scientific American* 257, no. 4 (1987): 136–45.

Iggers, Georg G. "The Crisis of the Rankean Paradigm in the Nineteenth Century." *Syracuse Scholar (1979-1991)* 9, no. 1 (1988).

Iggers, Georg G. "The Professionalization of Historical Studies and the Guiding Assumptions of Modern Historical Thought." *A Companion to Western Historical Thought*, 2007, 225–42. https://doi.org/10.1002/9780470998748.ch12.

Isaacson, Walter. *The Innovators: How a Group of Hackers, Geniuses and Geeks Created the Digital Revolution*. Simon & Schuster, 2014.

Jackson, Catherine M. "Chemistry as the Defining Science: Discipline and Training in Nineteenth-Century Chemical Laboratories." *Endeavour* 35, no. 2–3 (2011): 55–62. https://doi.org/10.1016/j.endeavour.2011.05.003.

Jackson, Catherine M. "The Laboratory." In *A Companion to the History of Science*, edited by Bernard Lightman, 296–309. Wiley-Blackwell, 2016.

Jackson, Steven J., Paul N. Edwards, Geoffrey C. Bowker and Cory P. Knobel. "Understanding Infrastructure: History, Heuristics and Cyberinfrastructure Policy." *First Monday*, 2007. https://doi.org/10.5210/fm.v12i6.1904.

Jänicke, Stefan, Greta Franzini, M. Faisal Cheema and Gerik Scheuermann. "Visual Text Analysis in Digital Humanities: Visual Text Analysis in Digital Humanities." *Computer Graphics Forum* 36, no. 6 (2017): 226–50. https://doi.org/10.1111/cgf.12873.

Jarlbrink, Johan, and Pelle Snickars. "Cultural Heritage as Digital Noise: Nineteenth Century Newspapers in the Digital Archive." *Journal of Documentation* 73, no. 6 (2017): 1228–43. https://doi.org/10.1108/JD-09-2016-0106.

Jeanneney, Jean Noël. *Google and the Myth of Universal Knowledge: A View from Europe*. Translated by Teresa Lavender Fagan. Chicago: University of Chicago Press, 2007.

Jenkinson, Hilary. *A Manual of Archive Administration Including the Problems of War Archive Making*. The Clarendon Press, 1922.

Jensen, Helle Strandgaard. "Digital Archival Literacy for (All) Historians." *Media History*, 2020, 1–15. https://doi.org/10.1080/13688804.2020.1779047.

Jockers, Matthew L. *Macroanalysis: Digital Methods and Literary History*. University of Illinois Press, 2013.

Jones, Steven E. *Roberto Busa, S. J., and the Emergence of Humanities Computing: The Priest and the Punched Cards*, 2018.

Kaltenbrunner, Wolfgang. "Reflexive Inertia: Reinventing Scholarship through Digital Practices." PhD thesis, Leiden University, 2015.

Kaplan, Frederic. "Linguistic Capitalism and Algorithmic Mediation." *Representations* 127, no. 1 (2014): 57–63. https://doi.org/10.1525/rep.2014.127.1.57.

Karasti, Helena, and Jeanette Blomberg. "Studying Infrastructuring Ethnographically." *Computer Supported Cooperative Work* 27, no. 2 (2018): 233–65. https://doi.org/10.1007/ s10606-017-9296-7.

Karasti, Helena, Volkmar Pipek and Geoffrey C. Bowker. "An Afterword to 'Infrastructuring and Collaborative Design.'" *Computer Supported Cooperative Work* 27, no. 2 (2018): 267–89. https://doi.org/10.1007/s10606-017-9305-x.

Kemman, Max. "Boundary Practices of Digital Humanities Collaborations." *DH Benelux Journal* 1 (2019).

Kemman, Max. "DHBenelux 2019 Submissions." *Max Kemman* (blog), September 3, 2019. http://www.maxkemman.nl/2019/09/dhbenelux-2019-submissions/.

Kemman, Max, Martijn Kleppe and Stef Scagliola. "Just Google It." In *Proceedings of the Digital Humanities Congress* 2012, edited by Clare Mills, Michael Pidd and Esther Ward. Sheffield, UK: HRI Online Publications, 2014.

Ketelaar, Eric. "Prolegomena to a Social History of Dutch Archives." In *A Usable Collection: Essays in Honour of Jaap Kloosterman on Collecting Social History*, edited by Aad Blok, Jan Lucassen and Huub Sanders, 40–55. Amsterdam University Press, 2014.

Kiesler, Sara, and Jonathon N. Cummings. "What Do We Know about Proximity and Distance in Work Groups? A Legacy of Research." In *Distributed Work*, edited by Pamela Hinds and Sara Kiesler, 57–82. MIT Press, 2002.

King, Gary, and Daniel J. Hopkins. "A Method of Automated Nonparametric Content Analysis for Social Science." *American Journal of Political Science* 54, no. 1 (2010): 229–47. https://doi.org/10.1111/j.1540-5907.2009.00428.x.

Kirschenbaum, Matthew. "Digital Humanities As/Is a Tactical Term." In *Debates in the Digital Humanities*, edited by Matthew K. Gold, Online. University of Minnesota Press, 2012.

Kirschenbaum, Matthew. *Track Changes: A Literary History of Word Processing*. Harvard University Press, 2016.

Klein, Julie Thompson. "A Conceptual Vocabulary of Interdisciplinary Science." In *Practicing Interdisciplinarity*, edited by Peter Weingart and Nico Stehr, 3–24. University of Toronto Press, 2000.

Klein, Julie Thompson. "A Taxonomy of Interdisciplinarity." In *The Oxford Handbook of Interdisciplinarity*, edited by Robert Frodeman, Julie Thompson Klein, Carl Mitcham and J. Britt Holbrook, 15–30. Oxford University Press, 2010.

Klein, Julie Thompson. "Evaluation of Interdisciplinary and Transdisciplinary Research: A Literature Review." *American Journal of Preventive Medicine* 35, no. 2 (2008): S116–23. https://doi.org/10.1016/j.amepre.2008.05.010.

Klein, Julie Thompson. *Interdisciplining Digital Humanities: Boundary Work in an Emerging Field*. Online. University of Michigan Press, 2014. https://doi.org/10.3998/dh.12869322.0001.001.

Klein, Julie Thompson, and Holly J. Falk-Krzesinski. "Interdisciplinary and Collaborative Work: Framing Promotion and Tenure Practices and Policies." *Research Policy* 46, no. 6 (2017): 1055–61. https://doi.org/10.1016/j.respol.2017.03.001.

Knorr Cetina, Karin. *Epistemic Cultures: How the Sciences Make Knowledge*. Harvard University Press, 1999.

Knorr Cetina, Karin. "The Couch, the Cathedral, and the Laboratory : On the Relationship between Experiment and Laboratory in Science." *Science as Practice and Culture*, 1992, 113–38.

Knorr Cetina, Karin. "The Ethnographic Study of a Scientific Work: Towards a Constructivist Interpretation of Science." In *Science Observed: Perspectives on the Social Study of Science*, edited by Karin Knorr Cetina and Michael Mulkay, 115–40. SAGE Publications, 1983.

Knorr Cetina, Karin. *The Manufacture of Knowledge: An Essay on the Constructivist and Contextual Nature of Science*. Pergamon Press, 1981.

Koeser, Rebecca Sutton. "Trusting Others to 'Do the Math.'" *Interdisciplinary Science Reviews* 40, no. 4 (2016): 376–92. https://doi.org/10.1080/03080188.2016.1165454.

Kohler, Timothy A., and George G. Gumerman. *Dynamics in Human and Primate Societies: Agent-Based Modeling of Social and Spatial Processes*. Oxford University Press, 2000.

Kortekaas, Simone, and Bianca Kramer. "Thinking the Unthinkable – Doing Away with the Library Catalogue." *Insights: The UKSG Journal* 27, no. 3 (2014): 244–48. https://doi.org/10.1629/2048-7754.174.

Kousser, Morgan. "Quantitative Social-Scientific History." In *The Past before Us: Contemporary Historical Writing in the United States*, edited by M. Kammen. Cornell University Press, 1980.

Krajewski, Markus. *Paper Machines: About Cards & Catalogs, 1548-1929*. Translated by Peter Krapp. MIT Press, 2011. https://doi.org/10.7551/mitpress/9780262015899.001.0001.

Kraut, Robert, and Carmen Egido. "Patterns of Contact and Communication in Scientific Research Collaboration." In *Proceedings of the 1988 ACM Conference on Computer-Supported Cooperative Work*, 1–12. ACM, 1988. https://doi.org/10.1145/62266.62267.

Krieken, Kobie van. "Using Digital Archives in Quantitative Discourse Studies: Methodological Reflections." *Tijdschrift Voor Tijdschriftstudies* 38 (2015): 43–50. https://doi.org/10.18352/ts.343.

Kuhn, Thomas S. *The Structure of Scientific Revolutions*. 2nd ed. International Encyclopedia of Unified Science Foundations of the Unity of Science. Chicago University Press, 1994.

Laite, Julia. "The Emmet's Inch: Small History in a Digital Age." *Journal of Social History*, 2019. https://doi.org/10.1093/jsh/shy118.

Latour, Bruno. "Give Me a Laboratory and I Will Raise the World." In *Science Observed*, edited by Karin Knorr Cetina and Michael Mulkay, 141–70. SAGE Publications, 1983.

Latour, Bruno. *Science in Action*. Harvard University Press, 1987.

Latour, Bruno, and Steve Woolgar. *Laboratory Life: The Social Construction of Scientific Facts*. SAGE Publications, 1979.

Lawson, Murray G. "The Machine Age in Historical Research." *American Archivist* 11, no. 2 (1948): 141–49.

Leetaru, Kalev. "Mass Book Digitization: The Deeper Story of Google Books and the Open Content Alliance." *First Monday* 13, no. 10 (2008).

Leezenberg, Michiel, and Gerard de Vries. *Wetenschapsfilosofie Voor Geesteswetenschappen*. 5th ed. Amsterdam University Press, 2001.

Lewis, Jenny M., Sandy Ross and Thomas Holden. "The How and Why of Academic Collaboration: Disciplinary Differences and Policy Implications." *Higher Education* 64, no. 5 (2012): 693–708. https://doi.org/10.1007/s10734-012-9521-8.

Liu, Alan. *Friending the Past: The Sense of History in the Digital Age*. Chicago; London: The University of Chicago Press, 2018.

Maag, Simon, Timothy J. Alexander, Robert Kase and Sabine Hoffmann. "Indicators for Measuring the Contributions of Individual Knowledge Brokers." *Environmental Science & Policy* 89 (2018): 1–9. https://doi.org/10.1016/j.envsci.2018.06.002.

Mäkelä, Eetu, and Mikko Tolonen. "DHN2018 – an Analysis of a Digital Humanities Conference," 1–9. CEUR-WS, 2018.

Malazita, James W., Ezra J. Teboul and Hined Rafeh. "Digital Humanities as Epistemic Cultures: How DH Labs Make Knowledge, Objects, and Subjects." *Digital Humanities Quarterly* 14, no. 3 (2020).

Manovich, Lev. *Software Takes Command*. Bloomsbury Academic, 2013.

Marcus, George E. "Ethnography in/of the World System: The Emergence of Multi-Sited Ethnography." *Annual Review of Anthropology* 24 (1995): 95–117.

Markus, M. Lynne, and Niels Bjorn-Andersen. "Power Over Users: Its Exercise By System Professionals." *Communications of the ACM* 30, no. 6 (1987): 498–505.

Marlow, Shannon L., Christina N. Lacerenza, Jensine Paoletti, C. Shawn Burke and Eduardo Salas. "Does Team Communication Represent a One-Size-Fits-All Approach?: A Meta-Analysis of Team Communication and Performance." *Organizational Behavior and Human Decision Processes* 144 (2018): 145–70. https://doi.org/10.1016/j.obhdp.2017.08.001.

Martin, Kim, and Anabel Quan-Haase. "Are E-Books Replacing Print Books? Tradition, Serendipity, and Opportunity in the Adoption and Use of e-Books for Historical Research and Teaching." *Journal of the American Society for Information Science and Technology* 64, no. 5 (2013): 1016–28. https://doi.org/10.1002/asi.22801.

Martin, Kim, and Anabel Quan-Haase. "The Role of Agency in Historians' Experiences of Serendipity in Physical and Digital Information Environments." *Journal of Documentation* 72, no. 6 (2016): 1008–26. https://doi.org/10.1108/JD-11-2015-0144.

Mayer-Schönberger, Viktor, and Kenneth Cukier. *Big Data: A Revolution That Will Transform How We Live, Work, and Think*. Houghton Mifflin Harcourt, 2013.

McCallum, Sally H. "MARC: Keystone for Library Automation." *IEEE Annals of the History of Computing* 24, no. 2 (2002): 34–49. https://doi.org/10.1109/MAHC.2002.1010068.

McCarty, Willard. "Collaborative Research in the Digital Humanities." In *Collaborative Research in the Digital Humanities*, edited by Marilyn Deegan and Willard McCarty, 1–10. Ashgate, 2012.

McCarty, Willard. *Humanities Computing*. Palgrave Macmillan, 2005.

McCarty, Willard. "The Residue of Uniqueness." *Historical Social Research/Historische Sozialforschung* 37, no. 3 (2012): 24–45.

McGillivray, Barbara, Thierry Poibeau and Pablo Ruiz Fabo. "Digital Humanities and Natural Language Processing: Je t'aime . . . Moi Non Plus." *Digital Humanities Quarterly* 14, no. 2 (2020).

Meyer, Eric T., and Ralph Schroeder. *Knowledge Machines: Digital Transformations of the Sciences and Humanities*. MIT Press, 2015.

Milligan, Ian. *History in the Age of Abundance?: How the Web Is Transforming Historical Research*, 2019.

Milligan, Ian. "Illusionary Order: Online Databases, Optical Character Recognition, and Canadian History, 1997–2010." *Canadian Historical Review* 94, no. 4 (2013): 540–69. https://doi.org/10.3138/chr.694.

Moretti, Franco. "Conjectures on World Literature." *New Left Review*, no. 1 (2000): 54–68.

Moretti, Franco. *Distant Reading*. Verso Books, 2013.

Morris, Sammie L., and Shirley K. Rose. "Invisible Hands: Recognizing Archivists' Work to Make Records Accessible." In *Working in the Archives: Practical Research Methods for Rhetoric and Composition*, edited by Alexis E. Ramsay, Wendy B. Sharer, Barbara L'Eplattenier and Lisa S. Mastrangelo, 51–78. Southern Illinois University Press, 2010.

Mounier, Pierre. *Les humanités numériques: Une histoire critique*. Online. Éditions de la Maison des sciences de l'homme, 2018. https://doi.org/10.4000/books.editionsmsh. 12006.

Mounier, Pierre. "Une «utopie Politique» Pour Les Humanités Numériques?" *Socio* 4 (2015): 97–112. https://doi.org/10.4000/socio.1338.

Müller, Philipp. "Understanding History: Hermeneutics and Source-Criticism in Historical Scholarship." In *Reading Primary Sources: The Interpretation of Texts from Nineteenth- and Twentieth-Century History*, edited by Miriam Dobson and Benjamin Ziemann, 21–36. Routledge, 2009.

Myers, Greg. "Centering: Proposals for an Interdisciplinary Research Center." *Science, Technology, & Human Values* 18, no. 4 (1993): 433–59.

Neubert, Anna Maria. "Navigating Disciplinary Differences in (Digital) Research Projects Through Project Management." In *Digital Methods in the Humanities*, edited by Silke Schwandt, 59–86. transcript Verlag, 2020. https://doi.org/10.14361/9783839454190-003.

Neumann, Laura J., and Susan Leigh Star. "Making Infrastructure : The Dream of a Common Language." In *Proceedings of the Participatory Design Conference*, 231–40. Cambridge, USA, 1996.

Nicholson, Bob. "The Digital Turn." *Media History* 19, no. 1 (2013): 59–73. https://doi.org/ 10.1080/13688804.2012.752963.

Niggemann, Elisabeth, Jacques De Decker and Maurice Levy. "The New Renaissance: Report of the 'Comité Des Sages.'" Luxembourg: European Commission, 2011.

Nyhan, Julianne, and Oliver Duke-Williams. "Joint and Multi-Authored Publication Patterns in the Digital Humanities." *Literary and Linguistic Computing* 29, no. 3 (2014): 387–99. https://doi.org/10.1093/llc/fqu018.

Nyhan, Julianne, and Andrew Flinn. "Hic Rhodus, Hic Salta: Tito Orlandi and Julianne Nyhan." In *Computation and the Humanities*, 75–86. Springer Series on Cultural Computing. Cham: Springer International Publishing, 2016. https://doi.org/10.1007/978-3-319-20170-2.

Nyhan, Julianne, and Andrew Flinn. "It's Probably the Only Modestly Widely Used System with a Command Language in Latin: Manfred Thaller and Julianne Nyhan." In *Computation and the Humanities*, 195–208. Springer International Publishing, 2016. https://doi.org/10. 1007/978-3-319-20170-2_13.

Nyhan, Julianne, and Andrew Flinn. "The University Was Still Taking Account of Universitas Scientiarum: Wilhelm Ott and Julianne Nyhan." In *Computation and the Humanities*, 55–73. Springer Series on Cultural Computing. Cham: Springer International Publishing, 2016. https://doi.org/10.1007/978-3-319-20170-2.

Oiva, Mila. "The Chili and Honey of Digital Humanities Research: TheFacilitation of the Interdisciplinary Transfer of Knowledge in Digital Humanities Centers." *Digital Humanities Quarterly* 14, no. 3 (2020).

Olson, Judith S., Stephanie Teasly, Lisa Covi and Gary Olson. "The (Currently) Unique Advantages of Collocated Work." In *Distributed Work*, edited by Pamela Hinds and Sara Kiesler, 113–36. MIT Press, 2002.

Ondercin, Heather L. "External Validity." In *The SAGE Encyclopedia of Social Science Research Methods*, edited by Michael Lewis-Beck, Alan Bryman and Tim Futing Liao, 360–62. Sage Publications, Inc., 2004. https://doi.org/10.4135/9781412950589.n318.

Owens, Trevor, and Thomas Padilla. "Digital Sources and Digital Archives: Historical Evidence in the Digital Age." *International Journal of Digital Humanities*, 2020. https://doi.org/10. 1007/s42803-020-00028-7.

Paju, Petri, Mila Oiva and Mats Fridlund. "Digital and Distant Histories: Emergent Approaches within the New Digital History." In *Digital Histories: Emergent Approaches within the New Digital History*, edited by Mats Fridlund, Mila Oiva and Petri Paju, 3–18. Helsinki University Press, 2020. https://doi.org/10.33134/HUP-5-1.

Pawlicka, Urszula. "Data, Collaboration, Laboratory: Bringing Concepts from Science into Humanities Practice." *English Studies* 98, no. 5 (July 4, 2017): 526–41. https://doi.org/10.1080/0013838X.2017.1332022.

Pawlicka-Deger, Urszula. "The Laboratory Turn: Exploring Discourses, Landscapes, and Models of Humanities Labs." *Digital Humanities Quarterly* 14, no. 3 (2020).

Pechenick, Eitan Adam, Christopher M. Danforth and Peter Sheridan Dodds. "Characterizing the Google Books Corpus: Strong Limits to Inferences of Socio-Cultural and Linguistic Evolution." Edited by Alain Barrat. *PLOS ONE* 10, no. 10 (2015). https://doi.org/10.1371/journal.pone.0137041.

Pfaffenberger, Bryan. "Fetishised Objects and Humanised Nature: Towards an Anthropology of Technology." *Man* 23, no. 2 (1988): 236–52. https://doi.org/10.2307/2802804.

Pickering, Andrew. "From Science as Knowledge to Science as Practice." In *Science as Practice and Culture*, edited by Andrew Pickering, 1–26. The University of Chicago Press, 1992.

Pickering, Andrew, ed. *Science as Practice and Culture*. The University of Chicago Press, 1991.

Piersma, Hinke, and Kees Ribbens. "Digital Historical Research: Context, Concepts and the Need for Reflection." *BMGN – Low Countries Historical Review* 128, no. 4 (2013): 78–102.

Pinch, Trevor J., and Wiebe E. Bijker. "The Social Construction of Facts and Artefacts: Or How the Sociology of Science and the Sociology of Technology Might Benefit Each Other." *Social Studies of Science* 14, no. 3 (1984): 399–441. https://doi.org/10.1177/030631284014003004.

Piotrowski, Michael. *Natural Language Processing for Historical Texts*. Edited by Graeme Hirst. *Synthesis Lectures on Human Language Technologies*. Vol. 5. Morgan and Claypool, 2012. https://doi.org/10.2200/S00436ED1V01Y201207HLT017.

Pipek, Volkmar, and Volker Wulf. "Infrastructuring: Toward an Integrated Perspective on the Design and Use of Information Technology." *Journal of the Association for Information Systems* 10, no. 5 (2009): 447–73. https://doi.org/10.17705/1jais.00195.

Ponomariov, Branco L., and P. Craig Boardman. "Influencing Scientists' Collaboration and Productivity Patterns through New Institutions: University Research Centers and Scientific and Technical Human Capital." *Research Policy* 39, no. 5 (2010): 613–24. https://doi.org/10.1016/j.respol.2010.02.013.

Poole, Alex H. "Now Is the Future Now? The Urgency of Digital Curation in the Digital Humanities." *Digital Humanities Quarterly* 7, no. 2 (2013).

Prescott, Andrew. "Beyond the Digital Humanities Center: The Administrative Landscapes of the Digital Humanities." In *A New Companion to Digital Humanities*, edited by Susan Schreibman, Ray Siemens and John Unsworth, 459–75. John Wiley & Sons, Ltd., 2015. https://doi.org/10.1002/9781118680605.ch32.

Prescott, Andrew, and Lorna Hughes. "Why Do We Digitize? The Case for Slow Digitization." *Archive Journal*, 2018.

Purvanova, Radostina K. "Face-to-Face versus Virtual Teams: What Have We Really Learned?" *The Psychologist-Manager Journal* 17, no. 1 (2014): 2–29. https://doi.org/10.1037/mgr0000009.

Putnam, Lara. "The Transnational and the Text-Searchable: Digitized Sources and the Shadows They Cast." *The American Historical Review* 121, no. 2 (2016): 377–402. https://doi.org/10.1093/ahr/121.2.377.

Quan-Haase, Anabel, Juan Luis Suarez and David M. Brown. "Collaborating, Connecting, and Clustering in the Humanities: A Case Study of Networked Scholarship in an Interdisciplinary, Dispersed Team." *American Behavioral Scientist* 59, no. 5 (2015): 565–81. https://doi.org/10.1177/0002764214556806.

Quinn, Patrick M. "Archivists and Historians: The Times They Are a-Changin'." *The Midwestern Archivist* 2, no. 2 (1977): 5–13.

Rabb, Theodore K. "The Development of Quantification in Historical Research." *Journal of Interdisciplinary History* 13, no. 4 (1983): 591–601.

Ramadier, Thierry. "Transdisciplinarity and Its Challenges: The Case of Urban Studies." *Futures* 36, no. 4 (2004): 423–39. https://doi.org/10.1016/j.futures.2003.10.009.

Ramsay, Stemphen. "On Building." *Stephenramsay.Us* (blog), January 11, 2011. https://web.archive.org/web/20170704144620/http://stephenramsay.us:80/text/2011/01/11/on-building/.

Real, Leslie A. "Collaboration in the Sciences and the Humanities: A Comparative Phenomenology." *Arts and Humanities in Higher Education* 11, no. 3 (2012): 250–61. https://doi.org/10.1177/1474022212437310.

Reynolds, John F. "Do Historians Count Anymore?: The Status of Quantitative Methods in History, 1975–1995." *Historical Methods: A Journal of Quantitative and Interdisciplinary History* 31, no. 4 (1998): 141–48. https://doi.org/10.1080/01615449809601196.

Rheinberger, Hans-Jörg. "Culture and Nature in the Prism of Knowledge." *History of Humanities* 1, no. 1 (2016): 155–81. https://doi.org/10.1086/685064.

Rider, Fremont. *The Scholar and the Future of the Research Library, a Problem and Its Solution.* N.Y.: Hadham Press, 1944.

Rieder, Bernhard, and Theo Röhle. "Digital Methods: Five Challenges." In *Understanding Digital Humanities*, edited by David Berry, 67–84. Palgrave Macmillan, 2012.

Risam, Roopika. "Beyond the Margins: Intersectionality and the Digital Humanities." *Digital Humanities Quarterly* 9, no. 2 (2015).

Risam, Roopika. *New Digital Worlds: Postcolonial Digital Humanities in Theory, Praxis, and Pedagogy.* Northwestern University Press, 2018. https://doi.org/10.2307/j.ctv7tq4hg.

Ritchie, Donald. *Doing Oral History.* Oxford University Press, 2014.

Robert Whaples. "Is Economic History a Neglected Field of Study?" *Historically Speaking* 11, no. 2 (2010): 17–20. https://doi.org/10.1353/hsp.0.0109.

Robertson, Stephen. "The Differences between Digital History and Digital Humanities." In *Debates in the Digital Humanities.* University of Minnesota Press, 2016.

Robinson, Peter. "Digital Humanities: Is Bigger, Better?" In *Advancing Digital Humanities*, edited by Paul Longley Arthur and Katherine Bode, 243–57. London: Palgrave Macmillan UK, 2014. https://doi.org/10.1057/9781137337016_16.

Roe, Glenn, Clovis Gladstone and Robert Morrissey. "Discourses and Disciplines in the Enlightenment: Topic Modeling the French Encyclopédie." *Frontiers in Digital Humanities* 2 (2016). https://doi.org/10.3389/fdigh.2015.00008.

Rogers, Richard. *Digital Methods.* MIT Press, 2013.

Rosenfield, Patricia L. "The Potential of Transdisciplinary Research for Sustaining and Extending Linkages between the Health and Social Sciences." *Social Science & Medicine,*

Special Issue Building Research Capacity for Health Social Sciences in Developing Countries, 35, no. 11 (1992): 1343–57. https://doi.org/10.1016/0277-9536(92)90038-R.

Rosenzweig, Roy. "Scarcity or Abundance? Preserving the Past in a Digital Era." *The American Historical Review* 108, no. 3 (2003): 735–62. https://doi.org/10.1086/529596.

Rossi, Giorgio, Jelena Angelis, Filipa Borrego, Joy Davidson, Elena Hoffert, Richard Wade and Patricia Postigo McLaughlin. "Supporting the Transformative Impact of Research Infrastructures on European Research." European Commission, 2020.

Ruggles, Steven. "The Revival of Quantification: Reflections on Old New Histories." *Social Science History* 45, no. 1 (2021): 1–25. https://doi.org/10.1017/ssh.2020.44.

Sample, Mark. "On the Death of the Digital Humanities Center." *@samplereality* (blog), March 26, 2010.

Schatzki, Theodore R., Karin Knorr-Cetina and Eike von Savigny, eds. *The Practice Turn in Contemporary Theory*. New York: Routledge, 2001.

Schellenberg, Theodore R. *Modern Archives. Principles and Techniques*. F. W. Cheshire, 1956.

Schlesinger, Arthur. "The Humanist Looks at Empirical Social Research." *American Sociological Review* 27, no. 6 (1962): 768–71. https://doi.org/10.2307/2090404.

Schmitt, Églantine. "Des Humains Dans La Machine : La Conception d'un Algorithme de Classification Sémantique Au Prisme Du Concept d'objectivité." *Sciences Du Design* 2, no. 4 (2016): 83–97.

Schreibman, Susan, Ray Siemens and John Unsworth, eds. *A Companion to Digital Humanities*. Online. Oxford: Blackwell, 2004.

Sharma, Anurag. "Professional as Agent: Knowledge Asymmetry in Agency Exchange." *Academy of Management Review* 22, no. 3 (1997): 758–98. https://doi.org/10.5465/AMR. 1997.9708210725.

Siemens, Lynne. "'It's a Team If You Use "Reply All"': An Exploration of Research Teams in Digital Humanities Environments." *Literary and Linguistic Computing* 24, no. 2 (2009): 225–33. https://doi.org/10.1093/llc/fqp009.

Siemens, Lynne. "'It's a Team If You Use "Reply All"': An Exploration of Research Teams in Digital Humanities Environments." *Literary and Linguistic Computing* 24, no. 2 (2009): 225–33. https://doi.org/10.1093/llc/fqp009.

Siemens, Lynne. "Project Management and the Digital Humanist." In *Doing Digital Humanities: Practice, Training, Research*, edited by Constance Crompton, Richard J. Laneand Raymond George Siemens, 1st edition., 343–57. New York, NY: Routledge, 2016.

Siemens, Lynne, and Elisabeth Burr. "A Trip around the World: Accommodating Geographical, Linguistic and Cultural Diversity in Academic Research Teams." *Literary and Linguistic Computing* 28, no. 2 (2013): 331–43. https://doi.org/10.1093/llc/fqs018.

Siemens, Lynne, Richard Cunningham, Wendy Duff and Claire Warwick. "'More Minds Are Brought to Bear on a Problem': Methods of Interaction and Collaboration within Digital Humanities Research Teams." *Digital Studies / Le Champ Numérique* 2, no. 2 (2011).

Smith, David A., and Ryan Cordell. "A Research Agenda for Historical and Multilingual Optical Character Recognition." NUlab, Northeastern University, 2018.

Smithies, James. "KDL, Established 2016." King's Digital Lab blog, October 21, 2016. https://www.kdl.kcl.ac.uk/blog/kdl-launch/.

Smithies, James, Carina Westling, Anna-Maria Sichani, Pam Mellen and Arianna Ciula. "Managing 100 Digital Humanities Projects: Digital Scholarship and Archiving in King's Digital Lab." *Digital Humanities Quarterly* 13, no. 1 (2019).

Smits, Thomas. "TS Tools: Problems and Possibilities of Digital Newspaper and Periodical Archives." *Tijdschrift Voor Mediageschiedenis* 139 (2014): 139–46.

Snow, C.P. *The Two Cultures and the Scientific Revolution.* Cambridge University Press, 1959.

Somers, James. "Torching the Modern-Day Library of Alexandria." The Atlantic, 2017.

Sonderegger, Petra. "Creating Shared Understanding in Research Across Distance: Distance Collaboration across Cultures in R&D." In *E-Research: Transformation in Scholarly Practice,* edited by Nicolas W. Jankowski. Routledge, 2009.

Speck, Reto, and Petra Links. "The Missing Voice: Archivists and Infrastructures for Humanities Research." *International Journal of Humanities and Arts Computing* 7, no. 1–2 (2013): 128–46. https://doi.org/10.3366/ijhac.2013.0085.

Speck, William A. "History and Computing: Some Reflections on the Achievements of the Past Decade." *History and Computing* 6, no. 1 (1994): 28–32.

Spiro, Lisa. "'This Is Why We Fight': Defining the Values of the Digital Humanities." In *Debates in Digital Humanities,* edited by Matthew K. Gold, Online. University of Minnesota Press, 2012.

Stanfill, Mel. "The Interface as Discourse: The Production of Norms through Web Design." *New Media & Society* 17, no. 7 (2014): 1059–74. https://doi.org/10.1177/1461444814520873.

Star, Susan Leigh. "The Ethnography of Infrastructure." *American Behavioral Scientist* 43, no. 3 (1999): 377–91. https://doi.org/10.1177/00027649921955326.

Star, Susan Leigh, and Geoffrey C. Bowker. "How to Infrastructure." In *Handbook of New Media: Social Shaping and Social Consequences of ICTs,* edited by Leah A. Lievrouw and Sonia Livingstone, 230–46. SAGE Publications, 2006.

Star, Susan Leigh, and James R. Griesemer. "Institutional Ecology, 'Translations' and Boundary Objects: Amateurs and Professionals in Berkeley's Museum of Vertebrate Zoology, 1907-39." *Social Studies of Science* 19, no. 3 (1989): 387–420. https://doi.org/10.1177/030631289019003001.

Star, Susan Leigh, and Karen Ruhleder. "Steps Toward an Ecology of Infrastructure: Design and Access for Large Information Spaces." *Information Systems Research* 7, no. 1 (1996): 111–34. https://doi.org/10.1287/isre.7.1.111.

Stevens, Rolland E. "The Microform Revolution." *Library Trends* 19, no. 3 (1971): 379–95.

Stokols, Daniel, Juliana Fuqua, Jennifer Gress, Richard Harvey, Kimari Phillips, Lourdes Baezconde-Garbanati, Jennifer Unger, Paula Palmer, Melissa A. Clark and Suzanne M. Colby. "Evaluating Transdisciplinary Science." *Nicotine & Tobacco Research* 5, no. Suppl_1 (2003): S21–39.

Stokols, Daniel, Shalini Misra, Richard P. Moser, Kara L. Hall and Brandie K. Taylor. "The Ecology of Team Science." *American Journal of Preventive Medicine* 35, no. 2 (August 2008): S96–115. https://doi.org/10.1016/j.amepre.2008.05.003.

Stone, Lawrence. "The Revival of Narrative: Reflections on a New Old History." *Past & Present* 85, no. 85 (1979): 3–24.

Stone, Sue. "Humanities Scholars: Information Needs And Uses." *Journal of Documentation* 38, no. 4 (1982): 292–313. https://doi.org/10.1108/eb026734.

Stovel, Katherine, and Lynette Shaw. "Brokerage." *Annual Review of Sociology* 38, no. 1 (2012): 139–58. https://doi.org/10.1146/annurev-soc-081309-150054.

Suchman, Lucy. "Located Accountabilities in Technology Production." *Scandinavian Journal of Information Systems* 14, no. 2 (2002): 91–105.

Sugimoto, Cassidy R., and Scott Weingart. "The Kaleidoscope of Disciplinarity." *Journal of Documentation* 71, no. 4 (2015): 775–94. https://doi.org/10.1108/JD-06-2014-0082.

Svensson, Patrik. "Envisioning the Digital Humanities." *Digital Humanities Quarterly* 6, no. 1 (2012).

Svensson, Patrik. "The Digital Humanities as a Humanities Project." *Arts and Humanities in Higher Education* 11, no. 1–2 (2011): 42–60. https://doi.org/10.1177/1474022211427367.

Tabak, Edin. "A Hybrid Model for Managing DH Projects." *Digital Humanities Quarterly* 11, no. 1 (2017).

Tasovac, Toma, Sally Chambers and Erzsébet Tóth-Czifra. "Cultural Heritage Data from a Humanities Research Perspective: A DARIAH Position Paper," 2020.

Terras, Melissa. "Disciplined: Using Educational Studies to Analyse 'Humanities Computing.'" *Literary and Linguistic Computing* 21, no. 2 (2006): 229–46. https://doi.org/10.1093/llc/fql022.

Terras, Melissa, Julianne Nyhan and Edward Vanhoutte, eds. *Defining Digital Humanities.* Ashgate, 2013.

Thaller, Manfred. "Automation on Parnassus Clio – a Databank Oriented System for Historians." *Historical Social Research* 5, no. 3 (1980): 40–65.

Thernstrom, Stephan. "The Historian and the Computer." In *Computers in Humanistic Research: Readings and Perspectives*, edited by Edmund A. Bowles, 73–81, 1967.

Thomas, William G. "Computing and the Historical Imagination." In *A Companion to Digital Humanities*, edited by Susan Schreibman, Ray Siemens and John Unsworth, Online., 116–32. Blackwell, 2004.

Thylstrup, Nanna Bonde. *The Politics of Mass Digitization.* Cambridge, MA: The MIT Press, 2018.

Tillett, Barbara B. "Catalog It Once for All: A History of Cooperative Cataloging in the United States Prior to 1967 (Before MARC)." *Cataloging & Classification Quarterly* 17, no. 3–4 (1994): 3–38. https://doi.org/10.1300/J104v17n03_02.

Tosh, John. *The Pursuit of History: Aims, Methods and New Directions in the Study of History.* 6th ed. Routledge, 2015.

Townsend, Robert. "Google Books: What's Not to Like?" American Historical Association blog, 2007.

Tsai, Chin-Chang, Elizabeth A. Corley and Barry Bozeman. "Collaboration Experiences across Scientific Disciplines and Cohorts." *Scientometrics* 108, no. 2 (2016): 505–29. https://doi.org/10.1007/s11192-016-1997-z.

Tuunainen, Juha. "When Disciplinary Worlds Collide: The Organizational Ecology of Disciplines in a University Department." *Symbolic Interaction* 28, no. 2 (2005): 205–28. https://doi.org/10.1525/si.2005.28.2.205.

Unsworth, John. "What Is Humanities Computing and What Is Not?" In *Defining Digital Humanities*, edited by Melissa Terras, Julianne Nyhan and Edward Vanhoutte, 51–63. Digital Research in the Arts and Humanities. Routledge, 2002.

Vaidhyanathan, Siva. *The Googlization of Everything (And Why We Should Worry).* Berkeley: University of California Press, 2011.

Vernon, James. "Who's Afraid of the 'Linguistic Turn'? The Politics of Social History and Its Discontents." *Social History* 19, no. 1 (1994): 81–97. https://doi.org/10.1007/s13398-014-0173-7.2.

VSNU, NFU, KNAW, NWO and Zon Mw. "Ruimte voor ieders talent: naar een nieuwe balans in het erkennen en waarderen van wetenschappers," 2019.

Wallace, Peggy. "Anonymity and Confidentiality." In *Encyclopedia of Case Study Research*, edited by Albert Mills, Gabrielle Durepos and Elden Wiebe, 22–24. SAGE Publications, Inc., 2010. https://doi.org/10.4135/9781412957397.n9.

Walsh, John P., and Nancy G. Maloney. "Collaboration Structure, Communication Media, and Problems in Scientific Work Teams." *Journal of Computer-Mediated Communication* 12, no. 2 (2007): 378–98. https://doi.org/10.1111/j.1083-6101.2007.00346.x.

Walsham, Alexandra. "The Social History of the Archive: Record-Keeping in Early Modern Europe." *Past & Present* 230, no. suppl 11 (2016): 9–48. https://doi.org/10.1093/pastj/gtw033.

Wang, Shenghui, Stefan Schlobach and Michel Klein. "Concept Drift and How to Identify It." *Web Semantics: Science, Services and Agents on the World Wide Web* 9, no. 3 (2011): 247–65. https://doi.org/10.1016/j.websem.2011.05.003.

Webster, Peter. "Digital Contemporary History: Sources, Tools, Methods, Issues." *Temp: Tidsskrift for Historie* 14 (2017): 30–38.

Weedman, Judith. "The Structure of Incentive: Design and Client Roles in Application-Oriented Research." *Science, Technology & Human Values* 23, no. 3 (1998): 315–45. https://doi.org/10.1177/016224399802300303.

Weingart, Scott. "Submissions to DH2017 (Pt. 1)." *The Scottbot Irregular* (blog), November 10, 2016. http://scottbot.net/submissions-to-dh2017-pt-1/.

Weiss, Gilbert, and Ruth Wodak, eds. *Critical Discourse Analysis*. London: Palgrave Macmillan UK, 2003. https://doi.org/10.1057/9780230288423.

Weller, Toni. "Introduction: History in the Digital Age." In *History in the Digital Age*, edited by Toni Weller, 1–20. Routledge, 2013.

Wenger, Etienne. "Communities of Practice and Social Learning Systems." *Organization* 7, no. 2 (2000): 225–46. https://doi.org/10.1177/135050840072002.

Wenger, Etiennef. *Communities of Practice: Learning, Meaning, and Identity*. Cambridge University Press, 1998.

White, Hayden. "The Question of Narrative in Contemporary Historical Theory." *History and Theory* 23, no. 1 (1984): 1–33. https://doi.org/10.2307/2504969.

Whitley, Richard. "The Rise and Decline of University Disciplines in the Sciences." In *Problems in Interdisciplinary Studies*, edited by R. Jurkovich and J.H.P. Paelinck, 10–25. Gower Publishing Company, 1984.

Williams, Robert V. "The Use of Punched Cards in US Libraries and Documentation Centers, 1936–1965." *IEEE Annals of the History of Computing* 24, no. 2 (2002): 16–33. https://doi.org/10.1109/MAHC.2002.1010067.

Winters, Jane. "Digital History." In *Debating New Approaches to History*, edited by Marek Tamm and Peter Burke, 277–300. Bloomsbury Academic, 2018.

Wyatt, Sally. "Mode 2 in Action : Working Across Sectors to Create a Center for Humanities and Technology." *Scholarly and Research Communication* 6, no. 4 (2015).

Yale, Elizabeth. "The History of Archives: The State of the Discipline." *Book History* 18, no. 1 (2015): 332–59. https://doi.org/10.1353/bh.2015.0007.

Zaagsma, Gerben. "On Digital History." *BMGN – Low Countries Historical Review* 128, no. 4 (2013): 3–29. https://doi.org/10.18352/bmgn-lchr.9344.

Zundert, Joris van. "The Case of the Bold Button: Social Shaping of Technology and the Digital Scholarly Edition." *Digital Scholarship in the Humanities* 31, no. 4 (2016): 898–910. https://doi.org/10.1093/llc/fqw012.

Zundert, Joris van, and Karina van Dalen-Oskam. "Digital Humanities in the Netherlands." *H-Soz-Kult*, 2014.

Zundert, Joris van, and Ronald Haentjens Dekker. "Code, Scholarship, and Criticism: When Is Code Scholarship and When Is It Not?" *Digital Scholarship in the Humanities* 32, no. suppl_1 (2017): i121–33. https://doi.org/10.1093/llc/fqx006.

Index